# Employee Assistance Programmes and Workplace Counselling

## JOHN BERRIDGE
## CARY L. COOPER
### AND
## CAROLYN HIGHLEY-MARCHINGTON

*Manchester School of Management*
*University of Manchester*
*Institute of Science and Technology*

## JOHN WILEY & SONS
Chichester · New York · Brisbane · Toronto · Singapore

# WILEY SERIES IN WORK, WELL-BEING AND STRESS

## Series Editor

## CARY L. COOPER

Manchester School of Management
University of Manchester Institute of Science and
Technology, UK

---

Creating Healthy Work Organizations
*Edited by Cary L. Cooper and Stephen Williams*

Employee Assistance Programmes
and Workplace Counselling
*John Berridge, Cary L. Cooper and Carolyn Highley-Marchington*

*Further titles in preparation*

*Other Wiley Editorial Offices*

John Wiley & Sons, Inc., 605 Third Avenue,
New York, NY 10158-0012, USA

Jacaranda Wiley Ltd, 33 Park Road, Milton,
Queensland 4064, Australia

John Wiley & Sons (Canada) Ltd, 22 Worcester Road,
Rexdale, Ontario M9W 1L1, Canada

John Wiley & Sons (Asia) Pte Ltd, 2 Clementi Loop #02-01,
Jin Xing Distripark, Singapore 129809

*Library of Congress Cataloging-in-Publication Data*
Berridge, John.
    Employee assistance programmes and workplace counselling / John Berridge, Cary L. Cooper, and Carolyn Highley-Marchington.
        p.   cm. — (Wiley series in work, well-being, and stress)
    Includes bibliographical references and index.
    ISBN 0-471-93805-X (pbk.)
    1. Employee assistance programs.   2. Job stress.   I. Cooper, Cary L.   II. Highley-Marchington, Carolyn.   III. Title.   IV. Series.
HF5549.5.E42B47   1997
658.3'8 — DC20                                                         96–34872
                                                                          CIP

*British Library Cataloguing in Publication Data*

A catalogue record for this book is available from the British Library

ISBN 0-471-93805-X

Typeset in 11/13pt Palatino from the authors' disks by
Dobbie Typesetting Ltd, Tavistock, Devon.
Printed and bound in Great Britain by Biddles Ltd, Guildford and King's Lynn.
This book is printed on acid-free paper responsibly manufactured from sustainable forestation, for which at least two trees are planted for each one used for paper production.

*This book is dedicated to the memory of
Mike Megranahan, Managing Director of EAR Limited,
a pioneer of EAPs in Britain,
a thinker and philosopher of employee counselling,
mentor and good friend to the authors,
who sadly was killed in a road accident
while this book was being written*

# Contents

# About the Authors

*John Berridge* has been at Manchester School of Management, UMIST (University of Manchester Institute of Science and Technology) since 1980, where he is currently Director of International Management Programmes. After an initial background in the chemical industry and management consulting, he has researched and taught in five British universities, two US universities, and a French business school, as well as being a visiting professor in Holland, Austria, the Caribbean and Australia. Since 1990 he has been editor of the journal *Employee Relations*. His research on EAPs has covered the US, Europe, Britain and Australia, and he has written on EAPs for *Work and Stress, Personnel Review, Employee Counselling Today*, as well as contributing on the subject to several books.

*Cary L. Cooper* is currently Professor of Organizational Psychology in the Manchester School of Management, and Pro-Vice Chancellor of UMIST. He has researched and written widely in the field of occupational stress, having published over 150 articles and 30 books on aspects of workplace stress. He is currently the co-editor of the medical journal *Stress Medicine*, and a Fellow of the British Psychological Society, the Royal Society of Arts and The Royal Society of Medicine.

*Carolyn Highley-Marchington* has degrees in Psychology and Occupational Psychology, and worked for two years in personnel management with Marks and Spencer. For three years she was a  Research Fellow at the Manchester School of Management, UMIST, where she conducted the first nationwide independent assessment and evaluation of British workplace counselling programmes, for the Health and Safety Executive. Carolyn now runs her own consultancy, the Highley-Marchington Consultancy, providing independent information and advice in the area of work stress and workplace counselling, as well as conducting audits and evaluations of EAPs and workplace counselling programmes. Since creating her own consultancy in 1994 Carolyn has successfully worked with both Government departments and blue chip organisations.

# Preface

Work stress is a feature of current economic activity — we all suffer from it at times and to different extents. At best, work stress can be a source of excitement and stimulus to achievement. At worst, it can seriously impair our quality of work life, and reduce our personal and job effectiveness. Work stress can result from the job itself and from the context and arrangement of work: equally it can originate from factors outside, such as personal or family matters. Whatever the origins, there is no doubt — work can be stressful.

This book is the result of three authors' wide-ranging interests in the quality of life at work, in the place of work as part of life, and how to achieve co-existence, if not synergy, between these two elements. When two occupational psychologists (Cary Cooper & Carolyn Highley-Marchington) come together with a human resources specialist (John Berridge), there is both an opportunity and a problem of synthesizing differing perspectives. We have attempted to do so in respect of a common interest in employee counselling and Employee Assistance Programmes (EAPs), as a means of coping with stress and improving the quality of life at work.

We retain an optimistic, yet realistic, view of employee counselling. We see it as having the potential to transcend its origins in employee rehabilitation and to pass through the intermediate stage of disseminating the skills of coping and adjustment. We can see EAPs as having the potential to promote individuals' positive contribution and wellness at work, and, as a consequence, to encourage organizational learning. In this context, counselling finds compatibility, if not alliance, with corporate strategy, as well as becoming incorporated into the organization's attitudes, discourse and practices. Counselling can thus become part of a corporate culture, and both a notionally quantifiable and an intangibly qualitative contribution to organizational effectiveness.

The EAP is a development of employee counselling which has grown up in the United States since the 1960s, and in Britain and other countries since the 1980s. While retaining the counselling of troubled employees at its core, it has moved that activity closer to the ongoing processes of the firm. The EAP includes the involvement of the employer who funds the counselling, involves management if appropriate, and is concerned that the outcomes of counselling can be related to the employee's job context as well as to her or his personal life. Within the EAP, solutions are sought simultaneously to individual and corporate problems in a professional and purposive, yet cost-driven, manner.

Much interest, and not a little concern, has been expressed at the considerable growth of EAPs in Britain during the 1990s. As a consequence, the Health and Safety Executive (HSE) funded at the Manchester School of Management at UMIST, the first major study in Britain into the evaluation of EAP provision, including the views of contractor provider firms, counsellors, and clients, both corporate and individual. Our thanks are due to the HSE for allowing us to discuss and interpret certain research findings from this study (Highley & Cooper, 1995).

We acknowledge our thanks to many persons within the employee counselling and EAP world and outside who have given generously of their time and thoughts. It would be invidious and even indiscreet to mention them all here, but we never fail to learn from their knowledge and practical wisdom. The book's merits derive from them in many respects, while the responsibility for errors rests with the authors.

The many respondents of our research survey deserve our warm thanks for the provision of information during the research and at other times:

- contractor provider companies of EAPs
- companies with operating EAPs, however provided
- individual counsellors working for EAP provider firms
- individual clients who completed many questionnaires, all of whose names have been omitted for reasons of confidentiality

Finally, we cannot overlook the back-up team without whom this book would never have been produced. We thank Sarah Teather, an original member of the research team, for numerous ideas that we subsequently explored; Linda Alker for statistical assistance on some of the original research data; Beryl Boswell and Jenny Ellison, whose expertise and equanimity in the organization of word processing and co-ordination of innumerable drafts never cease to amaze us; Gordon Lengden for his usual talent with graphics.

Our gratitude is due to our editors, Michael Coombs and Claire Plimmer, to Alison Mead our production editor, and to our publisher, John Wiley and Sons, for their faith in our capacity to eventually bring our research and thoughts on EAPs and workplace counselling together into what we hope is a coherent form.

Finally, we must recognize the contribution of our families, long-suffering to a fault, during the pains of authorship: you all have been heroes.

John R. Berridge
Cary L. Cooper
Carolyn Highley-Marchington
Manchester School of Management
University of Manchester Institute of Science
and Technology (UMIST)
P O Box 88
Manchester M60 1QD
England
November 1996

# Series Preface

The purpose of this series of books is to highlight the relationship between work, well-being and stress. It is intended that this series will explore topics such as managing organizational stress, worksite health programmes, burnout among human service professionals, Employee Assistance Programmes, the nature and control of violence in the workplace and many other topics. We anticipate that this series will appeal to both the academic community and practitioners in the fields of occupational health, human resource management and industrial/occupational/organizational psychology.

This book focuses on one of the most widely used approaches to organizational stress management in North America and Europe, Employee Assistance Programmes (EAPs). It highlights the history of EAPs, their place in human resource management, their different orientations and their impact on employee and organizational health. The book contains important research on employees' and organizations' perceptions of EAPs and their effectiveness, as well as information about workplace counsellors. An effort is made to outline the criteria that organizations should consider in deciding about the choice of an EAP provider, and the issues surrounding their use in organizations generally.

# 1
# Why Stress is a Corporate Problem

## THE COSTS OF STRESS TO UK PLCs

Against a growing body of international research evidence, there can be little dispute that stress is adversely affecting individual and organizational health (Cooper & Payne, 1988; Schabracq, Winnubst & Cooper, 1996). Links have been established between stress and the incidence of coronary heart disease, alcoholism, mental breakdown, poor health behaviours, job dissatisfaction, accidents, family problems and certain forms of cancer (Cooper, 1996). For UK companies in the 1980s, stress in the workplace was ten times more costly than industrial relations disputes. Recent figures released by the Confederation of British Industry (CBI) in 1995 calculate that in the UK alcohol and drink-related diseases cost the economy approximately £1.7 billion annually and 8 million lost working days, with coronary artery disease and strokes costing a further 62 million days lost and mental ill-health at £3.7 billion and 91 million days lost. With the great reduction in the 1990s of working days lost because of industrial relations issues, the relative incidence of working time lost because of stress has become all the more important.

Certain countries (e.g. the United States) are showing declines in their level of stress-related illnesses, such as heart disease and alcoholism. In contrast, the World Health Organization has published figures that indicate that not only is the United Kingdom near the top of the world league table in terms of mortality caused by heart disease, but it is also showing yearly increases. The British Heart Foundation has estimated that heart disease costs the average UK company of 10 000 employees 73 000 lost working days per year, the death of 42 of its employees (between 35 and 64 years old) and lost productive value to its products or services of over £2.5 million annually (Cartwright & Cooper, 1994).

The cost of stress for the nation is also currently extremely high. For example, the British Heart Foundation Coronary Prevention Group has calculated that 180 000 people die in the United Kingdom each year from coronary heart disease; that is, almost 500 people a day. In addition, MIND, the mental health charity, estimates that between 30% and 40% of all sickness absence from work is attributable to mental and emotional disturbance. The country has also suffered from increased rates of suicide amongst the young, increasing by 30% from the late 1970s to the early 1990s, particularly in the younger age groups of employees. The instability and life stress have led to annual divorce rates rising from 27 000 in 1961 to 155 000 divorces in 1988, and this rise still continues. Indeed, Relate estimates that by the year 2000 there will be four divorces in every ten marriages. And finally, Alcohol Concern estimates that one in four men in the United Kingdom drink more than the medically recommended number of units per week with 25% of accidents at work involving intoxicated workers (Cooper & Cartwright, 1996). So not only is British society in general suffering from stress, but also UK plc is suffering in its economic, financial and quality performance.

## PAYING THE COST

Why is it that many countries, such as the United States and Finland seem to be showing declines in their levels of stress-related illnesses (e.g. heart disease, alcoholism), while those in the United Kingdom are still rising? Is it the case, for example, that US employers are becoming more altruistic and caring for their employees, and less concerned about 'the bottom line'? Unfortunately, the answer is likely to be 'no'. Two trends in the United States are forcing US firms to take action. First, US industry assumes the cost for employee health care through direct payment of premiums for employees' insurance. As a consequence, it is facing directly an enormous and ever-spiralling bill for employee health care costs. Individual insurance costs have risen by 50% over the past two decades, but the employers' contribution has risen by over 140%. It has also been estimated that over $700 million a year is spent by US employers to replace the 200 000 men aged 45 and 65 who die or are incapacitated by coronary artery disease alone. Top management at Xerox estimate that the loss of just one executive to a stress-related illness costs the organization $600 000 (Cooper, Cooper & Eaker, 1988). The importance and cost of stress is brought home constantly to the employer in the size of health care insurance premiums and the rate of their increase. In the United Kingdom, however, employers can create intolerable levels of stress on their employees, and largely it is the taxpayer who picks up the bill through the National Health Service or Social Security payments. There is little direct accountability or incentive for firms to maintain the health of their employees. Of course, the indirect costs through taxation are enormous, but rarely does the firm actually attempt to estimate this cost. The firm treats absenteeism, labour turnover and low productivity as an intrinsic part of running a business (Dale & Cooper, 1992).

There is a second source of growing costs. More and more employees, in US companies at least, are litigating against their employers, through the worker compensation regulations and laws, in respect of job-related stress, or what is being termed 'cumulative trauma'. The United Kingdom is just beginning to see a move toward greater litigation by workers about their conditions of work. Several trade unions and professional associations are supporting cases by individual workers, and the trend is certainly in the direction of future mental disability claims and damages being awarded on the basis of workplace stress. The recent British cases are described to illustrate this trend.

## EMPLOYEE STRESS LITIGATION

Earnshaw & Cooper (1996) have highlighted many of the issues surrounding employers' liability for stress at work claims. Employers have always been under a duty to take reasonable care for the health and safety of their employees. The recent Walker case has reinforced this principle in respect of mental health (*Walker vs. Northumberland County Council*, 1995). John Walker worked for Northumberland County Council from 1970 until December 1987 as an area social services officer. He was in a middle management position and responsible for four teams of social services field workers. His area of responsibility included a high incidence of child care and child abuse problems, which he was in charge of manning and holding case conferences with all parties. In addition, there had been an increase in the workload because of a population rise in his area of responsibility, but without a corresponding increase in staff support.

Between 1985 and 1987 Mr Walker repeatedly complained (in writing) to his superiors expressing the need to alleviate the work pressure to which he and his social workers were subject. Recognizing that the Council would be unwilling to approve increased resources, Mr Walker made specific suggestions about how the situation could be dealt with. He was told this was not possible. During 1986 the workload continued to increase and in November 1986 Mr Walker suffered a nervous breakdown. In March 1987 Mr Walker resumed work, having negotiated for assistance to be provided for him on his return. As things turned out, support was provided to Mr Walker on only an intermittent basis, and was withdrawn by early April. During his absence a substantial backlog of paperwork had built up that took Mr Walker until May to clear. In the meantime, the number of pending cases continued to increase and Mr Walker once again began to experience stress symptoms. By September 1987 he was advised to go on sick leave, and was diagnosed as being affected by a state of stress-related anxiety. In the event, he suffered a second mental breakdown and was obliged to retire from his post for reasons of ill-health. The judge held that the Council was liable for Mr Walker's second nervous breakdown but not his first (full details of this case and its implications can be found in Earnshaw & Cooper, 1996).

It has always been the case in law that, as Earnshaw & Cooper (1994) highlight,

> if an employer breaches this duty of care and in consequence an employee suffers foreseeable damage in the form of personal injury, the employee may sue the employer in the tort of negligence in order to obtain compensation for the loss sustained (a tort is a civil wrong as opposed to a crime). Traditionally, such personal injury claims have come about as a result of workplace accidents in which, for example, the employee was trapped in machinery that was not securely fenced, or slipped on materials left on the floor, or was splashed by harmful substances because protective clothing was not provided.

The novel issue brought to the fore in the landmark case of *Walker vs. Northumberland County Council*, according to Earnshaw & Cooper (1996), was the attitude that the courts would take to the question of the employer's duty to protect against psychiatric harm generally. The judge's view was that:

> Whereas the law on the extent of this duty has developed almost exclusively in cases involving physical injury to the employee as distinct from injury to his mental health, there is no logical reason why risk of psychiatric damage should be excluded from the scope of the duty of care.

As Earnshaw & Cooper (1994) contend, even if employers were to avoid the risk of litigation by treating their workforce in a humane fashion by communicating effectively with them about their concerns, and by handling stressful situations such as redundancy exercises or mergers in a sensitive and caring manner, this would not of itself lead to the demise of occupational stress. Factors other than the behaviour of employers can play their part in causing stress at work, and these require more radical solutions. For example, unless the United Kingdom introduces minimum wage legislation, some employees may well 'choose', or even volunteer, to work excessive hours in order to earn a decent living wage. Whilst it continues to be regarded as 'macho' and a sign of commitment to the job for managers to take on more than they can cope with, they themselves are likely to be the authors of their own misfortune. And whilst we live in an era of recession and high unemployment, concern over job security will continue to generate anxiety and distress throughout the working population. Indeed, this is likely to grow as we enter the next millennium with more and more people on short-term and temporary-job sub-contracting or obliged to accept part-time work or other atypical employment patterns.

## THE CONTRACT CULTURE AND STRESS

During the 1980s the 'enterprise culture' helped to transform the British economy, following the notions of the market-driven economy and the individualized employee (Thatcher, 1993). But, by the end of the decade, substantial personal costs were being revealed in terms of major redundancies, heavier workloads, longer working hours, greater job insecurity, and greater pressures of work impinging on the family and personal life. At the time, an Institute of Management survey in the United Kingdom (Benbow, 1995) found that 77% of managers were distressed by their long working hours, a similar 77% were concerned by the effect of their work on their family life, and 74% were significantly worried as to how this was affecting their relationship with their partner. Stress, in other words, had not only found a firm place in modern business vocabulary (as much so as 'junk bonds', 'e-mail' and 'golden parachutes'), but also was becoming part of the demonology of managerial problems and dangers.

The 1980s was a decade of 'self-induced stress' with individuals pushing themselves toward the edge to achieve personal success and material gain. In much business rhetoric of the 1980s the emphasis was on individual opportunity such as that provided by the deregulation of markets, which led to high-earning, high-risk careerism and its consequent high-stress jobs, such as in financial services (Kahn & Cooper, 1990). The end of the 1980s and the beginning of the 1990s was also characterized by corporate 'imposed stress', where companies were attempting to survive the recession by cutting labour costs through downsizing (or as the Americans now colloquially call it 'right-sizing'), dumping more work on fewer shoulders and encouraging a culture of organizational commitment through long working hours. Coincidental with these developments, the British economy was shifting rapidly toward an aggressive commercial culture, especially in the considerable sectors of the economy that were privatized; also, in the new business ethics introduced into those remaining in the public sector, and even in the outsourcing of many activities within private sector companies. This has led to a new phase of organizational life, the 'contract culture', and one that is likely to have more profound effects on working people than those of the 'enterprise culture' or the downsizing activities of the recession.

Short-term contracts and part-time working are becoming the order of the day in Britain. In the last quarter of 1994 over 74 000 full-time jobs were lost while 173 000 part-time jobs were created. One in eight of British workers is now self-employed and from 1984 to 1994 the number of men in part-time work has doubled. This movement toward atypical contractual or part-time working will have dramatic effects on the individual as well as the organization. Most individuals up to now have not had to think about marketing themselves, developing their skill base, managing their time and careers, and living with the inevitable insecurity that this portfolio of jobs will entail.

What are the implications for the roles of men and women? Women are increasingly entering the world of work, with two out of every three women currently working, one of the highest proportions in the European Union (EU). But, more importantly, women have always pursued discontinuous careers, working part-time or on short-term contracts as they managed their careers and family life. Will this mean that men will become obsolete in this new 'contract culture', and that women will predominate because of their flexibility and ability to cope with insecurity and short-termism? If so, what impact will this have not only on the 'macho' corporate jobs and cultures but also on who takes what responsibilities in the family and domestic environment.

And finally, how will organizations cope with this development? How will they manage the new commitment of people to whom they are no longer committed long term? How will they manage part-time or portfolio employees, people who are no longer motivated by the carrot-and-stick approach to promotion or longitudinal career development? These are questions of profound significance to the corporate world and will necessitate even greater stress management resources by organizations. So what can organizations do to manage stress in their workplaces?

# MANAGING STRESS AT WORK

There are a number of options to consider in looking at the prevention of stress, which can be termed as primary, secondary and tertiary levels of intervention and address differing stages in the stress process.

*Primary prevention* is concerned with taking action to reduce or eliminate stressors (i.e. sources of stress) and to promote positively a supportive and healthy work environment. *Secondary prevention* is concerned with the prompt detection and management of mental concerns such as depression and anxiety by increasing individual and collective awareness of stress and improving stress management skills. *Tertiary prevention* is concerned with the rehabilitation and recovery process of those individuals who have suffered, or are suffering from, mental or physical ill-health as a result of stress (Cooper & Cartwright, 1996).

## Primary Prevention

The effective way of tackling stress is to eliminate it at source. This may involve changes in personnel policies such as improving communication systems, redesigning jobs, or allowing more decision-making and autonomy at lower levels. Obviously, as the type of action required by an organization will vary according to the kinds of stressors operating, any intervention needs to be guided by some *prior diagnosis* or *stress audit* to identify what these stressors are and who they are affecting.

Stress audits typically take the form of a self-report questionnaire administered to employees on an organization-wide, site or departmental basis. A widely validated example of such a diagnostic instrument is the Occupational Stress Indicator (OSI) (Cooper, Sloan & Williams, 1988). In addition to identifying the sources of stress at work and those individuals who are most vulnerable to stress, the questionnaire will usually measure levels of employee job satisfaction and coping behaviour, as well as physical and psychological health on a comparative basis with similar occupational groups and industries. Stress audits are an extremely effective way of identifying problematic areas and directing organizational resources into areas where they are most needed. Audits also provide a means of regularly monitoring stress levels and employee health over time, and provide a baseline whereby subsequent interventions can be evaluated.

Another key factor in primary prevention is the development of the kind of supportive organizational climate in which stress is recognized as a feature of modern industrial life and not interpreted as a sign of weakness or incompetence (Berridge, 1990a, 1990b). Mental ill-health is indiscriminate—it can affect anyone irrespective of their age, socio-economic class, hierarchical level or job function. Therefore, employees should not feel awkward about admitting to any difficulties they encounter, and that give rise to stress.

Organizations, with the co-operation of occupational health personnel, can also introduce initiatives that promote directly positive health behaviours in the workplace. Again, health promotion activities can take a variety of forms. They may include:

- the introduction of regular medical checks and health screening
- the design of 'healthy' canteen menus or restaurant facilities off-site
- the provision of on-site fitness facilities and exercise classes
- corporate membership or concessionary rates at local health and fitness clubs
- the introduction of cardiovascular fitness programmes
- advice on alcohol and dietary control (particularly cutting down on cholesterol, salt and sugar)
- smoking cessation programmes
- advice on lifestyle management, more generally

### Secondary Prevention

Initiatives that fall into this category are generally focused on training and education, and involve awareness-raising activities and skills training programmes. Stress education and stress management courses serve a useful function in helping individuals to recognize the symptoms of stress in themselves and others, and to extend or develop their coping skills and stress resilience. The form and content of this kind of training can vary immensely, but often includes simple relaxation techniques; lifestyle advice and planning; basic training in time management; and assertiveness and problem-solving skills. The aim of these programmes is to help employees to review the psychological effects of stress and to develop a personal stress control plan.

## Tertiary Prevention

One of the main aspects of tertiary prevention that organizations can consider to assist in the recovery and rehabilitation of stressed employees is workplace counselling. In this approach, organizations provide access to confidential professional counselling services for employees who are experiencing problems in the workplace or personal setting. Such services can either be provided by outside agencies who operate entirely independently of the organization, and to whom the employee is referred, or is advised to consult. In some instances, such counselling can be provided in-house, financed by the employer, although the independence of such a service is hard to ensure. A recent development of workplace-based professional counselling is the Employee Assistance Programme (EAP), which can be in-house or (more usually) delivered through an expert external agency or contractor. Normally it is fully-funded by the employer as an employee benefit. As such it is distinguished from other forms of workplace counselling and is relatively integrated into other organizational systems of human resources and line management. An EAP provides counselling, information and/or referral to appropriate internal or external counselling treatment and support services for troubled employees.

Workplace counselling and EAPs are the most common form of stress management, since they can be introduced quickly and provide a resource for dealing immediately with employee distress. Because they are widely used, the purpose of this book is to concentrate on their history, what services they provide, why organizations use them, how effective they are and what is the future in the context of human resource management.

# 2
# Defining and Describing an EAP

## WHAT IS AN EAP?

In essence, an Employee Assistance Programme (EAP) is a systematic, organized and continuing provision of counselling, advice and assistance, provided or funded by the employer, designed to help employees and (in most cases) their families with problems arising from work-related and external sources. The title of EAP is not universally used, and individual organizations may use other titles that meet local traditions or needs. While the EAP originated in the United States, some critics there find that the title of employee assistance is redolent of welfarism; the term 'Employee Counselling Programme' (ECP) is often used as a consequence.

To be effective, EAPs need to reflect not only the clients' needs in their work situation and in the wider context of kinship and society, but also to accord with the nature and needs of the organization in which they operate and with employers' motives, ranging from the purist altruism to the most calculated self-interest. Hence, a standardized model does not exist, and every instance of design and implementation should be treated individually (Davis & Gibson, 1994: 36–38).

EAPS in Britain have

> diversified into a range of systems, comprising different sponsorships, structures, processes, target populations, names and even objectives.

Nevertheless, despite this diversity, there is some agreement on what constitutes an EAP (Lee & Gray, 1994: 215–216, in the British context).

EAPs, however, have the capacity to defy routinization,

underlying the diversity of terms and organizational structures . . . the ultimate concern is with *preventing identifying* and *treating* personal problems that adversely affect job performance (Lee & Gray, 1994: 216).

Employee assistance also is highly influenced by national and organizational cultures; hence, it is manifested in very different forms in differing countries (Dessenne et al., 1992). In spite of the dominance of US practice, very varied patterns of employee counselling have developed in the industrialized countries, and US models do not ever overshadow practice in countries with divergent economic, social and health care delivery systems.

## DEFINITIONS OF EAPs

There are many definitions of EAPs, reflecting the wide range of participants in such programmes, the varying interest groups as providers or purchasers, and the differing views of professional commentators. In a sense, the diversity of all these stakeholders means that all the definitions have a degree of validity, however divergent may be the interests, beliefs or involvement that drive them.

The UK Employee Assistance Professionals Association (EAPA) defines an EAP as:

a mechanism for making counselling and other forms of assistance available to a designated workforce on a systematic and uniform basis, and to recognised standards (EAPA, 1994).

This definition highlights certain requisite characteristics of an EAP, i.e. its clear extent of coverage of all or selected employees and their dependants, its systematic provision of counselling as of right rather than by privilege or patronage, and its adherence to levels of service quality on an independent verified basis. It also emphasizes the drive for professionalism, necessary to confer occupational status and social recognition of an expert personal service in a confidential and fiduciary relationship.

A definition that brings out the EAP provider's viewpoint is:

> A confidential and professional service provided as an employee benefit which complements and extends in-company resources in the constructive and supportive management of people impacted by concerns in their personal and work lives (Megranahan, 1995).

The focus here is on the EAP's compatibility and integration with corporate goals and culture, and with managerial practices in the motivation and development of staff members. The provider contractor accepts working within the framework of the organization's structures and processes, while retaining professional standards of service.

The above definition tends to mirror US practice from which it draws its essence, and which is succinctly expressed in a recent formulation:

> . . . a program that provides direct service to an organization's workers who are experiencing many different types of problems in their personal or work lives (Cunningham, 1994: 5).

The progressional author of this definition goes on to explain further how this bland formulation demonstrates that employee assistance over the past twenty years has 'lost much of its original precision' that it had in its inception as industrial alcoholism and substance-abuse programmes. She sees occupational social work (a far wider field) merging into employee assistance, if not being dominated by it:

> It is sometimes hard to maintain the distinction between occupational social work and employee assistance, because the overwhelming majority of occupational social workers are employed in some type of EAP program (Cunningham, 1994: 6).

Hence, this commentator of the US scenario considers that it is valid to see 'employee assistance as the most significant area for occupational practice at this time' in respect of counselling professionals working in business and industry (Cunningham, 1994). This emphasis is not justified in the British context for many professional and corporate reasons, as will be developed at numerous points in this book.

A recent and relatively comprehensive definition developed by the present authors is:

a programmatic intervention associated with the work context, usually at the level of the individual employee, using behavioural science knowledge and methods for the control of certain work-related problems (notably alcoholism, drug abuse and mental health) that adversely affect job performance, with the objective of enabling the individual to return to making her or his full job contribution and reattaining full functioning in personal life (adapted from Berridge and Cooper 1993b: 89).

Such a definition attempts to reconcile the two potentially conflicting foci of attention of an EAP—the client *and* the employing organization—as it is widely found in British practice. The definition also draws out the expert and professional nature of the service provided, which is far removed from popular misconceptions of counselling being well-intended lay advice of an intuitive but unsystematic nature.

## THE OBJECTIVES OF EAPs

In Britain, EAPs tend to have two primary objectives:

1  To help the employees of organizations distracted by a range of personal concerns, including (but not limited to) emotional, stress, relationship, family, alcohol, drug, financial, legal and other problems, to cope with such concerns and learn to themselves control the stresses produced (EAPA, 1994).
2  To assist the organization also in the identification and amelioration of productivity issues in employees whose job performance is adversely affected by such personal concerns (EAPA, 1994).

The intended beneficiaries of the EAP hence are both the individual (the primary focus in British practice) and her or his employing organization (less directly in Britain, but more emphasized in US practice). At the personal level, the objective of employee counselling is not personal restructuring, as will be discussed in relation to psychotherapy. But the effect on individual coping and adjustment to work and non-work life can be considerable. At corporate levels, equally, the outcomes are intended as a corporate consultancy intervention, but:

... being more or less deeply embedded into the organizational processes of the firm, it becomes part of organizational discourse, it reflects and nourishes the organizational culture, and it becomes part of the organizational learning, problem-solving and adaptation mechanisms (Berridge and Cooper, 1994a: 5).

The attainment of such a level of pervasion by the EAP of the organizational culture would require a considerable period of time, if it were capable of being achieved at all in the face of a robust opposed formal culture. Equally, some EAP providers might well not regard this level of symbiosis as an objective that was professionally desirable or attainable. Their individual counsellors might be more antagonistic for reasons of therapeutic independence, an attitude that was criticized by Hoskinson & Reddy (1989: 4) as 'a failing on their part which enhances the general sense that they are not in touch with the shared reality of the workplace'.

## THE DELIVERY METHODS FOR EAPs

The variability of objectives for EAPs can result in many differing modes of programme delivery. The *modus operandi* of external contractor providers is often the main factor, since standardization of the mode of delivery is a key to their provision of a high-quality service with economic use of internal production factors. The choice of contractor provider may be central in determining whether the employer/organization adopts an EAP with a suitable delivery method. The main dimensions of delivery methods are shown in Figure 2.1.

The initial distinction between in-house and externally contracted provision was important at the outset of EAPs in the United States, when in-house services were the principal configuration. At that time a shortage existed of professional counsellors oriented toward workplace and employment-based practice, and an over-supply of enthusiastic but untrained lay counsellors—who often were reformed alcoholics or drug abusers. In the United States, in-house, on-site (cell 1 in Figure 2.1) provision is still widely found, especially among large employers and in government service. In Britain, the later development of EAPs in a different and more stringent economic

18

|  | In-house provision of EAP and counselling services | External contractor provision of EAP and counselling services |
|---|---|---|
| On-site EAP and counselling services | 1.<br>Often relatively direct control by Occupational Health (OH) or Human Resources Management (HRM) departments | 2.<br>Unusual, but may be found where many functions/services are subcontracted, or have been 'floated off' from former in-house services |
| Externally located EAP and counselling services | 3.<br>Unusual, but may occur for reasons of confidentiality, using an adjacent location, or as part of a 'mixed model' provision, as a partnership with a contractor | 4.<br>Customary delivery model in Britain, using provider company's offices, or affiliate counsellors' consulting rooms or home premises |

*Figure 2.1* Delivery methods for EAP and counselling services

climate has predisposed delivery methods to be by external contractor providers, who use a network of counsellors (cell 4) to provide services for a variety of large and smaller employer clients alike. In both countries, as the EAP industry matures and most major companies (that are going to) have adopted an EAP, the new market is found increasingly among small and medium-sized companies. The economies of scale render it unattractive for broad-brush, in-house provision of EAPs in British organizations employing less than 3000 persons (Reddy, 1993: 59). As a consequence, the trend, especially in Britain, is toward externally provided, externally located employee counselling services (cell 4). A 'mixed-model', as described in cell 3 of the diagram, being a combination of internal and external provision, may be the incipient trend in Britain as companies seek to maximize the advantages of the internal linkages of an in-house EAP, and those also of the external expertise of an externally contracted EAP. However, in general, EAPs in Britain currently are seen as being externally provided, with only a handful of internal in-house services describing themselves as full EAPs.

Although British EAPs typically emphasize an approach based on assessment plus 'brief' counselling or intervention, there are some EAP models based on assessment and referral services only (EAPA, 1994). British EAPs normally do not include any long-term therapy; those instances where such intervention is required are referred on to specialized professional psychotherapists or to NHS hospital-based services. In the United States, in circumstances of different health care funding, certain EAPs may include such long-term treatment.

## WHAT ARE THE ELEMENTS OF AN EAP?

The essential components of an EAP should reflect the provider's and the employer's preferred practice model, the resources available to the organization, the needs of its employees, as well as the size and the configuration of the organization (Davis & Gibson, 1994; Lee & Gray, 1994). Whilst all EAPs should be tailor-made to reflect the needs of the client organization, there are some EAP activities necessary to preserve the integrity of the service. The following list covers many of the essential elements that distinguish the EAP by its integrated approach and its systematic design, meshing with the administrative and social systems of the organization and its environment:

1  A *systematic survey* of the organization to determine the nature, causes and extent of problems perceived by individuals, taking also into account the viewpoints of all the stakeholders and functional specialists in the organization.

2  A *continuing commitment* on the part of the employing organization at the top level to provide counselling, advisory and assistance services to the 'troubled' employee on a no-blame and no-cost, totally confidential, basis.

3  An effective *programme of promotion and publicity* of the EAP to all employees as potential clients, emphasizing in particular its confidentiality, access and scope in issues covered.

4  A linked *programme of education and training* on the goals and methods of the EAP for all staff members, in terms of the definition of a 'troubled' employee, the individual's responsibility for well-being, the roles of managers, supervisors, and shop stewards within the design and implementation of the EAP, and the duties and capabilities of counsellors, including any limitations on their activities.

5  A procedure for *contact with the EAP and referral to counselling*, details of procedures for self-referral and (if appropriate) managerial referral.

6  A definition of *problem assessment procedures*, including diagnosis routes, confidentiality guarantees, timeliness, scope of counsellors' training, as well as their accreditation, competencies, and organizational knowledge.

7  A *protocol* outlining the extent of *short-term counselling and longer-term treatment* and assistance.

8  A statement of the *macro- and micro-linkages with other services* in the community, or with specialist resources or support mechanisms.

9  A procedure for the *follow-up and monitoring of employees* subsequent to their use of the EAP service, with the necessary provisions for their appropriate utilization and deployment.

10   An administrative channel for the *feedback of aggregated statistics* on the age and short- and longer-term outcomes of the EAP, provided by the provider.
11   An *evaluation procedure of individual and corporate benefits* of the EAP, on the most impartial basis that is practical (draws upon EAPA, 1994, EAPA, 1997).

These are the key activities that make EAPs as an entity distinct from other forms of workplace counselling services, whether internal or external. While desirable, these elements are not all to be found as part of most British EAPs.

The focus of other counselling services in the community is still on the provision of similar modes (but organizationally decoupled) and techniques of counselling. The distinctive features of EAPs by comparison with conventional individual employee independent counselling are their comprehensive nature, their organizational linkages to the 'troubled' employee's work context, and their inclusion of evaluation at both individual and corporate levels. This necessarily brief introduction to the key EAP activities will be expanded considerably in other chapters, particularly Chapter 4 on models of EAPs and Chapter 6 on EAP providers.


## WHAT ISSUES ARE COVERED BY AN EAP?


From the start, British programmes have provided counselling for a wide range of concerns, termed a 'broad-brush' approach in EAP terminology. This is in sharp contrast to the (formerly) alcohol- and (latterly) drug-focused programmes more commonly seen in the United States. Other distinctive features of EAPs in Britain include a very much higher proportion of 'self-referrals' than 'managerial referrals', the frequent provision of 24-hour access to telephone counselling services and the inclusion of family members. These and other differences expand the terms of reference of British EAPs, making them in general more broadly based than those typically found in the United States (Berridge & Cooper, 1994a).

It is difficult to identify a standardized range of issues in EAP provision but a 'broad-brush' EAP could include information, advice and counselling on:

**Table 2.1**    *Counselling issues included in a 'broad-brush' EAP*

| | | |
|---|---|---|
| Accident | Goal setting | Retirement |
| AIDS | Grievances | Risks at work |
| Alcohol abuse | Indebtedness | Smoking |
| Bereavement | Induction | Stress (work-extrinsic) |
| Career development | Job change | Stress (work-related) |
| Chronic illness | Job training | Substance abuse |
| Demotion | Lay-off | Suicide |
| Disability | Legal matters | Supervisory styles |
| Disaster | Legal problems | Technology changes |
| Discipline | Literacy | Test failure on job |
| Dismissal | Marital problems | Verbal abuse |
| Divorce | Mental health | Violence |
| Drug abuse | Performance evaluation | Vocational guidance |
| Family problems | Physical fitness | Weight control |
| Financial advice | Promotion | Women's issues |
| Gambling | Racial harassment | Young workers' problems |

*Source:* Adapted from Berridge (1993).

Individual EAP applications might well tackle a more limited range of issues, depending upon the provider's expertise and policies. Alternatively, the employer might identify a narrower range of issues to be covered in response to a wish to concentrate on key problems identified, a restricted range of employees (rather than dependants), or for reasons of cost limitation (Hoskinson & Reddy, 1989).

The potential list covers some of the more commonly found issues on what help may be available within an EAP. But the range of issues potentially capable of being brought to an EAP in modern employment, characterized by change, complexity and stress, can only be expected to grow (Berridge & Cooper, 1994a: 9–10). Given the employer's willingness to fund, and counsellors' training to tackle them, the list of potential issues is almost infinite in the view of one personnel management commentator (Dessler, 1984).

Within a 'broad-brush' EAP, a continuum of severity of presenting symptoms can be constructed as a guide to the appropriate response from the counsellor. This is depicted in Figure 2.2. Clearly, such a diagram cannot be inclusive of every issue, nor represent the client's perceived severity of the issue: it depicts a professional psychological view, and, even within that optic, the labelling of issues on a continuum or the existence of a continuum at all could be the subject of vigorous debate. Nevertheless, several interesting points can be extracted from the representation. First, it serves as an indicator of the wide range of presenting issues that are suitable for counselling within an EAP: these issues cover the great majority of employees concerned over a wide spectrum of troubling factors encountered in present-day employment. Secondly, the continuum is a reminder that the presenting issue in counselling may well not be the latent substantive issue. But it allows both the client and the counsellor to use the possible, or supposedly trivial, trouble or the request for relatively neutral information as a point of entry to the EAP, and as an opportunity to build confidence. Thirdly, it illustrates that the ethically constructed and supervised EAP cannot cope with certain severe issues within the EAP: razor-sharp assessment skills are needed among counsellors accurately to identify and refer on would-be clients whose conditions require therapeutic interventions in the fields of psychoanalysis and medicine, which are well outside the scope of short-term counselling.

## COUNSELLING AND THE ORGANIZATIONAL CONTEXT

The generic activity of counselling does not sit easily with many of the dominant values in organizations, such as those of aggression, entrepreneurialism, achievement and close control. Indeed, counselling or an EAP may be seen cynically as an organizational antidote or 'Bandaid' to mitigate the ravages of such values among the staff members.

Additionally, counselling in general is often misunderstood or viewed in a negative, stereotypical way in society, and consequent by management and those employees who have no experience of the process. One experienced commentator expressed it ruefully:

24

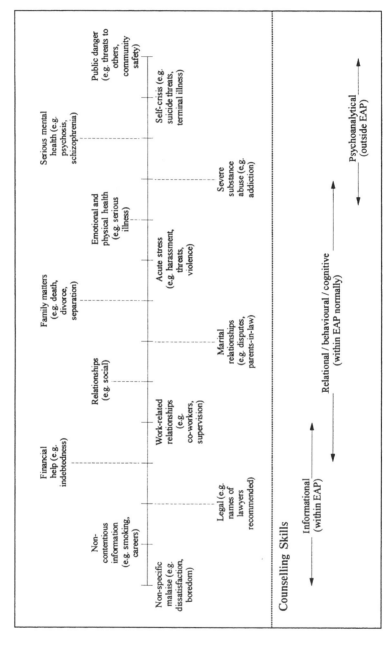

**Figure 2.2** *Presenting issues for EAP counselling and counselling techniques. Source:* Based on an idea and discussion with M. Megranahan

Current stereotypes of counsellors . . . are as varied as they are often wide of the mark. They range from the warm-hearted dispenser of tea and sympathy, to the Viennese accent, full beard and piercing eye of the stage analyst (Hoskinson & Reddy, 1989: 4).

The adoption of the word 'counsellor' by a myriad of occupations (usually sales-related, such as financial counsellor or beauty counsellor, for instance) has further debased its currency.

Another frequent misapprehension is that counselling is an offshoot of psychoanalysis, driven by a medical model that is concerned with treating mental illness by medical–scientific procedures. The counselling model is entirely different, viewing people as basically healthy, and not pathological. Counselling is optimistic and developmental, and assumes that most people in most situations have (or can learn with help) the ability to use their own internal coping to solve their problems. The British Association for Counselling (BAC) definition of counselling builds on this approach:

The task of counselling is to give the client the opportunity to explore, discover and clarify ways of living more resourcefully and towards greater well-being (BAC, 1989: 1.2).

Most counselling within employee assistance is short-term therapy, which accords with this social-psychological model. The counsellor brings professional training and knowledge, experience and skill and a range of perspectives and techniques to help a client at a time of change, choice or crisis. These times are not necessarily negative even for clients, although initially they may seem so: counselling can be an opportunity for the resourceful learning acquisition of problem-solving skills and the creation of new life choices. The counsellor is *not* concerned with passing judgement on the negative or deficit aspects of how people behave, nor aiming at the personal restructuring that can be effected by the psychoanalyst.

Nevertheless, as has been discussed earlier, the counsellor may encounter a situation that is clearly the result of a deep-seated disposition, or showing irretrievable or crisis characteristics. Such instances will need referral for psychoanalysis or other long-term medical treatment. In the British employee-counselling context, such referral will almost always be outside the EAP, and involve specialist facilities within the National Health Service or (if the employers' health insurance cover is extensive) calling upon specialist consultant help in the private health care sector.

## THERAPEUTIC COUNSELLING INTERVENTIONS AND EAPs

Most counselling professional models and interventions used in British EAPs are drawn from three major schools of psychotherapy.

1 Development psychotherapy (psychoanalytic/psychodynamic); for example, including perspectives drawn from Freud, Jung, Klein, Erikson and Winnicott.
2 Cognitive–behavioural; for example, including the contributions of Beck and Ellis.
3 Humanistic; for example, drawing on the work of Rogers.

In practice, most EAP providers, in-house and externally contracted services alike, use a mixed model, including elements from all three schools. The type of issue being worked upon with the client, and its severity of impact, is one significant factor in the choice. The professional training of the counsellor will also predispose the choice of professional model, and be likely to orient substantially those individuals coming from the occupational psychological tradition towards the cognitive–behavioural orientation. By contrast, persons coming from a lay or welfare background are probably more likely to identify with the Rogerian tradition, which has for such people the advantage of being more accessible. Nevertheless, the continuing rapid development of EAPs in Britain often means that the choice of therapeutic interventions is eclectic. Alternatively, in the event of more than one counsellor working with a client, an external contractor provider will have to rely upon the hope that the various professional inputs will prove to be integrated. Such an evaluation or judgment will be left to the contractor's supervising counsellor on a day-to-day basis, or be held over until a periodic review of an individual case either on a lateral (supervisor–counsellor) basis, or on a team basis.

An analytical discussion of the appropriateness of any one therapeutic counselling model is outside the scope of this book. Interested readers are directed toward the original works of the authors cited earlier in this section, and to the multitudinous commentators on their work. Nevertheless, in collaborating with counsellors (in-house or external), the HRM managers and the persons responsible for the EAP should have a clear understanding of the dominant models used, and their potential contra-indications.

## SHORT-TERM COUNSELLING

Traditionally, the majority of counselling (especially outside the work context) has taken place over a relatively extended period of time. Economic realities associated with EAPs' funding, and the ever-increasing waiting lists of clients (Winstanley, 1995) have made the adoption of short-term counselling an industry standard in EAPs. Indeed, very few employing firms will pay directly or indirectly for extended or open-ended counselling. The availability (or its absence) of longer-term counselling assistance within the community has also predisposed EAP providers toward short-term therapies.

Nonetheless, there is much professional evidence from research and practice that short-term therapies (typically three to eight sessions) can be effective with the great majority of clients and their presenting problems. This apparent effectiveness may be a function of clients' expectations or of the troubles that they experience in their current work life (Smith & McKee, 1993). But even if many traditional counsellors are uncomfortable with the notion and practice of brief therapy, the founding fathers were known to use it: Freud is reported to have treated the noted conductor Bruno Walter in six sessions. Whatever its driving forces, short-term therapy is developing its professional credentials as a suitable method in the panoply of therapeutic approaches.

## CONCLUSION

The EAP in Britain in less than two decades has demonstrated itself to be an enduring phenomenon of professional psychological practice, as well as being a functional technique available for management to provide as an employee benefit. Employee counselling is also an evolving phenomenon, whether in its practice models, or in its responses to emerging social problems. Ten years ago it would have been unimaginable to consider that employee counsellors would routinely be proficient in dealing with clients on issues like AIDS and HIV, or on negative housing equity. At the time of writing, the authors wonder whether counselling on troubles about BSE and CJD (supposed or confirmed) will be sources of clients' worries in five years' time. But EAP practice is developing solidity and robustness in both clients' and employers' perceptions, as well as in an increasing number of affiliate counsellors' eyes in professional terms.

# 3
# History of Counselling in the Workplace in Britain

## A BRIEF HISTORICAL PERSPECTIVE: FROM PHILANTHROPY TO EMPLOYEE ASSISTANCE PROGRAMMES (EAPs)

In Britain, the welfare of employees at work has a long history, dating back to the late eighteenth century, and is intertwined with British social, economic, technological and religious evolution in a complex and unique web of influences. Many of these original influences are still present, albeit in modified forms. A brief survey of the characteristics of Britain's early industrialization in the late eighteenth and nineteenth centuries can illustrate their nature and impact upon workpeople, and hence the need for welfare provision historically.

In social terms, from the early nineteenth century the demand for labour on the part of the emerging industries and the large towns provoked major movements of population, creating what Marx and many other commentators designated the rootless urban proletariat, whose family patterns and kinship networks had been severely disrupted, no longer serving as support mechanisms and role models. Economically, the competition for markets between manufacturers meant a downward pressure on wages, anti-social working hours and patterns, and risks to workers' physical health and safety. All of these were unfamiliar and upsetting conditions, especially to first generation industrialized employees. The increasing use of machine technologies demanded of workers a new intensity, exactitude and discipline in work, which was very different from the demands of an agrarian society. Finally, against such a backdrop of change in the world of work, Britain experienced a religious fervour, ranging from the relatively moderate Wesleyanism in the eighteenth century, to the often radical non-conformist protestant zeal of the nineteenth century industrial cities and towns. Such moral and religious concerns also extended to the well-being of the new factory classes and touched those employers who possessed religious convictions, as did many of the new non-conformist industrialists (such as Owen of New Lanark or the Gregs at Styal), or Quakers (such as the Frys or Rowntrees). These concerns also influenced philanthropists and politicians (such as Shaftesbury) or religious leaders (such as Booth) and were translated into legislation (such as the Factories Acts from 1802 onwards) or social action (such as the Salvation Army).

For the new factory working classes suffered work-related deprivation and stress, but in different ways from those experienced today by the typical white-collar tertiary employee. The symptoms were different, being more often those of physical ill-health, premature incapacitation or death, malnutrition, overwork and mental breakdown. The responses to such problems on the part of wider society and of employers (as far as they existed) were both humanitarian and economically oriented. They can be subsumed in their various guises under the generic label of welfare. Employment legislation was enacted, protecting especially young persons and women. Industrial accident and illness requirements, protection and reporting were instituted. Statutory provisions were put in place for public health. Religious and social crusades grew up, such as the Salvation Army. Civic initiatives, such as public sanitation, hospitals and education, were aimed at physical and mental health. All these measures and initiatives began to create the framework of employee protection.

But it was the employer who had the largest potential for focused employee welfare activity. Over and above minimal statutory compliance, employers had a vested interest in having a healthy, committed and compliantly-dependent workforce. If effort and money spent in calculated and controlled quantities on employee welfare could deliver these outcomes, the result could be productivity, continuity of production and quality, predictability of costs and an anticipation of control, authority and discipline. When welfare coincided also with employers' religious and humanistic principles, so much the better. Hence, from the early nineteenth century onwards, welfare provisions appeared in industry in the form of works' doctors and nurses, first aid, welfare helpers and social assistance, safety checkers, chaplains, almoners, employee self-help groups, even lay assistance from members of owners' families (usually the womenfolk). Gradually, during the nineteenth century, such provisions became more extensive and in the case of enlightened employers with moral principles (e.g. Cadburys, Lever, and Salt) they became comprehensive programmes.

But most of such efforts were usually little co-ordinated and relatively unsystematic, lacking a coherent unifying rationale or practice. Their practice was encouraged officially in the First World War, when welfare provision was legally required to support the employment of women in industry, notably in munitions production. Only a few years before, in 1913, the noted social reformer Seebohm Rowntree had led the formation of the Association of Welfare Officers, which was the direct ancestor of the Institute of Personnel Management (IPM) and Institute of Personnel Development (IPD) (Thomason, 1976; Anthony & Crighton, 1969).

In the period from the end of the First World War to the enactment of the programme of national social re-engineering by the Labour administrations between 1945 and 1951, the provision of industrial welfare was a regular feature of employee services and benefits in certain industrial firms, particularly the large bureaucratized companies like ICI or Shell, as well as in the Civil Service and other areas of the public sector. The motives for such an expansion of welfare included the economistic and humanitarian principles of the nineteenth century. But also new concerns were being expressed, such as a belief in corporate responsibility within a liberal democracy, and a desire to provide an employer-led initiative to offset the growing pull of trade unions on workers' loyalties and orientations. So a broad panoply of welfare was created among prominent employers covering occupational health, safety, advice and welfare officers, social and cultural amenities, housing, recreational and sports facilities, retirees' and family activities, and many other specific localized provisions. This period might be termed the 'high-water mark' of conventional welfare, especially in professionally managed large organizations operating in stable product and labour markets (Martin, 1967).

The creation in Britain of the welfare state by the Labour administrations of 1945–1951, and especially the implementation in 1948 of the National Health Service Act (1946), signalled a sea change in attitudes and provisions concerning industrial welfare. The focus of the Act was on physical medical treatment, free for all at the point of delivery, irrespective of the causation, including work injuries and disease. Mental health was included, but undoubtedly it was the Cinderella of the service—in spite of the growing evidence of a rising incidence of mental illness and stress, much of the latter being work-related. Additionally, other legislation covered social issues such as poverty, low incomes, housing, pensions, children's and family matters. Employers found themselves funding part of these new benefits through taxation, whether ostensibly through national insurance con-tributions or indirectly through increased corporate taxation. Hence, with an increasing abandonment of altruism, they began to expect employees to seek solutions to their own health and social welfare issues through the state provision. In practical terms, they objected to paying for such services, once in their budgets and then again in taxation, and consequently ran down their own welfare services, often to minimal levels of statutory observance of safety and health legislation.

By the late 1970s, welfare in Britain was not only a greatly reduced activity in volume, it was also a role to which personnel practitioners were extremely adverse, and with which they did not wish to be identified (Torrington & Chapman, 1978). Personnel staff viewed welfare as low level, low status, and low influence, and at variance with the business–professional image and function that they were in the process of creating. Welfare issues activities were further under pressure into the 1980s, as economic and financial demands for cost-cutting and demonstrable cost-effectiveness identified them as a soft target for abolition or further reduction as a routine provision of employee benefit. Welfare only came into prominence occasionally in conditions of downsizing, large-scale redundancies or closures, when special limited-term programmes were put in place—notably outplacement services, financial advice or retraining initiatives, as with the British Steel Corporation.

Yet these same corporate demands for economies had an obverse effect—that of requiring increased performance from those human resources that remained in work. The unintended results of such demands frequently were work-related stress and ill-health, an accentuation of anti-social behaviour, such as alcoholism and drug abuse, wider questions of social adjustment, such as family or relationship problems, and personal financial pressures, as well as issues of the rising incidence of lateness, absenteeism, accidents and injuries. The same economic pressures that had all but eliminated the welfare function had also greatly slimmed down personnel departments, which over and above a distaste for welfare, often now found themselves without the staff or expertise to tackle these newly-pressing issues. With the subsequent advent of Human Resources Management (HRM) and more transfer of responsibility for people-related matters back to line management, time and expertise were even more lacking. Furthermore, conflicts of interest and confidentiality arose if employees were to seek advice or help from the management staff members who were themselves in a position of power and authority and who were instigating some of the activities that led to stress.

Into this context in Britain in the mid-1980s, the advent occurred of the EAP. Many variations of provision exist, but broadly they can be considered as a contemporary version of welfare, adapted to current organizational needs and environments, and to individuals' perceptions of the wide variety of problems experienced as an employee in an advanced post-industrial society.

## THE INITIAL DEVELOPMENT OF EAPs IN THE UNITED STATES

The origins of the EAP are customarily traced back to US origins, and in particular to two seminal activities. The first of these is the foundation of Alcoholics Anonymous (AA) at Akron, Ohio in 1935 (Masi, 1984). The social pressure method and the subsequent development of the 12-step procedure of AA were at the heart of alcoholism campaigns in the United States from the 1940s onwards, which were usually led by lay people, often reformed alcoholics. From the 1960s, occupational alcoholism programmes became increasingly professionalized, being run more by social work specialists and extended into drug and substance abuse from about 1970 onward (Good, 1986). A substantial boost to employee counselling came with the passing of the Hughes Act (Alcohol Abuse and Alcohol Treatment Act) in 1970; it enabled the institution of programmes at federal and state level, and the foundation of the National Institute of Alcohol Abuse and Alcoholism (NIAAA). This state support and the NIAAA's publicity were central in transforming EAPs from a limited-scope activity in a few large corporations to a wide social movement (Pigors & Myers, 1977: 384–386). Subsequent refinements of the US corporate EAP have been increasingly 'broad-brush'—that is, extending coverage to a wider range of social issues, and broadening the field of therapeutic attention to the wider role set and familial context.

The second origin is arguably less procedural but more influential in attitudinal terms: it is one of the spin-offs of the celebrated Hawthorne studies of Mayo in the Chicago plant belonging to Western Electric, documented by Roethlisberger & Dickson (1939). A programme of employee advice and counselling grew out of the Hawthorne studies. It was manned [sic] by lay counsellors drawn from supervision and management, and was clearly aimed not only at promoting the social and psychological adjustment of the employee at work, but also at ensuring employee conformity and productivity within corporate objectives. As a result, the counselling link in EAPs in the United States also became seen as legitimately oriented toward achieving integration of corporate goals and individual employee behaviour.

The growth of EAPs in the United States has been impressive in extent at least. In 1972 there were 300 programmes recorded; in 1979, some 5000 programmes; by 1987 about 9000–12 000 instances were cited, mainly in the larger to medium-sized organizations (Berridge & Cooper, 1993b). Estimations from 1989 onwards persistently state that 75%–80% of the top *Fortune 500* companies operate an EAP (Luthans & Waldersee, 1989). Reportedly, the recent extension of EAPs into small- and medium-sized companies has been relatively slow (EAPA, 1992), yet about 25% of all US workers are covered by an EAP-type programme involving at least assistance with alcohol and drug abuse or mental health care.

## THE SPREAD OF EAPs OUTSIDE THE UNITED STATES

The introduction of US-model EAPs to other countries can be attributed (Roman & Blum, 1992) to a number of influences. First, there is the clear evidence of US international companies introducing EAPs with the goal of enhancing performance when faced abroad with opportunistic internalities similar to those at home, such as cost reduction, quality and reliability improvements and the increasing need for the adaptability of products and services to particular markets. Secondly, there are equally cogent instances of these companies turning to EAPs to tackle their problematic internalities, such as absenteeism, presenteeism, labour turnover, burnout, breakdown, maladaptation at individual and corporate levels, and general under-performance because of personal 'troubles' and 'stresses'. Other evidence instances the spread of EAPs in Europe to be owing to some extent to their use by the military and (especially) in US military hospitals; the internationalization of management and particularly US-style MBA training; and the trend to corporate imitation among self-designated top international corporations.

The direct, unmodified cross-national transfer of social institutions, in which the EAP can be included, is problematic and uncertain. Both anthropological theory and practical experience reinforce this conclusion. The anthropologist will point to the complex interaction of societal sub-systems that create and support any social institution. However admirable its characteristics and operation in one society, any contrived replication of any one country's social institutions to another country is unlikely to work as planned. For instance, the family system of modern China (a controversial case) would be almost certainly of extremely limited potential for establishment in (for example) Cuban society. However careful the transplantation and introduction from Shanghai to Havana, only a few elements of such social engineering would be likely to take root in the Caribbean, and very probably for other reasons than those prevalent in China.

Accordingly, it is not surprising to find that a time-lag appeared between the first widespread adoption of EAPs in the United States in the early 1970s, and the commencement of their significant presence in Britain in the mid-1980s. In spite of the outward similarities in corporate ownership patterns and employment markets, there was no rush into Britain of EAP contractors, nor of indigenous or implanted companies wishing to inaugurate their own in-house EAPs. The delay probably also reflected the deep extent of the cultural pervasion of the US-model EAP, the difficulty of its adaptation to other cultural and economic contexts, and the discouraging commercial results when contractor providers tried to export their unmodified EAP products to other countries. Even up to the mid-1990s, only a minority of commercial EAP providers in Britain have adopted US practice models in a virtually unchanged form. Certain US-owned companies operating internationally have followed (initially at least) the exemplars of their home-based EAPs in the creation of in-house EAPs.

## THE INITIAL GROWTH OF EAPs IN BRITAIN

No clear historical link is readily identifiable *at the programme level* between the EAP and the welfare and employee advice activity, as traditionally practised in Britain independently of work-instigated or related issues. At individual counsellor level, however, many instances occur of the same persons (whether counsellor or client) being involved in both activities. Indeed, the practice of individual client counselling outside EAPs, for instance, through general practitioner referral, continues strongly in Britain; sometimes such a referral is within organizational provision via occupational health or (more often) outside it. Additionally, many of the pre-existent intellectual, therapeutic and professional practice models of individual counsellors from pre-EAP days have been carried over entirely validly (if eclectically) into practice within EAPs. The programmatic aspects of EAPs and their integration with the workplace and performance issues, however, represent the distinctive difference between EAPs and earlier provisions of welfare.

In Britain, the first EAPs appeared on an in-house basis around 1980, notably in the electronics, chemicals and oil industries. They were closely linked to EAP practice in the US parent companies, but soon demonstrated, even at this developmental stage, characteristics that reflected programmatic adaptation to local conditions which included:

- a high extent of counsellor independence from corporate concerns, and a reluctance by affiliate counsellors to be exposed to corporate information
- a reluctance to encourage supervisors or managers to confront troubled employees or to instigate problem diagnosis at the referral stage
- a high proportion of self-referrals
- an absence of any role for the EAP in disciplinary or grievance procedures or other formal organizational strategies of control
- a 'broad-brush' scope, comprising counselling availability not only for the employee, but also for her or his immediate family
- further 'broad-brush' extensions, moving out from the narrow range of traditional major EAP issues of alcoholism, drugs and mental health into wider socio-economic, legal and family issues
- often being capitation-based for all current employees, covered without co-payments on the employee's part, nor cost-limited, nor insurance-funded, nor on a fee-for-service basis (as often in the United States), although this last characteristic is being introduced in Britain in some instances
- being usually characterized by 'brief counselling' (if necessary, referring clients on to other specialized services, often within the state-funded or not-for-profit sectors) rather than the US assessment *and* treatment model
- much initial client contact being through specialist counselling by telephone, available 24 hours per day

- little integration of the EAP into corporate personnel or human resources tactical activities, and a reluctance by employers to use it as a corporate tool
- a less routinized and less standardized routine sequence of stages for processing clients, by comparison with US practices of 'core technologies' (Blum & Roman, 1988)

These themes are developed further in various parts of the book, but this brief overview will serve to demonstrate initially that British practice is beginning to differentiate the British EAP as a 'uniquely British phenomenon' (Highley & Cooper, 1995).

## THE DEVELOPMENT OF THE EAP IN BRITAIN

From the mid-1980s onward, EAPs expanded considerably in Britain in many industrial sectors outside those in which they were originally introduced, and away from in-house employee counselling services. Employers' motives were various, as were the commercial contractor providers, since the majority of British EAPs became externally sourced. Some of the emerging EAP companies grew out of transatlantic parents (for instance, in electronics and computing), but most grew indigenously out of the entrepreneurship of occupational psychologists, occupational health staff and related professions. Other origins of British EAP provider organizations were extensions of existing companies in the insurance, health care and personnel consultancy fields.

The British Association for Counselling (BAC) has played a unique part in establishing professional codes of practice, training standards and definitions for counsellors and counselling. The Clinical Division of the British Psychological Society (BPS) equally played an important role in psychologist accreditation and training criteria. IPM, through a specialist group, assessed the contribution that EAPs could make to general and specialist objectives of managing people at work (IPM, 1992). But the dominant influence has come to be the UK Employee Assistance Professionals Association (EAPA). Created on the principles of the EAPA in the United States, and retaining close reciprocal links, the British association has made a major input to codes of practice and professional guidelines in the context of British EAP philosophy and operations (EAPA, 1994).

The take-up of EAPs in Britain has been slower and more sporadic than occurred in the United States during the period of expansion there in the decade from the late 1970s onward. A number of reasons may be cited for this relative hesitancy in Britain:

- an underlying worry that EAPs were an inappropriate import from the United States
- the lack of a cost incentive in terms of pressure on employers' health insurance premiums for employees' mental health treatment
- the lower awareness among employers of losses to the organization incurred as a result of employees suffering stress, or subject to alcohol or drugs abuse
- a reticence to adopt a comprehensive EAP-type approach to 'troubled' employees, because of a traditional (if perhaps misplaced) respect for individuals' independence and privacy
- a desire to obtain such services without cost or concern to the employer through the employee's family doctor or from the National Health Service
- a belief that such counselling services were sufficiently available in-house through other provisions such as the occupational health department, personnel department resources, or via line managers informally
- a lack of familiarity with counselling services on the part of employees, and a consequent distrust of them
- grave suspicions on the part of trade unions regarding the independence and confidentiality of work-related counselling, especially the potential link between EAPs and disciplinary and dismissal procedures
- a lack of compulsion from high awards for damages resulting from stress-based actions by employees instancing employers' deleterious actions or neglect as a basis for litigation
- an absence of positive official or governmental recognition of work-originated stress as a substantive and material origin of malfunction and under-performance at work—for example, on the part of the ministries responsible for health or

employment, or the Health and Safety Commission, until well into the 1990s

An additional factor that is less capable of being documented is the reluctance of certain professional psychologists to be involved with a mental health programme that was so closely associated with corporate objectives of productivity, discipline and cost-effectiveness. It was therefore relatively difficult for in-house programmes and independent contractors alike to receive appropriate professional recognition and status, and hence to attract able professional colleagues and to establish distinctive British standards of practice.

## THE CONFIGURATION OF THE EAP INDUSTRY IN BRITAIN

The extent of the EAP industry in Britain is hard to quantify and to describe, since no comprehensive standardized and undisputed statistics exist. No procedure or requirement exists for the registration of EAP providers, nor does the term EAP have any legal protection for its use. The UK EAPA seeks to unite providers with a business–professional framework, but has some significant absentees from membership. The reasons may range from provider firms' inability or unwillingness to stand scrutiny of their activities, to highly principled professional objections to joining an organization that has a commercial function in promoting the EAP industry. Neither do other organizations keep a reliable record of the EAP industry. Professional bodies such as the BAC, United Kingdom College of Psychiatrists (UKCP), or Institute of Personal Development (IPD) could assume such an overall registration role. By extension, governmental ministries and agencies such as the Departments of Health, Trade and Industry, Education and Employment, or the Health and Safety Executive (HSE) could keep records, if not assume a regulatory role.

The statistics given below are based on the HSE survey data, (Highley & Cooper, 1995) gathered in 1995 by the Manchester School of Management and extrapolated to provide an estimation of the total industry characteristics. Responses were gathered from most major providers of EAPs in Britain, as well as from certain smaller or restricted scope providers of EAPs, including counselling-only services.

All known external providers were contacted with a request for information on various parameters of the EAP industry. In all categories of enquiry, a majority response was obtained, in some cases over 80%. The following data on the EAP industry in Britain are computed from the HSE Report (Highley and Cooper, 1995) on the basis of the authors' judgment, with extrapolation of the statistics and interpretation of missing values. Considerable caution is therefore recommended in regarding this statement of EAP coverage as definitive. In particular, it was problematic to distinguish between full-scale EAPs, and varying degrees of employee counselling programmes, which could approach EAPs in various respects of scope of provision and integration into the client organizations.

The size of the EAP industry in Britain and its configuration is given in Table 3.1. The calculated overall coverage in 1995 of external EAP and employee counselling contractors amounts to 1 285 000 employees, which represents between 5% and 6% of the working population in Britain who potentially have access to EAP provision—excluding the self-employed, agricultural and military employees. This estimation is in line with the opinion of Reddy (1994) that:

> improbable as it may have seemed . . . around one million UK employees (and their families in many cases) will by the end of 1994 be included under the EAP umbrella—however flimsy or primitive some early UK models remain in design and capability (Reddy, 1994: 61).

By comparison with the United States, where up to 25% of all employees are covered by EAPs, this current proportion of coverage in Britain apparently allows considerable scope for future EAP expansion. Information was not collected on the extent of concentration of EAPs in certain industrial sectors, or in large and high-profile organizations. But interviews with EAP and provider companies indicated that larger organizations were the most likely to institute EAPs. Estimates of EAPs in the US *Fortune Top 500* companies, regularly indicate that 75% to 80% of such firms have EAPs (US Department of Labor, 1990). The evidence of such trends in Britain suggests that the concentration

**Table 3.1** Extent and configuration of EAP and employee counselling provision in Britain—1995

| EAP and employee counselling providers | Number of employees covered by EAP | Number of contracted organizations | Average number of | | Per capita (employee) fee structure per year | | |
|---|---|---|---|---|---|---|---|
| | | | employees per contract | contracts per provider | High | Low | Mean |
| Major providers (n = 11) | 768 000 | 282 | 2723 | 25.6 | £40.00 | £15.00 | £24.00 approx. |
| Other EAP providers (n = 25) | 517 000 | 317 | 1631 | 12.7 | £57.00 | £21.00 | £25.00 approx. |
| Total providers (n = 36) | 1 285 000 | 599 | 2145 | 16.6 | n.a. | n.a. | £23.92 (weighted) |

*Source:* HSE Report (Highley & Cooper, 1995).
*Notes* 1  All figures computed with extrapolation of missing values.
      2  Figures on 'other providers' include some counselling-only provisions.
      3  In-house EAP and employee counselling provisions not included.

does not yet approach the US density. Nevertheless, there is evidence that industrial concentration of the British EAP industry is starting to appear, based on disaggregation of these figures, as shown in Table 3.2.

The three leading EAP providers (in terms of the number of contracts held) are beginning to build a dominant position in the industry. Their coverage of employees is 2.34 times proportionately more than their numerical presence among providers. By comparison, the next eight providers' ratio is 1.81, and that of the remaining 25 providers is 0.58. Such a configuration of the EAP industry indicates that the leading three providers do not have a marked numerical superiority of provision over the following eight providers—although the position of the leading single provider is clearly dominant in the leading three companies.

It is to be expected then that market forces will dictate that rationalization will occur among the following eight EAP provider companies by means of mergers or withdrawals from the industry. In this manner, the industrial configuration will begin to show the characteristics of a more mature industrial sector. It is likely that provider companies will exploit factors such as economies of scale, development of professional and marketing expertise, and linkages with parent companies and associated providers of other human services, such as general health care, specialized hospitals, and personnel advisory and information services.

**Table 3.2**  *Industrial concentration in British EAP and employee counselling providers*

|  | Total identified providers (%) | Total contracts held (%) | Total employees covered (%) |
|---|---|---|---|
| Top three external providers | 8.3 | 28.9 | 19.5 |
| Following eight external providers (excluding top three) | 22.2 | 18.2 | 40.3 |
| Remaining other 25 external providers | 69.5 | 52.9 | 40.2 |

*Source:* Highley & Cooper, 1995.

Among the following 25 providers (in size of provision terms), some will probably remain in this final category for reasons, for instance, of original conception, tied clients or individual corporate strategy or owners' personal wishes. The EAP industry is remarkably open to individual professional entrepreneurs, given its lack of demands for a large and complex fixed capital structure as a condition of entrance. Neither are revenue cost implications a deterrent factor preventing entry of new small firms, since professional counselling services can be sourced on a part-time, fee-for-service basis. But a degree of structural fluidity can be expected to occur in the future, in an industry where both entry costs and exit costs are relatively small.

The propensity of professionals in the psychological disciplines to networking (which is at the heart of counselling provisions for the referral and treatment) will always ensure the opportunity for new entrants to the EAP industry on a localized basis, in a specialist sector of counselling, or in response to new needs from client organizations. Equally, companies operating in industrial sectors contingent to EAPs (for instance, insurance companies, business consultancies, health care providers, legal or financial professional firms, etc.) may seek a presence in the EAP field as a support to their core business, and to be able to provide a wide and seamless service to clients.

Such hypotheses of the future industrial configuration of the EAP and employee counselling industry assume no major environmental change in the industrial sector. Nevertheless, such environmental turbulence could be occasioned by a radical change in National Health Service (NHS) provision and funding, or by a major revision in the NHS basis of charging clients referred from EAP or employee counselling providers. Another potential discontinuous change could be a more onerous legal liability on employers for compensation to be made to 'troubled' employees as a result of an extension of current health and safety statutes, or landmark judgements in civil actions. A final future threat could lie in employers' insurance cover, provided as an employee benefit, or as part of pension provisions. If claims rise as a result of employment-related causes, then premiums will do so also. The consequence will be pressure by insurers and the employers alike for a managed care approach towards the employees' well-being and assistance (Reddy, 1994).

The financial dimensions of the EAP and employee counselling industry remain enigmatic. The principle is of a commercial activity in which income is on a capitation basis, and expenditure on counselling fees (the major outgoing) is largely on a fee-for-service basis in arrears. One respondent in a provider contractor company described it as currently having the appearance of a licence to print money (Highley & Cooper, 1995). Additionally, as has been discussed, the institutional barriers to entry to the EAP market remain almost non-existent in Britain—in the absence of mandatory statutory professional certification, and the weakness of enforcement of criteria of best practice. Equally, the financial obstacles to entry are small, providing that the new business operates on a small scale, or in a protected market (such as the NHS), or in a restricted geographical or industrial segment. Nevertheless, there have been financial casualties in the EAP market, with amalgamations or withdrawals of financial support by a powerful patron organization. So far, no bankruptcies have occurred among major provider organizations, confirming the underlying optimism concerning the financial opportunities in the EAP and counselling industry in Britain.

An analysis of the financial situation of EAP and employee counselling providers was only a secondary objective of the HSE-sponsored research. The tentative results on this dimension are given in Table 3.3.

**Table 3.3**   *Financial dimensions of the EAP and employee counselling industry*

| Provider | Estimated percentage of market (%) | Estimated annual average total revenue (£m) | Estimated annual average revenue per provider (£1m) |
|---|---|---|---|
| Top three providers in size (volume) | 19.5 | 6.0 | 2.0 |
| Next eight providers in size (volume) | 40.3 | 12.3 | 1.5 |
| Following 25 providers by size (volume) | 40.2 | 12.2 | 0.5 |
| Total | 100.0 | 30.5 | 0.85 |

*Source:* HSE Report (Highley & Cooper, 1995).

The authors' impression is that these statistics understate considerably the extent of the British EAP and employee counselling industry. The industry has almost certainly grown since the collection of this data in 1994. It is revealing to note that the considerable development of the industry in Britain has occurred since 1985 in economic conditions that were generally adverse. The capacity of the EAP industry to 'buck the trend' must surely be a recognition of the highly functional nature of the EAP in stringent economic conditions.

The size of the EAP industry in Britain (estimated at £30.5 million annually) probably is a shortfall on the actual annual revenue, since it was difficult to contact smaller providers of employee counselling services. The estimate also does not take account of independent counsellors, for whom employment-related counselling is a part (sometimes a significant proportion) of their professional activity. Neither does the estimation include the in-house EAP or employee counselling services, which are central programmes in prominent organizations such as British Telecommunications, the Post Office, British Airways, Conoco, Zeneca, Customs and Excise, DTI or Barclays Bank as well as many others at times of crisis. If the estimates from the HSE Report survey are valid and the extent of EAP (or similar) coverage in Britain is around 5%–6% of all employees, then the prospects for expansion of employee counselling are very considerable. Should the overall EAP coverage of around 25% be obtained (as found in the United States), then the potential market for externally sourced EAPs in Britain is around £150 million annually, apart from in-house provisions, which probably represent a further 25%–30% of the market.

Should the extent of this potential market be widely known among companies specialized in the provision of human services, it is very possible that major new entrants to the industry will appear. Given the capacity for the profitable operation of EAPs in conditions of economic stringency, and for the rationalization and routinization of professional services and subsequent cost reductions, major investors could be attracted from contingent sectors (such as health care and legal or financial services) where margins are under pressure, regulation is increasingly oppressive, and profits are even more hard to win.

At the same time, it is always likely that a number of small specialist or limited-scope providers with low overheads will always challenge the market leaders in defined sub-sectors. As in other service industries, the companies likely to feel the financial squeeze are the medium-sized companies, who lack both the economies of scale and the resources to engage in the research and product development that characterize the large providers. For such companies the necessary conditions for survival are likely to be either a captive market or the continuing support of a parent organization for whom they represent an essential complementary business function. Otherwise, for the medium-sized companies, merger or take-over by a major provider appear to be the main hope of ensuring survival.

## CONCLUSIONS

Welfare in British industry has moved a very long distance from its nineteenth-century image and origins. New technologies and new jobs have produced needs that are very different from Victorian times. The balance between state provision and employers' initiatives has fluctuated over the period. Social problems (and public attitudes toward them) have changed considerably. New therapeutic approaches and occupations have evolved, as have the costs of helping employees. Such changes do not mean that welfare must disappear completely. In some companies and communities, old patterns are still valued, as with the industrial chaplaincy movement or some traditional areas of occupational health and safety.

Yet the advent of the EAP and its impact on present forms of employee counselling probably mean that disinterested welfare, loosely and only distantly linked to organizational needs is unlikely again to have a large place among employee benefits in Britain. The new EAP model will undoubtedly evolve in future environments. But while it is functionally relevant to employers and employees, it looks set to acquire greater prominence and to be more widely adopted in Britain in the future.

# 4
# Models of EAPs

## INTRODUCTION: REASONS FOR ABSENCE OF EXPLICIT MODELS IN PRACTICE

Most analysts of Employee Assistance programmes (EAPs) comment that there are no universally accepted models of EAPs, and that a wide diversity of approaches can be found in practice. No dominant model can be argued to exist, and it would probably be unrealistic to assert that EAPs are clearly moving in a single direction (let alone convergence) toward acceptance of some pattern of preferred practice, other than in the most general sense. In Britain, professional associations such as the British Association for Counselling (BAC) or the Employee Assistance Professionals Association (EAPA) are seeking to promote standards of professional conduct, and standards of practice responsibility within the industrial or service sector of EAPs. While laudable and, indeed, necessary, both these bodies and those like them, especially in the United States, either take for granted, or regard as outside their scope, the programme models that underpin the provision of the EAP service in a professional manner.

This relative neglect may be due to a number of reasons:

1  The cross-disciplinary nature of the EAP, combining as it does such diverse inputs as psychology, sociology, medicine and politics, renders the formulation of over-arching theoretical

models both complex and disputed on speciality lines (Berridge & Cooper, 1993a: 93–94).

2 The origin of much EAP practice was in the occupational alcoholism movement, which was characterized in its early days by lay leadership by persons with no clinical training: the result was an emphasis on process skills rather than on model and theory construction, other than in limited and short-range terms (Murphy, 1995: 43).

3 EAPs are close to corporate fortunes, fads and fashions, so that specificity of design and pragmatism become the drivers of individual programmes in companies, and the determinants of success for professional providers of EAPs outside the organization (Cunningham, 1994: 14).

4 The ownership of EAPs was often disputed between personnel (or human resources, HR) managers, professional counsellors and financial officers and, and as a consequence, a compromise between opposing viewpoints had to be sought conceptually and operationally. This compromise is usually more of an empirical 'fix' and less of a rigorously constructed model based on principles.

Additionally, professional EAP counsellors are likely to be more concerned with their therapeutic theoretical models at the interface with the client, rather than at their interface with the EAP system, or the system's interface with the organization. Hence, basic explanatory theory, change theory and practice theory are likely to be prime concerns for the counsellor. Practice models of the EAP at the organizational level are likely to be seen as constraints at worst or opportunities at best, but not central to the core of individual practice. This may explain in part why individual counsellors in private practice can also work with equanimity on a part-time basis within EAPs of widely differing natures. Unfortunately, managements who are considering adoption of an EAP rarely consider the underlying models, other than in the most utilitarian manner. Their concern tends to be with economic and financial consequences, with control and insurance aspects, perhaps even with industrial relations, personnel management or even with humanistic cultural messages given to employees.

The following sections will deal first with procedural–classificatory models of EAPs, based largely on their structural–administrative characteristics. Next, the 'core technologies' model will be examined with its concentration on a programmatic sequence of types of intervention. Finally, the ideal typical approach will be discussed, using a structural–functional approach in a systems optic.

## PROCEDURAL–CLASSIFICATORY MODELS OF EAPs

The procedural–classificatory models analyse the difference between EAPs on the basis of a number of criteria that can be aggregated into various commonly found combinations. As a result, a classification of EAPs can be constructed as a basis for analysis. The criteria can include:

- the physical location of the service (on or off the worksite)
- the locus of direct control of the service (provided by in-house employee counsellors, or by external counsellors)
- the extent of counselling services provided (whether referral and assessment only, or extended into short- or long-term counselling)
- the period of time over which counselling normally is provided (whether constrained in the number of sessions or open-ended within the programme)

These criteria have a number of implications that will often follow in the case of an EAP showing particular procedural characteristics, but that are not regarded as *defining* characteristics in this model. The implications include:

- whether the EAP is staffed by lay counsellors or professional staff, and at which stage of the EAP sequence
- whether the EAP procedure involves corporate line management, and in what role
- whether the EAP has a connection (input or output) with other organizational control mechanisms, such as the performance review and appraisal, development, and disciplinary processes

Such secondary and downstream considerations are essentially technical choices that are internal to the operation of the

EAP, rather than initial definitional characteristics. In practice these matters can assume large proportions in the eyes of the decision-makers or actors within the system.

The classificatory model of Hellan (1986) in Table 4.1 illustrates well the procedural approach to models of EAPs, and is based on the criteria listed above in this chapter.

The identification of the key actors in the EAP process and their roles is made by this model, but the wide range of their values and practice modes renders this model useful only as a preliminary classification (Berridge & Cooper, 1993b: 93).

This model is not to be interpreted as a sequence along which a particular EAP progresses, although numerous US examples have done so. In Britain, type 1 is a less frequently found origin, because of the lower prominence in Europe of the industrial alcoholism movement. Type 2 often is a product of an age of corporate affluence dating from the 1970s when EAPs were in the embryonic stage in Britain, except in a few US-owned corporations. Type 3 has long existed informally, but from the 1980s has been under considerable pressure from two sources—larger numbers of more-troubled employees in more highly stressed organizations, and a run-down of state-funded community health provision, especially in mental health. It is not a formal provision in Britain at the present time, and open-ended treatment is not a typical British concept in employee counselling. Type 4 accordingly tends currently to be the favoured model by employers in Britain, (see Chapter 7) meeting as it does their imperatives of devolution of non-core activities,

**Table 4.1**  *Models of EAP—procedural classificatory approaches—1*

| Type no. | Characteristics | Commentary |
| --- | --- | --- |
| 1 | In-house, lay assessment and referral if needed | Reflects origins in industrial alcoholism movement |
| 2 | In-house professional assessment and referral | 'Classic' US model of earlier EAPs |
| 3 | Open-ended treatment often with self-referral | Reliance on community health resources in many instances |
| 4 | Closed-end full service, usually short-term counselling | Cost-effective EAP model, external contractors used |

*Source:* Based on Hellan (1986); Fleisher & Kaplan (1988).

market testing for quality, cost, benefit and flexibility in continuation of EAP provision. But all types continue to be found in Britain, even if type 2 tends to be associated with a few larger corporations, particularly those that are US-owned.

A development of the procedural classificatory model is provided by Masi & Friedland (1988) in Table 4.2 who use many of the same elements as Hellan (1986) does with a less implicit sequence of types.

This model is driven primarily by the nature of the provider of the EAP, being less centred on the nature of the counselling service. It is not axiomatic that a certain type of provider will *sui generis* furnish a certain type of EAP service. Nonetheless, the authors of the model may well have assumed that they are very likely to do so in the context of a mature EAP industry and a high level of professionalization among providers' staff members. One of the main insights resulting from the distinctions between the types in this model lies in the extent of integration of the EAP into corporate objectives and even procedures. Alternatively, whether it is operated independently, with little awareness or consideration of corporate goals, by comparison with the needs of the individual client. Current British practice tends to be a mixture of categories 2 and 4.

***Table 4.2***   *Models of EAP—procedural approaches—2*

| Type no. | Characteristics | Commentary |
|---|---|---|
| 1 | In-house: integrates with corporate policies, and all staff are directly employed | Employer-controlled, hence may lead to conflicts of interest and ethics |
| 2 | Out-of-house: objectives may fit into corporate goals, but provision contracted to external provider | Problematic linkages and inter-knowledge between provider and organization |
| 3 | Consortium: several firms pool resources using external contractor | Smaller firms share overheads this way: co-ordination and premises come through contractor |
| 4 | Affiliate: resembles type 2, but provided more loosely by co-operating independent professionals for a group of firms | High client focus, and reduced organizational involvement, if any |

*Source:* Based on Masi & Friedland (1988).

A very different classificatory model is provided by Straussner (1988), as an incidental product to her study of the relative benefits of in-house and out-of-house EAPs. This is less a procedural model than a classification on a *cui bono* basis, as applied to organizational bureaucracies by Blau and Scott (1962). The distinguishing criteria are the balance of relative benefits to the principal organizational stakeholders, as shown in Table 4.3.

The employer-favouring EAPs might initially be assumed to be exclusively those found in-house, which Straussner's study showed to be more coherent with the social and operational systems of the total organization, more cost-effective and more likely to endure through the vicissitudes of corporate fortunes. But in times of intense competition between EAP external contractors, relatively low market entry costs, and easy availability of financial backing, contractors may be tempted to keep business by appearing to meet management's bidding. However, in a harsh corporate environment, it is unlikely that employers will knowingly or willingly finance an EAP that was overtly employee-favouring. Business goals and social responsibility come sharply into conflict if the balance is seen to be more than

**Table 4.3**  *Models of EAP—procedural classificatory approaches—3*

| Type no. | Organizational stakeholder who benefits from EAP | Commentary |
|---|---|---|
| 1 | Employer-favouring EAPs | Associated more with in-house EAP. Organizational knowledge and integration provides flexible, dedicated EAP—at expense of clients' needs? |
| 2 | Employee-favouring EAPs | Associated more with externally provided EAPs and professional identification with clients as individuals; tends to produce less managerial satisfaction |
| 3 | EAP staff-favouring EAPs | May result from a need to avoid polarization, or from a lapse into bureaucratic routinization. Best practice or merely its continuance can lead to excessive internal focus, and consequent dysfunctionality |

*Source:* Based on Straussner (1988).

marginally favourable to the employee, unless EAPs have official backing (as in Australia) or form part of a collective agreement. Thirdly, the EAP staff-favouring EAP will tend to become a dysfunctional variant—whether slipping into excessive professionalism at the expense of the financing employer or (less likely) of the client-employee, or falling into bureaucratic routinization leading to a less than demanding standard of quality or integrity.

All the three procedural–classificatory models that have been described have considerable limitations in analytical terms. This is because of their lack of precision in definition, and of their basis in a diverse range of practices. Few operational EAPs fit easily into the specified types, and hybrids or mixed types are often likely to be found. Since EAPs have to be (or become) tailored to organizational contexts, they also show immense diversity. The consultants or contractors who devise EAPs to meet the needs of individuals and corporations tend to do so pragmatically, for they lack standardized training or officially sanctioned universal models. In US practice, however, a more prescriptive model has emerged from research and professional training, and has come to exercise a considerable influence there over practice—although, so far, less so in Britain.

## A PRESCRIPTIVE EAP MODE: CORE TECHNOLOGY

The looseness of analytical definitions of EAPs has led not surprisingly to attempts to produce a definitive statement of the EAP, that could serve as a practice yardstick. Its principal authors are two US academics Roman and Blum, latterly working in the University System of Georgia. They see it as a route out of a 'Babel syndrome' or an 'EAP bedlam' for nascent EAP professional organizations, for governments and policy-makers, and for contractor providers (Roman & Blum, 1992). The authors do not claim 'rightness' for the model. But they argue that it is data-based, has shown robustness in refinement (not modification) since the mid-1980s, and is capable of application only with 'scrutiny and imaginative consideration' of its utility on a much wider geographical extent than its US and Canadian origins (Roman & Blum, 1992). It is claimed that the 'core technologies' represent the 'unique contribution of EAP presence in the workplace'. These seven cores are listed in Table 4.4:

**Table 4.4**    *Seven 'core technologies' approach to EAPs*

| No. | Description of core technology | Commentary |
|---|---|---|
| 1 | Indentification of problem employees via documented evidence of impaired job performance | Clear performance standards are required to avoid vague 'labelling' of employees with supposed behavioural problems |
| 2 | Provision of consultative assistance to supervisors, managers and shop stewards by the specialist designated to operate the EAP | Training and education at all levels of employees prepares a climate in which the EAP becomes part of HR policy |
| 3 | Constructive confrontation of the problem employee by management to obtain recognition of troubles and a willingness to act | This unique aspect of EAP derived from the occupational alcoholism origins, but has of late taken on a 'softer' nature |
| 4 | Creation of micro-linkages between the employee and community resources most appropriate to assist | Both clinical and practical community knowledge can ensure effective direction of employees to sources of help |
| 5 | Creation of long-term macro-linkages between workplaces and service provider systems in the community | Workplaces can thus become informed consumers of treatment—leading to more effective managed care |
| 6 | Promulgation of an organizational culture to provide constructive assistance in dealing with employees' problems | Neither benign neglect nor punitive discipline, but a culture of responsible cooperative mutual help |
| 7 | Evaluation of employee and EAP in terms of job performance adequacy | Resolution of job-related problems rather than judged on clinical or other criteria |

*Source:* Roman & Blum, (1992).

This brief tabulation of the seven carefully developed 'core technologies' indicates the programmatic nature of this approach, which has a heavy methodological bias. Other EAP activities are termed 'supporting technologies' and include policy statements, training and education initiatives, joint union–management co-operation, incorporation into individual conduct codes and into collective agreements. These activities are seen as secondary, since in essence they could equally apply to a variety of employee services and labour relations procedures.

The programmatic nature of the 'core technologies' approach is further emphasized in the 'core functions' statements of the benefits of such EAPs. These are stated to be:

- retention of employees, especially key staff members
- reduction of load on managers in coping with 'troubled' employees
- provision of 'due process' for such employees, thereby ensuring fairness in the event of subsequent legal proceedings
- improved control of employers' liability for health care and insurance costs
- monitoring of employees' recourse to mental health provisions, thereby tracking stress and dissatisfaction within the enterprise
- enhancement of employees' morale and the employer's reputation for caring and assistance (Roman & Blum, 1992)

These benefits are not necessary characteristics of an EAP; but taken with the 'core technologies' they represent a powerful and coherent statement for an EAP on these implicitly prescriptive lines. They are a persuasive argument for corporate adoption of this corporately focused type of EAP.

The authors of the 'core technologies' see them neither as constraining (as if all other activities were either relatively superfluous or peripheral) nor as necessarily present (EAPs can operate validly in certain contexts with other characteristics). Indeed, Roman & Blum recognize the cultural context of their US-derived model. They cite that in different countries different patterns will be recognized of the troubled employee definition, different patterns of health care provision and community support, changing patterns of abuse, varying salience of work and organizational values, as well as variations in modes of EAP delivery from state sponsorship to prevalent entrepreneurialism (Roman & Blum, 1992).

In spite of the insistence by the authors that the model is not a statement of 'rightness', in its application it tends to so appear, or to be so interpreted, by certain EAP contractors in particular. It is difficult to envisage that an EAP application on 'core technologies' principles could realistically exclude any one or more of the components without becoming intellectually or operationally incoherent. Hence, for some EAP purchasers, it tends also to define the EAP essentially—in spite of claiming only to be a generalized statement of characteristics.

Nevertheless, the 'core technologies' model is a basis for practice for many US professional–commercial providers of EAPs. One major British EAP provider has successfully operated on this model for a number of years, although it should be added that this provider's organizational origins were in US practice. A considerable body of professional opinion in Britain opposes a 'core technologies' approach as being too business focused, and insufficiently cognizant of the needs and wishes of the individual client, and less appropriately developed to the British socio-economic context. The implicit heavy emphasis on achievement of employer objectives *along* with employee outcomes is perhaps redolent of unitarist HR philosophies. These may be well-adapted to the US context of their origin. But in a long British tradition of industrial relations pluralism, the arguable bias toward the realization of employer objectives through employee compliance may well appeal more to new companies in emergent technologies or new sectors of service, or to foreign-owned enterprises. In more traditional sectors of British industry and commerce, where pluralist values and adversarial industrial relations remain or are close to the surface, a less closely coupled programme of counselling-only provision, based in the community, may prove much more acceptable.

## AN IDEAL–TYPICAL MODEL OF EAP

All the EAP models discussed so far are either typologies or taxonomies, or are prescriptive in the case of the US-based 'core technologies' model. The critical social scientist may well still be looking for a practice model of an ideal–typical nature, which eschews these two orientations.

An introduction to this approach is offered by Shain & Groeneveld (1980), who aim to create a systems-based practice model. Their desire is not to categorize or prescribe, nor to create a perfect model for emulation and imitation. But rather they seek to identify, but *in systems terms*, the essential elements of the EAP that are necessarily present, resembling the core technologies in this respect or the listing approach of the UK EAPA Standards (EAPA, 1994). Additionally, they seek to analyse the nature of the interrelationships between the elements of the model, thereby bestowing a critical dynamism to the overall system. Practice can then be evaluated against such a model, not in a judgemental manner, but in an examination to what extent the postulated elements are present, and the pattern and nature of the interactions that occur.

Developing Shain & Groeneveld's original concept of an EAP, the EAP model in Figure 4.1 can be constructed as a basis for the initial creation of an EAP, or for its analytical comparison where an existing EAP is under scrutiny. It will be noted that the 'technical' elements of the EAP itself compose only a relatively small part of the total system, which, of course, itself functions in a wider organizational and societal environment. The research-based analysis of the need for an EAP, its constitutional basis in the enterprise, and the nature of preparation or education are all essential prerequisites for the effective installation of an EAP. The monitoring and evaluation elements equally are central in ensuring (in this model) that the structural–functional nature of the EAP is maintained. Any EAP cannot stand still, and it will change continually by means of the imports and exports to its system (e.g. new problems, new counselling techniques or rehabilitated employees, newly convinced managers) across its various boundaries with the organizational stakeholders, the community and the economic environment. The model shows how the EAP is in no way an isolated or encapsulated organizational intervention. Nor is it a short-run 'Bandaid' but a considered intervention in the organization's cultural and efficiency processes, which has to be woven into the web of organizational mechanisms, values and beliefs.

## OTHER MODELS

This discussion has focused on three main approaches to the construction of EAP models. The approaches outlined have more analytical power and interpretive capacity than alternative approaches to be outlined below. Nonetheless, it must be

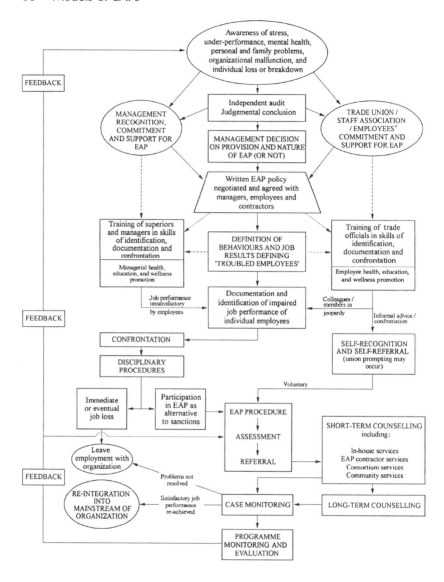

***Figure 4.1*** *Ideal typical model of an EAP. Source:* Some elements derived from Shain & Groeneveld (1980); von Bertalanffy (1950)

acknowledged that EAPs are arguably best explained and understood critically as a 'technology', in the way exemplified in Roman & Blum's work (1992). EAPs are not embellished by high theories or an advanced level of conceptualization in their design—up to date, at least. It may be that in the future, a theoretical view of this cross-road of disciplines will be achieved in a critical synthesis.

The aspect of EAPs in which theoretical perspectives are most highly developed is that of the therapeutic approaches used by counsellors. In principle, almost any of the major schools of psychology can contribute to EAP therapeutic practice, and psychiatry contributes its corpus of knowledge and techniques. It is outside our remit to develop these theoretical perspectives at this point, although brief reference was made to them in Chapter 2. The EAP in itself, however, provides a framework within which such advanced theory can be applied by the counsellor in numerous instances of the troubled employee-client's intervention.

At a more utilitarian level, qualitative distinctions can be made between EAPs on various criteria. First, the funding basis can be a source of variation in orientations and practice between EAPs, which can be:

- directly and wholly employer-funded (the main instance in Britain)
- insurance-funded wholly (as in many US EAPs)
- shared funding between employee and employer or insurance company (varying proportions and levels of co-payment)
- state-funded in part or whole (whether *de facto*, as with Britain's NHS where provision exists, or through state sponsorship, as in the Australian model)
- third party, independently funded in part (as with independent agencies such as Britain's Citizens' Advice Bureau, or independent charitable services such as Gamblers Anonymous)
- unfunded in part (for example, using the help of industrial chaplains, community priests, members of parliament, etc.).

The diversity of such approaches will inevitably entail a gamut of social, economic, political, religious, and financial beliefs, which are likely to colour the nature of the intervention or assistance offered.

A second type of definitional approach to EAPs (which arguably has some model-like properties) is that based on the scope of counselling offered to employees or to the organization. The developing scope of counselling follows a historical sequence to some extent, but such a sequence is not a limiting factor as such, since contemporaneous organizations may opt for a stage that is relatively early in the evolution of counselling in that enterprise (see Figure 4.2).

The distinctive features of this depiction of the counselling sequence of development are:

1  The broadening scope of counselling activities, widening out from organizational alcohol programmes to the 'broad-brush' approach, to recognition of the need for simultaneous organizational adjustment to the occupational/professional

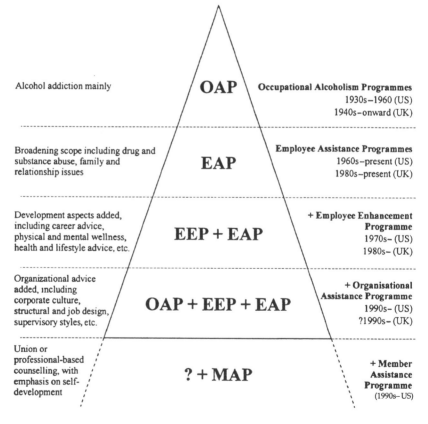

**Figure 4.2**  *Developing the scope of counselling in organizations. Source:* draws upon Dickman (1984)

development stage, which is becoming salient in times of demanding employment and employers, job obsolescence and career change.

2 The recognition that the differing stages are pervaded by widely differing values and ideologies, which shape the outcomes of the counselling process, regardless of the therapeutic models used, or counsellors' individual values: in increasingly complex employment contexts, a variety of counselling and assistance provisions may be necessary to deal with troubles and dysfunctions at many levels.

Strictly speaking, this approach is a classification with relatively imprecise borders between categories. But, even so, the validity of the pluralism of viewpoints imposed by the widening scope of EAPs is valuable in highlighting the dichotomies between the five developmental stages. Whether all the viewpoints are capable of being reconciled within a single programme, or through a single provider (external or internal) is far from clear. Whether it would be desirable to attempt this raises fundamental issues of the organization as a polity, which are outside the scope of this chapter.

## CONCLUSIONS

Any employer considering the installation of an EAP, and any employee considering enrolment in an EAP, could do well to first consider the connotations and consequential implications of an EAP. These may well not be obvious from the commercial promotion of the service emanating from the EAP contractor. The 'troubled' employee who is enrolling on the EAP, whether voluntarily or not, may have little understanding of the complex system into which she or he is agreeing to enter, nor how to exercise control once within it.

But,

if the different elements of the overall EAP service delivery system represent different practice approaches, or if they are poorly coordinated, problems can develop (Cunningham, 1994: 22).

The critical description and analysis of the socio-economic and organizational–political context of any EAP adoption is clarified by the comprehensive use of an 'ideal-type' model. By examining every element in the system in its contexts mentioned above, and, even more importantly, by examining the nature of the linkages between elements (as depicted in the model), malfunctions, conflicts, overloads, discontinuities or gaps can be identified. Finally, the congruity of the system as a whole can be checked against other sub-systems, and with overall organizational and wider systems. It is in the resolution of such latent incompatibilities that are potentially inherent in an EAP, that the value of the time and thought devoted to the scrutiny of any proposed EAP application can prove to be resources well spent.

# 5
# Employers' Rationales for the Adoption of EAPs

## INTRODUCTION

The motives of an employer in considering the adoption of an Employee Assistance Programme (EAP) are rarely altruistic in totality. Nor are they often purely economic—however strongly the EAP may be justified on such grounds by its providers. Most employers have motives that fall somewhere between these two poles, which have a twin focus of enhancing the work contribution and also providing an employee benefit, as well as disinterestedly helping troubled employees.

The reasons for adopting an EAP may well not be explicitly articulated, at least not as they appear to the employer at the time. The advocacy of a single articulate EAP champion in the firm may sway corporate opinion, and typically this could come from the Human Resources Management (HRM) or Occupational Health (OH) functions. Alternatively, a chairman or influential non-executive director could play a decisive role in airing the advantages that an EAP could bring to the organization. For a case-study illustration of influences for EAP adoption, see Berridge (1996b). Recent research quoted elsewhere in this book reveals a surprising lack of detailed knowledge and prior evaluation of EAPs (see Chapter 11) on the part of British employers adopting them (Highley & Cooper, 1995). In addition, 30% only of British enterprises instituting an

EAP did so on a systematic basis of research into the provision in its various patterns and models.

Because of companies' widespread prior lack of comprehension of EAPs, there may be a tendency to see them as a *deus ex machina*, when companies are faced with an unfamiliar or inchoate problem of staff members' morale and contribution. The adoption of an EAP can be 'a knee-jerk reaction' triggered by a critical event that is disturbing to the employer, such as 'restructuring redundancies, a merger or move, or perhaps the response to an [adverse] attitude survey' (Finn, 1995: 29). The dilemma at the centre of a corporate adoption decision is frequently that of bounded rationality: the company's decisional processes are logically and economically sufficient within their customary parameters. But neither the dimensions of the perceived problem nor the philosophical and operational nature of the EAP accord with the organization's decision-making model, criteria or mind-set. This condition of confusion probably explains in a more critical manner the comment by a practitioner:

> Companies tend to be woolly about their reasoning, especially when there is an element of panic in the decision . . . they rush into the market . . . (Steddon, cited in Finn, 1995: 29).

Given that the adoption of an EAP is a 'step into the unknown' for many companies, the advice of an independent EAP consultant could prove to be wise in making a decision. The consultant can help the organization to perform several of the key steps in assessing the extent of a 'good fit' between the enterprise and the potential EAP. This match (or mis-match) of dimensions can include:

- the nature of perceived problems, collectively and individually, as well as on a corporate basis
- the nature of the organization, and the resources already in place within it for resolving problems
- the potential EAP provider's staff, clinical and operating practices

This list excludes the downstream elements, such as take-up, economic justification, repercussions (anticipated and unanticipated) and other issues dealt with in Chapter 11.

But however much an EAP provider may attempt to sell his product in marketing terms, it is the client company ultimately that buys according to its needs, whether explicitly articulated or more latently felt. Accordingly, the remainder of this chapter will concentrate on the motives and dynamics of this process on the part of the key decision-makers, whether owners, directors or managers. The subsequent sections will discuss first the employer's underlying motives within the corporate culture for adopting an EAP; secondly, the linkages between personnel management and HRM, respectively, and an EAP; thirdly, the industrial relations and trade union aspects of EAP provision; and, finally, the EAP's role in future organizational contexts such as high performance work design, quality-pervaded organizations, and future configurations of organizational structures and societies.

## UNDERLYING MOTIVES FOR ADOPTING EAPs

Employers' motives for adopting EAPs often defy the tidy labels that can be applied to them or spill over the defined boundaries that can be identified for them. Nevertheless, a variety of rationales on the part of employers will be examined in this section of the chapter, with the proviso that pure types rarely exist. Most employers' motives will either be confused or intermingled, or may explicitly contain more than one type of rationale.

### The Humanistic Motive

The *humanist rationale* for an EAP is rooted in a complex of interrelated concerns and beliefs. A disinterested desire to help, improve and even reform individual employees may have religious or ideological origins—as exemplified, in particular, by the industrial alcoholism movement. Conspiracy theorists may well maintain that no true entrepreneur ever acts in such a manner (Braverman, 1974; Friedman, 1980). Entrepreneurial zeal is, however, in practice often tinged with social conviction, and such beliefs may prompt an interest in the EAP, especially in the owner-managed firm.

In addition, professional managers in bureaucratic firms may identify sufficiently with their fellow employees, and show such sentiments, in spite of Friedman's (1980) moralizing strictures that any managerial action that does not unequivocally create wealth for stockholders is tantamount to theft. Research evidence shows equally unequivocally that managers are potential candidates for EAPs. Yet a caring approach to the content and context of work can be humanistically extended to a caring attitude to the whole family, as in a 'broad-brush' EAP, which is typically found in British practice. This stance equally is questioned in a cynical mind-set on the premise that 'contented cows give the creamiest milk'. Such humanism is not only patronizing to employees, but as such diverts their attention from the more fundamental issues of their powerlessness in the overall organizational context (Blauner, 1964).

Within the humanistic case for EAPs, both ideological beliefs about the employment relationship and also those concerning the employer's legal and moral duty of care play a part. Within this concern, the employee (in the Anglo-Saxon socio-judicial tradition, at least) undertakes to devote her or his best physical and mental endeavours to the work task. In return, the employer is normally bound to mitigate the damaging aspects of work, to treat the employee with reasonable consideration, and (if required) to compensate the individual for detriment or suffering so caused. The ideological basis for such concern might be religious, such as Robert Owen's non-conformist Protestantism in the nineteenth century, or latterday Cadburyism in the twentieth century (Smith et al., 1990). Alternatively, its mainspring could be secular, as in the capitalist egalitarianism of the John Lewis Partnership or the counselling programme of General Electric's Hawthorne plant in Chicago (Roethlisberger & Dickson, 1939).

This major originating factor for EAPs lies in the prescient employer's possession of a conscience over the damaging effects of work on the individual. As a result, the employer feels an obligation to offset or rectify these effects—one of which methods is enrolment in an EAP, without cost or blame to the employee. Tackling the issue as close as possible to its work-related source, and relating action (whether organizational or employee-centred) directly to problems, can be seen both as a responsible and effective employee approach. Unfortunately, it is the employer who is most cynically exploitative, manipulative and oppressive of the employee who is most likely to create the intra-organization context that most calls for an EAP. Conversely, it is such an employer who is most unlikely to adopt an EAP. Nonetheless, the orientation of the conventional personnel function often accords well with such a humanist orientation, reflecting well with elements in the industrial social worker tradition (Thomason, 1976; Torrington, 1978).

Another strand of the pervasive humanistic orientation is the pressure exerted by the members of the caring professions. As frequently occurs, such persons are employed in the personnel function, or in the occupational health (OH) role in particular. They may well accept the argument of social responsibility in the wide sense for the problems experienced by the 'troubled' employee. The enhanced social awareness and critical analysis that such experts can bring to bear on an enterprise over a period of time can build up to a substantial pressure of internal opinion in favour of counselling or EAP provisions as part of organizational culture. Provided that the status of the personnel, OH or HR function is high, the chances of an EAP being advocated or adopted are increased. Alternatively, where commercial interests dictate pressure on employees (as in the case where staff reductions are required to justify a merger), top management may decide to inaugurate an EAP in order to handle the inevitable distress among staff members.

A negative version of this social responsibility is where the personnel function is cast in the role of organizational conscience—in this instance raising the problem of the individually damaging effects of work in the employing firm. If work is harmful to physical or psychological health as a result of inadequate job design or oppressive control mechanisms, it is the employer's moral duty to help staff members to recover from it by providing a coping or recuperative service. Such a moralistic stance, of course, is a tertiary-level intervention, doing nothing to remove the origins of the damage to the individual.

The numerous facets of the humanist rationale for the adoption of an EAP are demonstrated through the considerable extent of their discussion, and, in practice, how influential and how persuasive they are in an organization's decision to institute an EAP. But, at the same time, their moralistic and philosophical foundations render any rational-economic justification for an EAP all the more problematic and contested among the various organizational stakeholders. After all, both stakeholders and investors have a moral and institutional voice.

## The Efficiency Motive

The *efficiency rationale* for EAPs is based upon a more or less precise calculation of financial return. On one side of the equation are the set-up costs and the annual operating costs of the EAP. On the opposite side are firstly hard demonstrable savings (reduced insurance premiums/productivity increases, etc.), secondly reduced costs that are more or less closely causally linked (health care expenses, early retirements, staff turnover, accident costs, absenteeism, etc.) and thirdly, intangible positive gains (enhanced quality, greater innovation and creativity, reduced presenteeism, etc.). It is inevitable that a positive economic advantage needs to be proven in almost all organizations, and most EAP providers have impressive justifications to present to potential EAP adopters. These issues are dealt with more fully in Chapter 11, as part of the evaluation of EAPs.

## The Political Motive

The *political and organizational rationale* for EAPs is a more subtle qualitative case, which will vary greatly from one organization to another, reflecting the uniqueness of each enterprise and its environmental context. Most managements complain about employees' motivational level. Complaints typically centre on organizational goals and the impression that employees are not motivated towards them, or at best, are partially motivated, or even worse are counter-motivated. The EAP allows each employee to explore and try to resolve her or his preoccupations impinging on work performance and the key areas of individual and team results and contribution to corporate goals. The potential gain is a more focused employee who has worked through at least some of the most acute work-related stresses and individual adjustments to the job. Where supervisory referral occurs, or there is co-optation of management in problem resolution within the EAP, the classic managerial principle of resolving problems as close as possible to their origins is fulfilled. But, at the same time, supervisory referral or co-optation increases the management's knowledge and involvement in the problem solving process—and more importantly, it adds to management's control within the organization of employees' attitudes and behaviour.

Another aspect of the economic rationale for EAPs lies in the part that they can play in systems of staff appraisal and training. As part of a positive strategy of staff retention, motivation and maximization of contribution, the information and action resulting from an EAP provides a feedback and correction loop that helps to ensure the effectiveness of the overall strategy. This aspect of appraisal applies particularly in the case of the under-performing employee, who may suffer heightened levels of stress from both their personal contexts and from the centrality of the job to the firm's fortunes. The advice and support coming from the EAP aids the employee in working with the counsellor, and perhaps with the informed supervisor or manager, in focusing on the key results areas of work, and on building an appropriate career through achievement and commitment. Hence, the EAP *does* play a part in the labour supply and control function within the organization. But this role certainly should not be oppressive or exploitative. Instead, the EAP becomes a means of mutual exploration of differences and deviations with a view to reconciling them and creating individual self-reliance and mutual trust.

### The Excellence Motive

A *cultural rationale* for EAPs can be argued on a more qualitative basis, but with culture being cited with Chief Executive Officers (CEOs) frequently as the critical performance factor between competing organizations, it is clearly an important rationale. The arguments of the 'excellence' theorists (e.g. Peters & Waterman (1982), who identify that top-performing organizations do so through a strong culture of paying attention to human resources) are clearly supportive of EAPs. The search for excellence in products or markets, quality or customer service must inevitably tie in intimately with the desire to provide excellence of treatment for those employees who aspire to such standards.

It would be a source of serious cognitive dissonance for staff members if their employing organization was not to also apply internally the demanding criteria (which it insists on for customers) for its own employees. Additionally, an organization's public image can be enhanced internally by the existence and effective operation of an EAP that denotes a caring ethos in parallel with the need for performance (see also Chapter 6). Such an ethos goes further than accepting that the work pressures that can cause individual dysfunctions should be compensated for and mitigated at the expense of the employer. It also includes a belief that successful coping with work problems can be a source of personal growth that extends into the wider circles of non-work, family and increased social integration.

The enhancement of the work organization into a learning organization is promoted implicitly, if not positively, by the EAP. By integrating the employee into taking responsibility for identifying, analysing and tackling his or her own problems in the process of short-term counselling, the EAP provides a practical framework for problem-solving in less troubling contexts within everyday situations at work. Hence, a resilient approach and a flexible, developmental mind-set can be encouraged. A co-operative attitude to receiving advice and accepting help can be seen widely as the normal way to work through difficulties, to foster innovation, and to engender creativity. The non-judgemental nature of the EAP is an important element in such a culture, and accords well with an increasing de-emphasis on hierarchy in knowledge-based organizations.

The collegiate involvement of the counsellor, and the shared responsibility of the troubled employee's supervisor are both at the centre of EAP philosophy. Both relationships need to be non-authoritarian if problems are to be resolved with learning and commitment to future effectiveness. The relationships so created align well with current thinking on the forms of work organization needed for high-achievement work teams in unfamiliar environments or in leading-edge situations of knowledge. Team management, participative structures and process-centred, autonomous working groups all pose new problems of working relationships, and shared responsibility assumed under conditions of uncertainty and ambiguity. While such contexts may even, on occasion, produce stresses that lead to individuals having recourse to the EAP, a stronger influence will be the supportive behaviour strategy inherent in the EAP. Many of the counselling techniques underpinning the EAP can equally be applicable and effective in solving the tensions of team-centred management and autonomous team working. The supervisor or team member who has learned about EAP methods (or even experienced them) will be able to bring the same perspectives to interpersonal problems or difficulties in everyday managerial issues. In such a way, the EAP supports and validates current non-hierarchical structures, such as matrix organizations and autonomous working. It helps to draw attention to the methods of organizational effectiveness through individual helping and social facilitation in problem resolution in a co-operative relationship of trust and mutual respect.

Any *HRM rationale* for an EAP has to start with a consideration of the relationship between the HR function and the EAP system. As a confidential, 'no blame' counselling process, both HR and counselling professional standards require that the organization has no involvement in the EAP client–counsellor relationship, unless the client employee has explicitly agreed willingly for this to occur. Only in exceptional cases does the British Association for Counselling (BAC) Code of Ethics (1989) allow for a breach of confidentiality in instances of grave physical or moral danger or breach of the law. The HR function owes its power and relevance to its possession of information (quantitative and qualitative) about the employee, with the intention of maximizing the utilization of the individual's skills and knowledge, and minimizing the negative effects of influences producing any lack of individual commitment or effort. Clearly, the EAP with its access to sensitive and significant information about the individual is at the crossroads of these two views on confidentiality. In analysing the potential directions in which the EAP could tend to lean, the *confidentiality principle* must remain intact if the programme is to retain integrity. But the degree of integration with other human services in the organization, and its overall direction, will depend on whether the EAP is provided in-house, or supplied through an external contractor.

The in-house EAP typically will report to the Director of Human Resources, through a director of the EAP. The latter's role will have considerable safeguards of independence, supplemented by the views and the support of an expert impartial advisory group. But even where the counselling process zealously protects its detached status in all client-related matters, the in-house EAP can be integrated relatively into other social and administrative processes within the enterprise. For example, supervisors may be ready to suggest and facilitate an employee's first contact with an EAP; the corporate culture may approve it; appraisal programmes and procedures may offer it routinely in the case of markedly diminished performance; career development programmes may customarily use it for reinforcement (particularly, for instance, for young employees or disadvantaged groups); and many other routine instances such as pre-retirement plans or occupational health issues may activate it. So while the EAP remains independent and confidential, formal routes legitimately may be set up, and informal patterns will supplement them in practice. As the EAP becomes part of the organization's 'normal' culture, such linkages will come to reinforce each other mutually. With growing confidence in the EAP on the part of employees, they may well consent to the release of specified information from the EAP to (for instance) line supervisors or training and development advisers. Only if a pervasive organizational culture exists of the ethical use of sensitive EAP information will such a symbiotic situation be capable of arising, and its construction may require a considerable period of time over which to build trust. Such integration is aided by the inclusion of the EAP as a division (albeit privileged) of a human services function in a company, providing a comprehensive and mutually-consistent range of philosophies and technical inputs to the maintenance of human resources at a high level of effectiveness.

The externally sourced, out-of-house EAP offers a different rationale in HR terms, being one that is more aligned to developmental objectives on the part of the individual. As a result of counselling experience of joint problem-solving, the employee can learn or enhance her or his capacity to be a resourceful person when faced with problems. This ability is then available to be transferred to work-related issues for the benefit of the organization and the satisfaction of the individual. The close concatenation of organizational mechanisms (such as performance appraisal or discipline procedures) with the EAP may well not be possible, as a result of the physical or attitudinal distance between the firm and the external EAP provider. Often, counsellors are given some organizational background, but, by definition, their understanding of the whole work context cannot be as detailed as that of the in-house provider. The HR manager may see such separation as a desirable form of independence and impartiality in the counselling process, thereby ensuring that the conventional internal past culture of the firm is not applied to future problems.

It has been discussed how the HR rationale for EAPs may bifurcate according to the practice model adopted. For either type, however, the EAP offers the personnel or HR manager a way out of the long-detested 'welfare' image (Torrington & Chapman, 1978). The EAP represents a modern, expert, cost-effective and independently responsible way of handling welfare issues in a manner that relates to work and its accomplishment, and which offers a closed-ended, financially predictable and legally prudent format. When we add in the socially responsible and confidential elements, the wide spread of issues covered (by broad-brush EAPs at least), and extensive family coverage, then the EAP could look like the answer to an HR manager's prayer after struggling with the welfare role.

The 'hard' variant of HRM (Legge, 1995a; 1995b) with its emphasis on quantitative and programmatic integration with business results, might well be achieved more consistently through an in-house EAP. The interrelationships between the administrative systems of 'hard' HRM (especially appraisal, performance-related pay and total quality management (TQM) can be designed more specifically to line up with participation in an EAP, whose counsellors have a close and acute knowledge of the organization's culture. The 'soft' variant of HRM (Storey, 1995: 34–36) with its emphasis on development, organizational identification and managerial trust might well accord more with an externally sourced EAP, provided by a specialist contractor or through a consortium. Although such counsellors' focus on the particular context of a business may be lacking, the generalized values of the 'soft' variant in many ways are capable of being encouraged through counselling philosophies that are based on wider humanistic principles.

The introduction of an EAP poses numerous attractions for the HR function; in particular, the realization that the traditional disinterested, unintegrated welfare role will no longer be suitable for continuation. It is quite practicable that former welfare officers, who often possessed only very generalized social work training or who were lay persons in counselling terms, can be trained for certain in-house EAP responsibilities. Many former personnel officers, who carried out some welfare work along with their other more technical functions, will probably have been entirely willing in different socio-economic contexts to shed the 'softer' welfare aspects. When asked to reorient themselves to the business results-driven HRM role, they could find that their previous welfare and counselling duties are discordant (if not opposed) to their new role. But, finally, the low status of much of the welfare activities performed by the former personnel function made them willing and ready to discard it in favour of the more strategic and higher-reputed role of HRM; practitioners may be less enthusiastic to abandon (and possibly reject) such roles. Professionally educated and trained human resources practitioners may well have fewer hesitations.

## The Industrial Relations Motive

The *industrial relations rationale* for employers to adopt an EAP is based on both ideological and practical bases. Both types of rationale are connected with the current dominance in Britain of HRM models in the management of people at work, within the socio-economic environment of the 1990s and beyond.

The first industrial relations characteristic that accords well with EAPs is the trend towards individualism in employment, as reflected in such employer tactics as personal contracts, performance-related pay, personal appraisal and development methods. These are also ideological and economic strategies, encouraged by the political notions of the Conservative administration in Britain since 1979 of the 'enterprise culture' (Thatcher, 1993) but found also more widely in the industrialized economies (Bean, 1995; Kessler & Bayliss, 1995). There is no intention to contend simplistically that EAPs have an ideological basis in individualism or enterprise culture as a political philosophy. It is undeniably true that the EAP addresses individualized issues and troubles (rather than collective concerns) within a perspective of individual psychology, not social psychology. The concepts of individual employees' resourcefulness and self-reliance undoubtedly find resonance with employers' industrial relations strategies, while at the same time being one of the bases of the therapeutic models of short-term EAP counselling. But this socio-political point is not one that counsellors or their employing or representative organizations would often wish to espouse formally.

An extension of the EAP-and-individualism argument is that the EAP provides the employer with a weapon against the collectivity represented by the trade union. Traditionally, the solidarity of the union has provided the individual member with a source of support and a general frame of reference within which to base his adjustment to troubles at work, or in relation to the wider context of work. This union-based foundation has been massively eroded in most industrialized countries in the 1980s and 1990s, with great reductions in union membership and density. In Britain, from the high point of membership of 13.4 million (55% density) in 1979, the 1996 figure is probably under 8 million (a little over 30% density) based on realistic estimates (Goodman et al., 1997). Hence the basis of moral reinforcement at work for the individual employee has been severely weakened, even in firms still recognizing unions. In the many non-union new enterprises, greenfield sites, and smaller firms that have been set up in emergent industry and service sectors, there is no basis for employee role models based on workers' representatives, or informed by any popular source of solidaristic advice for the troubled employee among her or his peers. The breakdown of traditional working communities based around an industry or single employer has contributed to an increased awareness of such anomic states (MacInnes, 1987; Routledge, 1993). Consequently, the conscientious employer may feel an increased duty to provide advice and counselling for employees in the absence or exclusion of the union. The widely recognized accentuation of work pressures and more demanding societal expectations add relevance to such motives on the employer's part. The suggestion is not being made that EAPs are anti-union in intent or philosophy, or that counsellors' actions are in any sense subversive or corrosive of union solidarity: they may advise clients to seek advice or services from their union if they are members. But it is equally difficult to refute the individual orientation in EAPs toward personal problem resolution and the individual taking of control of one's work-related concerns.

Trade unions in Britain have not been active in promoting member counselling and advice services as a counterweight to employer-funded EAPs (Reddy, 1993: 52). This situation is unlike that in the United States, where a number of member advisory services have been set up (Kemp, 1989). One of the few services, and one that is unusual in developing beyond a telephone-based advice hotline, is that offered by the Royal College of Nursing (RCN). Originating in 1981 on a telephone basis, it now provides regionally based, face-to-face counselling as well as London-located services to members of the principal nursing trade union in the much-stressed health services. For reasons primarily of cost it is not heavily promoted, since the potential take-up among the RCN's membership of over 300 000 could be very high, and many health service employing authorities in fact themselves possess an EAP or similar counselling facilities in-house (Somerville, 1990).

An emerging aspect of the industrial relations rationale for EAPs is whether the existence of an EAP provides a legal defence in the instance of a contested dismissal as unfair or constructive dismissal. This topic is dealt with in detail in Chapter 12, and the industrial tribunal precedent is certainly not yet unequivocally established. Neither is the Health and Safety at Work Act 1974, or the Code of Practices a safe guide to the existence of any specific employer's liability in the absence of an EAP. To go further, opinion from the United States suggests that an attempted defence on the grounds that the employer operated an EAP could be challenged substantially on issues such as its coverage, the accreditation and competence of counsellors and any potentially discriminatory nature of its operation (Nobile, 1991). So the notion of the EAP as insurance in a dismissal case appears not to be the catch-all defence that it is sometimes argued to be, but the matter remains inconclusively tested in the British context.

The use of an EAP as an element in disciplinary and grievance procedures within an organization remains an important element in justifying an EAP, in US practice at least. During satisfactory participation in an EAP, an employee may indeed claim to be 'in sanctuary' in terms of on-going disciplinary procedures. This state will usually be supported by counsellors, and may even be included in the official definition and terms of operation of the EAP. An employee, anticipating possible disciplinary action may voluntarily refer her or himself to the EAP, or be advised by a union to do so, in order to protect her or his employment status. Accordingly, a defence put forward by a defendant at a disciplinary hearing will be that to impose any sanction would be prejudicial to a positive outcome from that person's EAP participation, and would be contrary to the principles of employee counselling. Alternatively, at an internal disciplinary hearing, the decision may be made to suspend action, dependent on successful completion of an EAP. If the individual concerned failed to enrol, or discontinued the EAP without the agreement of the counsellor, or failed to resolve her or his problems or to modify behaviour, then the original sanction would automatically apply. The case for linking EAPs and discipline at work is made more strongly in the United States than in Britain, perhaps reflecting the greater weakness of unionism in much of US employment. In Britain, only a minority of EAPs have this provision, an indication of the unease that many professional counsellors have with such a conflation of two very different types (punishment and development) of ethos. But from the viewpoint of an industrial relations professional, the EAP provision has advantages of avoiding summary judgements, obtaining union officials' support by taking action only on confirmed, repeated evidence, and avoiding unnecessary loss of skilled employees passing through a temporary (if unacceptable) phase of grossly inappropriate behaviour or inadequate performance.

## SUMMARY OF EMPLOYERS' MOTIVES FOR ADOPTING AN EAP

Should employers institute an EAP? What pressures to do so should they see as valid or cogent? Every instance of EAP implementation is difficult. As will be indicated in Chapter 11, the formal justification of an EAP is contestable on ethical grounds, and problematic on financial-efficient criteria. The economic certainty found in many other corporate initiatives may well not be present in decision-making about EAPs. However, if we subscribe to the cultural theories of organizational pre-eminence (Peters & Waterman, 1982), then the EAP has much to offer in creating a high-quality contribution from employees at all levels. Any institution of an EAP is, at base, a statement of faith and trust in employees. Any EAP needs careful use of technical skills (Roman & Blum, 1992) in its preparation, design, introduction or negotiation, operation and evaluation. The organization's motives (as categorized in this chapter) need discerning interpretation to its executives and managers—a task that also includes the EAP provider firm. If this clarification is not done, unrealistic expectations may be raised among employees, and deviant role perceptions may be fostered among managers. The EAP is far from being a universal panacea or a miraculous 'Bandaid' for a troubled organization or for a concerned employee. It may well not suffuse an enterprise in rose-coloured light, but may, in contrast, bring employees at all levels to see employment-related problems in a very cold light of day.

# 6

# EAP Provider Organizations in Britain

## EAPS IN BRITAIN

Employee Assistance Programmes (EAPs) in Britain have diversified into a range of systems, comprising different sponsorships, structures, processes, target populations, names and even objectives. Nevertheless, despite this diversity, there is some agreement on what constitutes an EAP (Lee & Gray, 1994) as well as increasing divergence and distinctiveness from the US models of the EAP.

The UK Employee Assistance Professionals Association (EAPA) defines an EAP as

> a mechanism for making counselling and other forms of assistance available to a designated workforce on a systematic and uniform basis, and to recognised standards (EAPA, 1994).

This definition was used in Chapter 2 and can include many different programme models. *Internal* EAPs are worksite-based, whereas *external* EAPs are located outside the workplace and are usually administered by providers who are independent of the organization. Some EAPs can be a combination of internal and external provision. However, in general, EAPs in the United Kingdom are generally seen as being externally provided, with only a handful of internal services describing themselves as EAPs.

Many of the original EAPs, especially in the United States, were set up and provided on an in-house basis, often based originally around the occupational health function. Their counsellors and managers were direct employees of the firm or organization, and there was considerable corporate control of the programme. While some of the pioneering company EAPs in Britain were instituted in this manner, the trend in Britain has been for external specialist EAP contractor companies to provide services to a range of client organizations, not necessarily in the same industrial or geographical sector. The 'consortium' EAP is found in the United States, where a diverse group of professionals in the health and personal social services group together to provide a comprehensive EAP service on a referral basis to a range of firms, often based around a locality. This model is not frequently found in Britain, although it fits the drive for commercialization being experienced by health care trusts in Britain, and hence may become more widespread.

A full definition and discussion of the nature of the EAP, with particular reference to the British context is given in Chapter 2. But before examining the characteristics and practices of British EAP provider organizations, it is worth re-stating certain key points that influence their operation:

- British EAPs emphasize brief counselling and intervention
- British EAPs tend to be 'broad-brush' in coverage of topics and employees' families
- British EAPs primarily receive self-referrals rather than managerial referrals
- British EAPs concentrate on the individual client rather than the organization
- British EAPs are employer-funded rather than insurance-funded

The primary aim of this chapter is to highlight the main characteristics of British EAPs, from the perspective of providers, both internal and external. The needs and views of purchasers will also be introduced in order to throw light on providers' practices and motives. Up to the present, no large-scale independent studies had been conducted. Consequently, little was known about the diversity of programmes in Britain.

Accordingly, in 1992, the Health and Safety Executive (HSE) decided to fund a three-year research project at the Manchester School of Management (UMIST) on the nature of British EAPs, their providers, their purchasers and their independent evaluation. The following part of this chapter is based closely on the findings of the research project (Highley & Cooper, 1995). This discussion of the findings will be made in particular conjunction with the statements of the UK EAPA Standards, in order to contrast prescription of good professional practice with those actually achieved.

## INTRODUCTION TO THE EAP PROVIDERS

Most of the current major British EAP providers were established between 1979 and 1993, with the greatest number emerging between 1989 and 1993. This time-scale coincides with the massive growth of externally provided workplace counselling programmes as a result of their mass marketing during this period. Most British EAP contractors are not EAP-only specialists, but see themselves as general providers of counselling services, of which the EAP is one, albeit one of their most commercially significant activities. The survey revealed that 69% of workplace counselling providers describe themselves as providing EAPs, but only 6% see this as their only business. The remaining 63% offer workplace counselling on an *ad hoc* basis, in addition to providing EAPs. Of the 31% of providers who do not offer EAPs, 19% provide both workplace counselling programmes and counselling on an *ad hoc* basis, whilst 12% offer specialist workplace counselling programmes. Figure 6.1 depicts these percentages.

About 56% of external providers offer a nation-wide service, with 44% providing essentially a local service. Those providers offering a nation-wide service do so either by having offices located throughout Britain (in 34% of cases); or by having a head office and a network of affiliate counsellors throughout Britain (in 66% of cases). Only 40% of providers have 24-hour access to

84

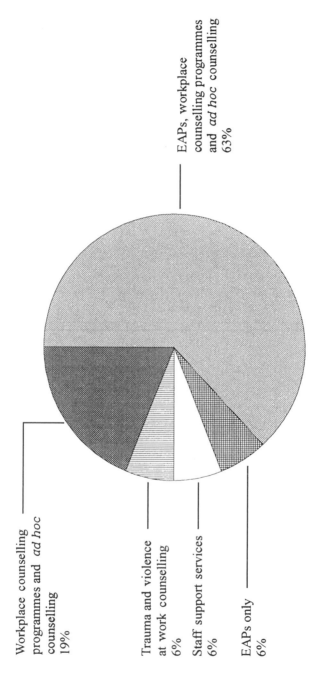

**Figure 6.1** *EAP and counselling services offered by external providers. Source:* Highley & Cooper (1995)

their counselling service and some of these are via an answerphone.

EAPs tend to be charged on a per capita basis, with the average price (1994–1995) being about £25 per employee per year. Most providers base their per capita fee on a number of factors, including the number of employees covered, the number of face-to-face counselling sessions available per client, and other services provided to the organization, such as training or consultancy.

The average number of face-to-face counselling sessions per client offered by providers is about six, which is about the professional norm for short-term therapy. There is a great deal of variation in the number of sessions provided amongst providers, the lowest being three and no limit being placed in a few cases. However, a three-session model should not be classed as a counselling service because, in practice, it is simply an assessment and referral service, with clients being referred on to often over-stretched agencies (e.g. Relate) without any attempt at therapeutic intervention.

## KEY EAP ACTIVITIES

About 63% of the British organizations surveyed that provide a counselling service for their employees do so via an EAP. However, there is a general lack of understanding amongst organizations as to the differences between external counselling services and EAPs, even after companies have bought an EAP. For example, many organizations did not realize that EAPs provide a confidential advice service for managers (to help them deal with difficult issues or staff problems), despite the fact that this is seen by EAP providers as a core EAP activity. Reportedly, one major British clearing bank has a counselling service offering assistance in coping with stress among staff, but open to managers only (BIFU, 1996).

This lack of clarity amongst organizations is to be expected to some extent, because there is still very little consensus amongst providers as to what an EAP really is. However, from the providers' perspective, the core activities of EAPs can be seen, in general, as being: (1) initial and on-going advertising of the EAP (by 80% of providers); (2) orientation sessions for managers and employees (by at least 80% of providers); (3) the provision of face-to-face counselling (by over 90% of providers); (4) advice to managers (by nearly 70% of providers); and (5) statistical and detailed feedback to the client organization (by approximately 70% of providers). Legal and financial advice, 24-hour access, telephone counselling and crisis back-up are not seen as essential ingredients for an EAP by the providers. This is summarized in Table 6.1.

**Table 6.1**   *Summary of key and peripheral EAP activities*

| Key activities | % of providers citing this activity | Peripheral features |
|---|---|---|
| Initial and on-going advertising | 80 | Financial and legal advice |
| Orientation sessions for managers | over 80 | 24-hour access |
| Orientation sessions for staff | over 80 | On-going telephone counselling |
| Face-to-face counselling | over 90 | Crisis back-up |
| Advisory service for managers | nearly 70 | |
| Basic statistical feedback | 70 | |
| Detailed feedback | 70 | |

*Source:* Highley & Cooper (1995).

But one of the most effective and acceptable methods of advertising counselling services is by word of mouth. A satisfied client will often be a person who can recognize symptoms of troubles in colleagues, and who will have the discretion to raise the subject of aberrant behaviour (e.g. alcoholism, under-performance or lateness) in an acceptable manner. While being aware of the dangers of over-zealous proselytization reminiscent of early days of lay occupational alcoholism programmes, the personal recommendation of a sympathetic and non-authoritative co-worker is a major stimulus to self-referral. The EAPA Standards (1994) state that:

> The EAP should be prepared to respond to emergencies and urgent situations in a timely fashion, consistent with organisational policies. Timely intervention may prevent or lessen long-term problems.

In addition, they say that:

The EAP should be able to provide crisis intervention and other appropriate professional services, 24 hours a day, 7 days a week.

The fact that the majority of providers do not see the provision of 24-hour access or crisis back-up as essential ingredients of an EAP is clearly not in line with the EAPA Standards, although indicating a fair level of consensus among providers themselves. Numerous other providers believe that training (e.g. stress management, relaxation, assertiveness) should be an integral part of an EAP.

A clear majority of providers feel that detailed feedback to the company is essential, as this can highlight both policy issues and general areas of operational concern, which the company can then attempt to change structurally; hence, reducing the stress imposed on employees by the organization. This latter point is a very important one that warrants further consideration. EAPs aim only to address stress at the individual level. There is also a need to address stress at the organizational level. But to do so within the framework of an EAP risks compromising confidentiality according to some providers (Lee & Gray, 1994). For this reason, most workplace counselling programmes and EAPs concentrate on individuals with personal problems, and attempt to provide a service in helping to reduce anxiety derived from financial, marital and family issues. These activities are obviously fundamental to helping an employee in terms of both his or her personal happiness and work performance. Stress at work, however, is often caused by a complicated combination of both personal and work-related issues. Thus, in order to be effective, counselling programmes at work must address jointly both personal and work issues (Cartwright & Cooper, 1994).

This joint approach is clearly not the case, and even the recently published EAPA definition of a British EAP does not allude to this combination of issues. The only mention of the workplace is in terms of 'employees who are not being productive enough'; hence, the focus is still at the individual level. Using counselling programmes in the traditional individualized way, as espoused by the EAPA definition, can lead to the responsibility for employee mental health being shifted from the company on to the individual employee. If a counselling programme operates purely at the individual level, then clearly the organizational sources of stress are not being tackled and the organization can conveniently 'forget' such employment-generated problems, because they provide a counselling service to help employees to cope. The organization is, in effect, distancing itself from the programme and, hence, from the need to address problems of stress generation within the organization.

Any EAP or workplace counselling programme should identify sources of stress within the organization, and advise the organization on appropriate resources to help deal with these sources of pressure. We should not see EAPs and workplace counselling programmes as a short-term, individual-based 'sticking plaster' solution, but rather as a way of feeding back problems to the organization (within the bounds of confidentiality) and empowering that organization to help itself.

## SELECTING AN EAP PROVIDER

The selection of an external EAP provider is a decision that is likely to have long-term and deep consequences upon the internal culture of an organization. It should, therefore, be a well-informed and clearly structured decision taken at the right level with the appropriate decision support mechanisms. Yet 56% of organizations report that there is not enough *independent* advice available about workplace counselling. Neither is there sufficient independent information specifically about EAPs and the benefits they can bring to organizations. In addition, organizations have difficulty in identifying all the providers of counselling services and EAPs, and when they do identify a provider they have no independent information about how effective that provider is at delivering the claimed levels of service and quality.

Many organizations do not initiate a careful procedure for selecting an EAP provider, but either buy the first EAP they came across or use the provider recommended by another company. Given the weighty potential impact of the EAP, and the heavy marketing engaged in by the major EAP providers, this shortfall of informed decision-making often contrasts markedly with decisions in other sectors of corporate activity.

Only 30% of companies carry out any form of needs analysis or stress audit before deciding to introduce counselling. Even those companies who attempt to do so do not use a rigorous procedure to identify whether or not there is a need for a counselling service. However, the EAPA standards clearly expect some form of need assessment to be carried out:

> Programme design should be based on an assessment of organisational and employee needs, as they relate to EAP utilisation (EAPA, 1994).

An assessment of the needs of the employees and the organization is a vital part of programme planning and development and is primarily the responsibility of the organization. This assessment will help the organization to determine the most appropriate method of providing counselling services. The EAP provider should assist the organization in assessing expressed needs and help in reviewing existing company policies (e.g. alcohol or wellness), and their relationship to the EAP.

The factors that are considered by organizations important reasons for introducing a counselling service, are assurances to employees about confidentiality and independence. The choice between an external and an internal service will be discussed in further detail in Chapter 7, along with organizational issues and problems.

After the decision to institute an EAP has been taken (in 50% of companies at a very senior level), responsibility for the EAP is usually passed back down to a less senior hierarchical position. This is not the most appropriate level at which the EAP can operate. A senior person is far better placed to institute changes as a result of feedback. Indeed, the EAPA Standards state that:

> The EAP needs to be positioned at an organisational level where it can be most effective and where it will gain support and endorsement from all levels of management, including Board Directors. The EAP should establish working relationships with a variety of internal departments (e.g. Human Resources, Occupational Health) (EAPA, 1994).

Programme acceptance and utilization is directly related to the degree of support from top management, and also to the involvement of employees, supervisors, line management, personnel, unions, welfare, and occupational health. One technique for maximizing the potential for a highly effective programme is to form an advisory committee representing the different levels, functions and sectors within the organization. This committee can formulate a policy statement, as well as specific strategies for implementation and evaluation. Indeed, the EAPA Standards document maintains that:

> The organisation needs to have an advisory committee with a high level executive mandate and this committee needs to involve representatives from a cross-section of the workforce (EAPA, 1994).

## INTERNAL VERSUS EXTERNAL SERVICES

As discussed in Chapter 3, fee structures for British EAPs are predominantly based on a per capita payment system, the average being about £25 (US $40.00) per employee per year. In contrast, other forms of employee counselling-only services tend to be charged on an as-used basis, ('fee for service' in US terms) with a management fee payable annually. Whether this can be managed more cheaply in-house depends largely on the size of the company. It has been estimated variously that 3000 to 10 000 employees is the cut-off point, above which contracting out is more expensive than an internal alternative (Reddy, 1993: 59). Most companies take the decision whether to provide counselling in-house or to contract out on grounds other than cost, assuming that they are committed to the expenditure.

The advantages of contracting out are: confidentiality may be seen to be greater; for small companies it may be more cost-effective; and external counsellors may have more expertise in specialized counselling situations. Against this, the main advantages of providing the service in-house are: counsellors know the company culture; and as problems are identified, it is easier for counsellors to influence managers, whether to help the employee affected, or, if appropriate, to modify their own behaviour or the company's practice. Despite the smaller proportion of in-house counselling services, their counsellors appear to have a better appreciation of the organization's policies, procedures and 'culture'.

The greater confidence that employees have in the confidentiality of the counselling service, the more likely they are to consult it. All EAP services guarantee confidentiality in general, with only certain exceptions in instances of severe physical or moral risk, public danger or very serious other breaches of the law. Companies with externally-sourced EAPs generally expect to be told less than companies with internal counselling services. However, this tends to lead to a lack of organizational feedback from EAP providers, even though such feedback does not in any way compromise confidentiality.

## INTRODUCING A COUNSELLING SERVICE

The EAP needs to be carefully positioned in order to maximize not only its contribution to individual employee-clients, but also its value as an employee benefit, and its role in organizational change and development. The EAP functions as an integral, yet independent, part of the organization. It needs to ensure that it offers support to all involved in achieving performance, encouraging change, and other company developments within corporate goals, policy and culture.

The feedback loop is an essential component of a responsive and constructive EAP. An EAP provider should report to the internal co-ordinator within the organization on any current or emergent organization trend which has been distilled quantitatively or qualitatively from problems presented by users of the EAP. As a corollary, providers should be proactive in suggesting steps which an organization might take to minimize any adverse impact of organizational developments, thus moving closer to primary prevention. Services that combine the best of internal and external provision are likely to function most effectively in this sense. An effective combination appears to be that of an internal company counsellor who has the back-up of an external service, either for cases which she or he feels unable to deal with, or, in some cases, for employees to contact directly, if they wish to.

However, a different type of service that is not really prevalent in the United Kingdom as yet could well be the best option. This type of counselling service would involve the company funding an external counselling provider to supply them with their own dedicated company counsellor or team of counsellors. These counsellors would visit the company regularly and become conversant with its culture, policies and procedures. Clinical responsibility would be held by the external provider thereby ensuring confidentiality and quality. In addition to combining the positive aspects of internal and external provision, this type of service would also address not only the negative aspects associated with external provision (e.g. possible lack of integration with the company) but also those of internal provision (e.g. lack of perceived confidentiality). A key aspect of this type of service would be the ability of the counsellor to give effective and timely feedback to the organization on cultural, structural, or operational managerial issues that may need attention.

## PUBLICIZING THE SERVICE

The formal aspects of publicizing an EAP service can be handled by the external contractor's routine communications of booklets or videos targeted at employees and introduced in briefing sessions or on a self-service basis. An explanatory letter about the EAP is sent to each employee and to their home address, if family is covered. With EAPs, a laminated card is also often given, detailing contact methods, and articles in the company newsletter also communicate the service. Counselling services are often also effectively advertised by word of mouth.

If publicity is not constantly reinforced, then usage rates may fall, so companies usually take steps to keep the interest and awareness of employees high. One publicity measure adopted by companies with an external EAP is to send out regular leaflets dealing with particular issues, e.g. alcohol problems, financial worries, family or relationship difficulties.

There is a need to emphasize to managers that the provision of the counselling service does not restrict their role. Usually, seminars are arranged to alert managers to the existence of the scheme and explain how they can identify when deteriorating job performance might be due to personal problems, and how to refer staff to the counselling service in these instances. In instances where unions participate in promoting an EAP, such seminars can also be run on a joint basis in order to maximize their contribution in avoiding or resolving individual industrial relations problems through mutuality.

## SERVICE AUDIT AND EVALUATION

The subject of audit and evaluation is addressed in detail in Chapter 11. However, a brief discussion is pertinent here in the context of EAP provider organizations' practices.

> An EAP provider needs to evaluate the appropriateness, effectiveness and efficiency of its internal operations. This could be achieved by identifying measurable objectives for both process and outcome evaluation. Evaluation needs to take place at least annually (EAPA, 1994)

Meaningful evaluation of an EAP depends upon having measurable programme objectives and data collection mechanisms. These should be developed early in the programme planning process. In addition to guiding the implementation of the EAP, measurable objectives allow the organization to judge the programme's progress and usefulness, and to identify the need for programme modifications. The procedures for achieving each objective need to be reviewed periodically to ensure that the objectives are obtainable. Data that measure programme effectiveness should be gathered routinely and analysed, in order to evaluate the extent to which the programme is achieving each objective. At the outset of the programme, a written evaluation plan should be developed, directly relating to the programme's goals and objectives, and stating the techniques by which the data will be collected.

The HSE Report research revealed that 47% of EAP providers do not set clear performance objectives before implementing an EAP (Highley & Cooper, 1995). Therefore, they are unable to monitor the performance of the EAP against agreed objectives or outcomes. The 53% of providers who set objectives do so to varying degrees. Providers routinely ask employee-clients to complete satisfaction questionnaires, but many providers do not evaluate or audit their EAPs in any consistent way. One provider expects an annual service uptake of at least 5% of employees, whilst another sets various objectives including 'speed of response from first contact to first session', 'user satisfaction levels at the end of counselling and after three months', and 'changes in performance levels'. Performance objectives are agreed with each customer company at the outset, according to one provider, and another indicated that client companies often specify in advance their own parameters (e.g. a decline in sickness absence, a desired level of uptake of the service).

In terms of evaluation, one client company itself sends out its own questionnaires annually to verify the number of employees who have used the service, whereas another relies on the feedback obtained from the provider. One provider evaluates its services by looking at 'usage rates', 'reports from counsellors' and 'feedback from client companies and individuals', whilst another provider says that it undertakes its own evaluation surveys amongst users. The same provider works with corporate clients in order to conduct research in organizations, as well as working in partnership with client companies to plan and conduct evaluation programmes. Company and client feedback, in conjunction with individual case monitoring, forms the evaluation of another provider's service.

A review of the daily operation of the programme does not necessarily measure its total impact on the organization and the effectiveness with which its fulfils its mandate. Therefore, a well-run EAP continually reassesses the needs of the organization. To assess the efficiency and quality of the service, process measures should be monitored. This essential audit procedure helps to identify the integrity of the programme both internally and comparatively.

The EAPA Standards document suggests that:

> EAPs should be audited by external, independent, professional auditors to agreed UK Standards, as laid down in the Standards document (EAPA, 1994).

Only a minority of providers, however, (40%) report that client organizations have commissioned an independent audit of their EAP, although what the audit consisted of is not clear. Whilst 45% of organizations report having evaluated or audited their counselling service, the rigour of the process may be in question, because, in fact, the services have not been audited or evaluated in any systematic and independent way. One provider who has not been audited believes that many companies are reluctant to formalize their monitoring procedures.

It is also the case, however, that EAP providers have traditionally resisted any form of cost evaluation by stating that EAP benefits cannot be quantified. The importance of justifying an EAP cannot be overestimated. Many social programmes must be evaluated to justify their existence to some external authority and even if this is not the case for an EAP, it should be evaluated, or at least audited, to ascertain the extent to which it is reaching its objectives and to find ways to improve the effectiveness of its performance. The goals of an EAP should be built in from the beginning and it is essential for organizations to be able to evaluate whether or not those goals are being met.

In the first place, companies need to know that the EAP is running smoothly and that the efficiency and quality of the service is high. Whilst such process evaluation, or audit, is an essential basis for continued improvement and development of the service, it does not measure 'value for money'.

Companies rarely actively attempt to quantify the cost savings made by the counselling service. There is a belief that the counselling service pays for itself in terms of reduced absenteeism, improved morale and a lower staff turnover, although this confidence is based on anecdotal evidence rather than hard data. Most companies provide a counselling service as an uncosted benefit for employees, and will continue to do so as long as it is believed to be useful, even if it costs more to operate than it saves.

Organizations are also often reluctant to audit or evaluate services for a number of reasons. First, some organizations still implement an EAP as a public relations exercise to 'show they care'; they may not, therefore, be particularly interested in its effectiveness. Secondly, most organizations take it for granted that programmes are effective, being assured by providers that EAPs are effective and, because other organizations have EAPs, companies do not perceive a need to invest in their own audit or evaluation. Thirdly, a frequently perceived problem with audit and evaluation is that of confidentiality, raised as a defence, in spite of the fact that a professional audit or evaluation carried out independently does not in any way threaten confidentiality. Fourthly, EAP counsellors and managers can feel threatened by the thought of being evaluated and will try to think of reasons why an evaluation of the EAP cannot be done.

As a consequence of the lack of audit and evaluation, once externally provided EAPs are put in place, few changes are made, and, if so, they tend to be minor or cosmetic. In contrast, internal counselling services are much more likely to have changed over the period of time they have been in place, and these changes are likely to have been more fundamental.

The haste and enthusiasm that often accompany the development and implementation of an EAP mean that audit and evaluation planning is usually either ignored or assigned a low priority. However, as EAPs become more of an everyday occurrence in Britain, organizations will increasingly be expected to justify their spending on an EAP, and evaluation and audit are essential for this verification.

## THE COUNSELLORS

### Introduction

This section examines the practices of counselling provider organizations in respect of the counsellors whom they employ directly and whose services they use in providing EAPs and counselling-only services in Britain. This material is drawn from the HSE Report data, and from provider organizations' responses. It is, therefore, illustrative of policies, practices and perceptions of contractor-providers alone. The perceptions of counsellors working for EAP providers are detailed in Chapter 8.

The findings of the HSE Report (Highley & Cooper, 1995) did not entirely accord with the recommendations put forward by the EAPA Standards document (1994); in particular, with regard to the minimum levels of qualifications and experience that an EAP's counsellors should have. The EAPA states that:

> The minimum professional standards for EAP counsellors are: training and experience to a level required by the registration and accreditation systems of the different professional bodies (e.g. BAC, BPS).

Another Standard relates to the fact that:

> EAP counsellors should have training and experience in work-related and organisational issues, and EAP practice.

Such experience is surely a prerequisite, along with recognized training in brief counselling and experience over an appropriate period of time.

> An EAP counsellor must be trained in short-term counselling and problem management (EAPA, 1994).

It is against a background of such professional criteria, that provider organizations' policies and practices will be addressed in respect of counsellors.

### Numbers Employed

The number of counsellors employed by individual providers varies from one up to 670. Only 10% of these counsellors are employees, with the other 90% being affiliates who are paid on an 'as used' basis. Affiliates may be independent practitioners or may have part- or even full-time employment in another sector of counselling. In a few instances, affiliates are paid an annual retainer, regardless of their activity level.

Only 70% of counsellors are actually described as counsellors by the providers, 17% are clinical psychologists, 8% are debt counsellors, solicitors or money advisers, 2% are registered Neuro-Linguistic Programming (NLP) psychotherapists, 1% are occupational psychologists, 1% are counselling psychologists and 1% are systemic psychotherapists. These proportions are depicted in Figure 6.2.

98

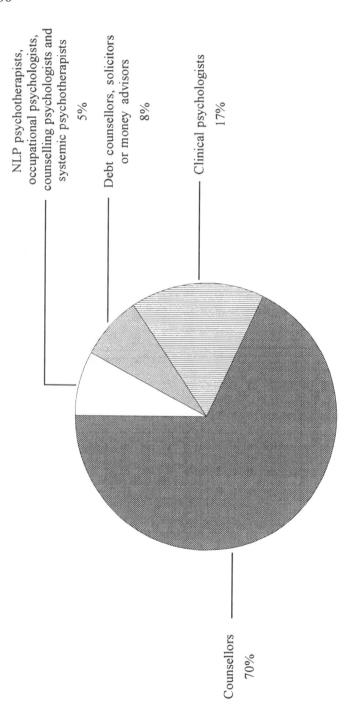

*Figure 6.2* Background of EAP counsellors. *Source:* Highley & Cooper (1995)

## Qualifications and Training

The training and experience that providers require of their counsellors vary widely. At one end of the spectrum one provider requires all counsellors to be United Kingdom College of Psychiatrists (UKCP) registered psychotherapists and to have at least six years' experience. However, this provider has some client companies who insist upon counsellors who work with their employees having a degree in psychotherapy and at least ten years' experience. Another provider uses only clinical psychologists, with the requirement that they must be chartered by the British Psychological Society. One provider insists upon all counsellors having a professional formal qualification in addition to their counselling qualification, such as psychiatric nursing, occupational therapy or psychology. Another provider simply requires a Diploma in Counselling, but demands that all counsellors have a minimum of 250 hours of supervised face-to-face counselling experience, with specific expertise in 'brief counselling'. A different provider has a similar requirement in that they insist upon counsellors having the equivalent of British Association for Counselling (BAC) accreditation, in addition to a minimum of two years' post-qualification experience. Yet another provider expects all counsellors to have completed at least 200 hours of classroom training plus 200 hours of supervised counselling experience. One provider even demands that all counsellors have been in private practice for at least five years. However, some providers only require counsellors to have a Diploma in Counselling and do not insist upon counsellors having gone through therapy themselves. It will be seen, therefore, that as the variety of qualifications and training specified of counsellors by providers is wide, client companies have a considerable range of training and qualifications from which to choose.

## Brief Therapy

The majority of providers say that they expect counsellors to be experienced at 'brief therapy'—an introduction to which was given in Chapter 2. One provider expects counsellors to produce evidence (e.g. a professional supervisor's reference) of their ability and willingness to do short-term counselling, whilst another provider ideally thinks that counsellors should be trained in 'brief therapy'. A similar provider gives all counsellors who do not have training in short-term work at least two days' training, during which their suitability is assessed. One provider prefers counsellors who have worked with a general medical practitioner (GP) or Relate, and a second provider, who believes that experience of short-term counselling is essential, states that the systemic psychotherapy approach fits this requirement perfectly. The provider who uses only clinical psychologists does so because 'brief therapy' forms part of the standard Chartered Clinical Psychology training. Finally, one provider points out that the ability to do short-term counselling is necessary because client companies cannot afford extended counselling, and with short-term counselling most cases reach resolution within four sessions. Only 63% of providers report that they check the counsellor's suitability for EAP work (i.e. brief therapy) with their professional supervisors. Again, a variety of practices is revealed by the research, showing a considerable concern for training in short-term counselling, with much specific reference to brief therapy.

### Experience in Workplace Counselling

A surprising finding from the research was that only 25% of providers expect their counsellors to have prior experience of workplace counselling, with 75% saying that this is not necessary. One provider who does insist upon all counsellors having experience of counselling in the workplace says that it is essential as it is the only way in which counsellors can gain credibility, especially where counsellors may be supporting managers.

Although the majority of providers do not insist upon their counsellors having such experience, some do expect counsellors to be able to demonstrate an understanding of the workplace. One provider states that experience of workplace counselling is not necessary because the provider trains counsellors for this type of work, whilst another gives at least two days' training in which workplace issues are addressed. One provider feels that because 95% of the counselling takes place at the provider's own premises, such experience is not necessary. Another provider suggests that although experience of workplace counselling is desirable, the relatively low rates of pay make it financially difficult to recruit such counsellors. Yet another provider says that such experience is not necessary because many problems are straightforward in counselling terms and would apply to any environment: all of this provider's counsellors do, however, train in business counselling issues such as redundancy, workplace law, and job-related stress.

## Recruitment of Counsellors

The ensurance of quality in counselling provision depends greatly on the recruitment of suitable persons, and their possession of suitable premises for the reception of clients. With the high level of use of affiliates and the wide geographical spread of clients, the control of quality in these two dimensions is crucial to the service to individuals and client companies.

According to the providers, the general method of recruitment for affiliate counsellors is the interview, even if this is only conducted over the telephone. A majority (63%) of providers say they interview all counsellors before placing them on their network. Two providers who do not interview all their counsellors say that interviews are superfluous because all the counsellors are 'hand picked' and are therefore already known to them. One provider feels that interviews (which poor counsellors can be very good at) are inappropriate and prefers to rely on professional supervisory reports. However, this provider does 'meet' all counsellors *after* selection. Two further providers explain that all counsellors are interviewed over the telephone and one also follows up references. The final provider who does not interview counsellors states that it only uses network counsellors very rarely, but before a client is referred to one the counsellor is interviewed and her or his professional supervisor contacted.

Two providers who do interview all counsellors say they have comprehensive formal interview and assessment procedures, and one also verifies counsellor qualifications. Another provider initially interviews counsellors informally but at induction conducts a formal interview. One provider insists on a minimum of two interviews with its representatives, followed by an interview with the counsellor's supervisor.

The subject of judging counsellors' assessment and diagnostic skills yielded some interesting comments. One provider says that it attempts to do so initially by interview and references, which it then monitors through in-depth supervision; whilst another seeks professional supervisors' references as well as including a case study at the interview stage. One provider says it is extremely difficult to judge the assessment and diagnostic skills of counsellors, but conducts rigorous checks on qualifications, supervision and case notes. Another two providers ask all counsellors to do a 'case study' presentation at interview. A different provider insists upon all counsellors providing three professional references. Most providers say that the best way of ensuring that counsellors maintain standards and quality is to carefully supervise their work initially, and subsequently by ongoing case management.

In a decentralized counselling service, the quality of professional premises used by network counsellors can have a considerable effect on clients' expectations. Only 31% of providers inspect all their counsellors' premises before placing them on the network. However, 25% of those who do not inspect premises feel that it is not necessary because their organizational structure means that all counselling is done at the provider's premises. One provider says that they do not inspect premises because of the geographical spread of counsellors, whilst another says it does not inspect premises until a referral is made to an individual counsellor. One provider claims to know all the counsellors personally, and so believes that inspection is not needed. Another 'has the intention' of inspecting all premises in the future, and a final provider relies on reports from 'other professionals' as to the suitability of counsellors' premises.

## Telephone Counsellors

The survey showed that 56% of providers use trained counsellors to answer their clients' contact by telephone. One provider says that in addition to being trained counsellors, all their telephone counsellors have the necessary skills to provide telephone support for raid, robbery and hostage victims. Another provider, however, says that experienced secretaries are entirely suitable for answering the telephone, whilst two different providers consider that the role of the receptionist is simply to verify the right of the client to access the service. They are then transferred directly to a trained counsellor.

Quality assurance in clients' contact by telephone with the counselling service is an important element, whether in initial contact via a hot-line or as part of ongoing counselling.

### Ensuring the Quality of Counselling

Some providers attempt to ensure the quality of counselling by giving questionnaires to clients and asking for feedback. Other providers tend to place more emphasis on case management and supervision. One provider states that it has counsellor guidelines that must be adhered to and there is also a complaints procedure. Some providers expect counsellors to submit detailed case notes that are monitored by a clinical review team, and one provider has fortnightly formal case discussions and peer review sessions.

### Training

A large majority (81%) of providers say that they train counsellors once they have been recruited, but this training varies in terms of content and depth. Some providers simply say that they provide extra training as required, but give no further details and one provider says that all BAC accredited counsellors, if they wish, have access to basic NLP training. Another provider trains counsellors in techniques for dealing with symptoms arising out of violent experiences, and some providers run quarterly workshops on topics and issues of particular interest. One provider says that it expects all its counsellors to abide by the BAC code in relation to continuing professional development. The provider that employs solely clinical psychologists states that each psychologist has a personal development programme that is continually reviewed.

### Information Provided to Counsellors
### about Client Companies

It is a matter for concern that (according to the survey) most providers do not give information to counsellors about client companies on a routine basis. If, for some reason, it is felt necessary, then this type of information is given to counsellors.

Most providers say they *sometimes* give counsellors some information about client companies, including culture, policies and procedures. One provider says that this is done in accordance with the client company's wishes and is usually on a 'need-to-know' basis. However, the telephone counsellors who work for this provider receive full briefings at the start of the scheme and up-dates as necessary. Most providers, however, do *not* give this type of information to counsellors as a matter of course, doing so only if the information may be useful. One provider arranges for its counsellors to visit client companies at the introduction of the programme and meet with key personnel in the organization, as well as doing site tours. Another provider asks client organizations to provide a 'brief for counsellors' and two providers believe it is essential for counsellors to know all about the company as standard practice.

### EAP Usage Rates

As with any administrative procedure, good practice dictates that an organization's system of counselling has a built-in feedback mechanism with both quantitative and qualitative measures.

> EAPs should provide the company with a breakdown of the types of calls received (EAPA, 1994).

The feedback typically splits calls between the various problem categories and also by age, sex, length of service, grade and location.

Usage rates are typically between 4% and 8% of staff, although there is some variation. Often, rates start low and then rise as employees begin to trust the service and respect its confidentiality and usefulness.

In terms of usage, there is an approximate 50%–50% split between males and females, and 91% of clients are employees, the remaining 9% being families or dependants. Clients from managerial positions represent 30% of all clients, with the other 70% being spread across a variety of non-management categories. In addition, three-quarters of all referrals are self-referrals, re-emphasizing the British tradition of individual (not organizational) assistance and the reluctance on the part of supervisors to incorporate EAPs into the management process of unsatisfactory employees. Provider organizations themselves differ in their attitudes toward the mode of referral, with 20% believing that self-referral is the only suitable method of referral for an EAP, and 80% saying that management referral also has a place, providing it is within strictly controlled boundaries.

The survey showed that for British counselling services, nearly a third of presenting problems are categorized as being emotional, nearly a quarter are work-related, a fifth stem from marital or family problems and nearly a further fifth of problems have legal or financial origins. Only a small number of clients report having alcohol (4%) or drug (1%) problems. The figures are shown in Figure 6.3.

Such proportions differ from US reported figures of usage, particularly of the extent of EAP usage on alcohol (4%) or drug (1%) problems. Any explanation of such differences is complex and capable of being contested, reflecting the cultural connotations inherent in transplanting a social intervention mechanism such as the EAP (Berridge & Cooper, 1994a). However, the indication is that the proportion of work-related problems is much higher (nearer 50%) for in-house counselling services, which may be the result primarily of the fact that in-house counselling services tend to be very organizationally aware. Counsellors will, therefore, focus on work-related issues, as well as on personal ones. In contrast, some external providers' EAP

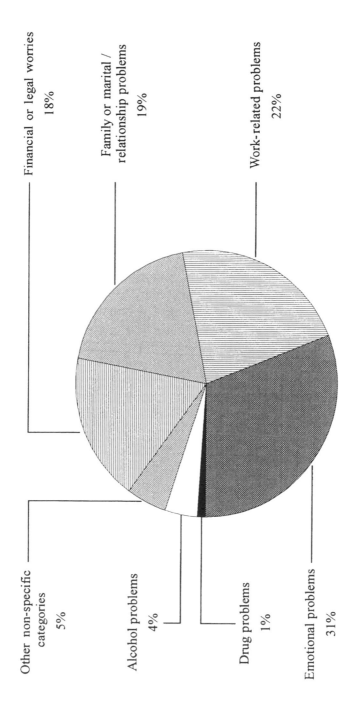

*Figure 6.3* Categories of problems presented by clients. *Source:* Highley & Cooper (1995)

counsellors see themselves as personal independent counsellors and actively dissuade the client from talking about work issues — an issue that is discussed in detail in Chapter 8 on counsellors as part of the survey on counsellors.

EAPs tend to be used only rarely at night, with 95% of calls being received between the hours of 7.00 a.m. and 11.00 p.m. The fact that few calls are made at night suggests that EAPs tend not to be used as an emergency service, and perhaps justifies certain providers' reluctance to offer a 24-hour service, in spite of EAP standards.

The majority of clients who contact the EAP go on to have face-to-face counselling (80%) with the average number of sessions being four. Such a progression argues for two observations related to EAP providers' coverage and practice. First, it illustrates the need for qualified counsellors to receive the initial contact from the client, and to respond to it according to the client's needs and expectations, making the decision over referral on informed criteria. Secondly, the relatively small number of four sessions may be seen as an indication of the philosophies and techniques of brief therapy. But care is essential, however, to ensure that system imperatives (such as cost, overload on counsellors) are not driving an excessive limitation on the number of counselling sessions.

## CONCLUSION

The practices and (implicitly) the supporting philosophies of British counselling provider organizations and (less comprehensively) in-house counselling services have been revealed by the HSA Report research data. The comparison with the UK EAPA Standards reveals broad agreement among providers concerning the coverage suitability and pertinence of the Standards. Such acceptance is not entirely surprising, since the EAPA is, in essence, a trade association to which all but one major provider belong.

At the same time, it is also noticeable that slavish or total conformity to the Standards was not demonstrated by providers. Most contractor organizations diverged markedly from standards in numerous aspects of their practice. Variability amongst competitors in the EAP industry may be argued to connote that the market principle is working in an industry that is still at a relatively immature and unconsolidated stage. The variability could be functional, enabling the testing-out of service provision and practice in the eyes of fellow professionals and the purchasers. But in the absence of widespread acceptance of even minimum practice standards on the part of the key firms that compose the EAPA, it is certainly risky for an intending purchaser of an EAP to make an informed and discerning decision about instituting a counselling service and through which method of provision.

# 7

# Workplace Counselling Purchasers

## INTRODUCTION

The research carried out at the Manchester School of Management between 1993 and 1995 (Highley & Cooper, 1995) was designed in part to discover the extent of employers' use of Employee Assistance Programmes (EAPs) in Britain, and to measure some of the main dimensions of such usage. A questionnaire was distributed either directly to organizations possessing their own counselling service of any type, or via the EAP provider, to the key decision-maker on this issue employed in the client organization. The results of 168 returned questionnaires were analysed, representing a response rate of 72%: as far as can be estimated, the returned questionnaires were representative of British practice.

## CHOICE OF COUNSELLING SERVICE: EAPs VERSUS COUNSELLING-ONLY SERVICES

One of the basic distinctions among models of counselling provision made in Chapter 4 was that between in-house provision against external provision. This distinction gave rise to issues of independence from management, expertise of counselling provision, and economies of scale and expertise.

The percentage of all organizations offering employee counselling who had opted for some form of EAP totalled

68%, and the various forms of counselling-only services totalled 32% (see Figure 7.1).

This twofold proportion of EAPs over counselling indicates the rapid advance made by EAPs over the more traditionally found counselling in Britain. But care needs to be taken with this proportion since some organizations claiming to have a full EAP service in practice probably only possess an enhanced counselling service. Also, it should be recalled that some organizations currently having an EAP may *not* have previously operated a counselling-only service for employees. No data are available on this point, but, also, there was no evidence that organizations were reverting to counselling only after having tried out an EAP. It is unlikely that counselling only will disappear completely since its underpinning values are central to the internal culture of certain organizations. But a further swing toward EAPs can be a confident prediction.

## CHOICE OF TYPE OF COUNSELLING SERVICES: INTERNAL VERSUS EXTERNAL

In theory, it could be expected that in-house EAPs and externally provided EAPs could functionally provide the same services. The internal corporate environment and the external socio-economic environments of organizations will, however, produce

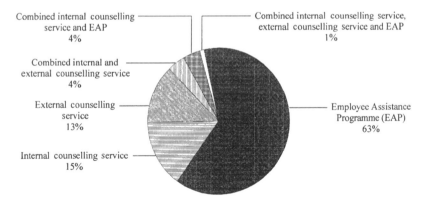

**Figure 7.1** *Different types of counselling services within organizations. Source:* Highley & Cooper (1995)

differing rationales for opting for external or internal provision of the service. The reasons put forward in favour of having an externally provided EAP include the factors set out in Table 7.1, which are not necessarily in order of frequency.

In-house counselling services were not felt necessarily to be less effective in delivering on the above points, but there was a widespread belief that they were more expensive per capita. Nevertheless, some firms with in-house provision saw them as more cost-effective, more accountable and more flexible. Importantly, firms with in-house counsellors felt that such people possessed a better appreciation of corporate procedures, policies and culture than external counsellors could do, and any potential loss of detachment was not mentioned. Hence, there appears to be uncertainty about generalizing overall on the comparative merits and advantages of in-house and externally provided counselling services, and the circumstances of individual organizations were often the key factor in the perception of an EAP.

## INITIAL IMPETUS FOR THE ADOPTION OF AN EAP

The initial impetus for an EAP in an organization proved to have a definite effect on whether an in-house or external programme

**Table 7.1**  *Main factors cited in favour of externally provided EAPs*

Confidentiality ensured for employees
Independence ensured
National coverage available
Wide range of issues covered
Higher skills of counsellors
Higher take-up encouraged
Flexibility and reliability of service
Set-up and development costs minimized
Lower per capita operating cost than in-house EAPs
Frees up HR professionals from counselling role
Frees up line managers from advisory role
Foreign parent company has external EAP
Company policy of external sourcing for services

*Source:* Highley & Cooper (1995).

was adopted. The initial 'champion' for an organizational innovation such as an EAP may be expected to gain internal political leverage over its nature and control, which will flow to a considerable extent from its internal or external location.

Figure 7.2 demonstrates that in 60% of organizations, the social science and medical professionals (personnel or human resources, occupational health, and welfare staff) promoted or inaugurated counselling services. Senior or line management, or trade unions, initiated counselling services in only 40% of organizations. Such sponsorship tends to indicate that traditional personnel management and welfare values, particularly humanistic and developmental values, may underpin the adoption decision and arguably the operational principles of such EAPs in a majority of organizations.

It is not surprising, then, with 48% of counselling being sponsored by the human services professionals (HR, personnel staff), that such organizations preferred externally sourced services. Such EAPs are typically less integrated with other organizational control systems and processes, because of counsellors' lack of detailed knowledge of the firm's economics, politics and culture. Organizational professionals with a highly developed, external frame of reference may well prefer specialist employee services (such as counselling) to have a large degree of autonomy from corporate philosophies and interests.

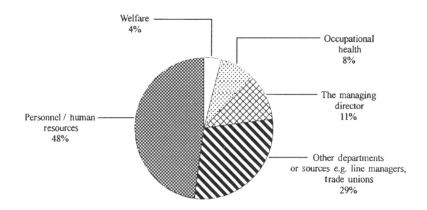

**Figure 7.2** *Who within the organization initiated counselling? Source: Highley & Cooper (1995)*

A more detailed analysis of sponsoring functions and the decision between in-house and externally sourced EAPs and counselling reveals a further dichotomy in provision (see Table 7.2). These figures suggest that if the personnel or HR function initiates the EAP or counselling service, it is twice as likely to be external as to be in-house. The reasons for such a trend are likely to include the developmental rather than control nature of the external service (as already mentioned), the problems of confidentiality with an EAP integrated with the HR function, and the personnel professional's wish to differentiate the HR and counselling roles as far as possible in practice.

The occupational health function's sponsorship of counselling or EAPs was four times as likely to correlate with in-house provision as with external provision. Explanations for this preference may lie in occupational health professionals' strong concerns for confidentiality and belief that it is most securely maintained internally, as occurs with occupational health and medical services. An additional reinforcement for the internal preference could lie in these professionals' feeling that they

**Table 7.2** *Sponsoring department or function and choice of in-house or externally sourced EAP or counselling*

| | Percentage of organizations making: | | |
|---|---|---|---|
| Sponsoring or initiating function or department | choice of in-house counselling/EAP | choice of externally sourced counselling or EAP | Total (weighted) |
| *Social science or medical professions* | | | |
| Personnel or human resources | 26 | 53 | 48 |
| Occupational health | 23 | 5 | 8 |
| Welfare | 19 | 1 | 4 |
| Sub-total | 68 | 59 | 60 |
| *Senior or line management* | | | |
| Managing director (or equivalent) | 1 | 12 | 11 |
| Other departments (e.g. line managers, unions, parent firm) | 31 | 29 | 29 |
| Sub-total | 32 | 41 | 40 |
| Total | 100 | 100 | 100 |

*Source:* Highley & Cooper (1995).

already possess counselling skills or can further acquire them, without the need for contracting out such sensitive, medically related services.

Unsurprisingly, where the welfare function initiates counselling or EAP services, such practitioners themselves are unlikely to advocate external contracting-out, even in times of outsourcing being a corporate fashion. This trend has had considerable significance in the US context, where a former emphasis on lay counsellors may well have resulted in current EAP emphases being in employee alcohol and drug/substance abuse counselling. This trend contrasts with the current British emphases on EAPs being broad-brush, broad-scope counselling.

The reverse situation, however, applies with managing directors (or equivalents) who are twelve times as likely to opt for external provision—a tendency that reflects boards of directors' concerns for concentrating on core business retaining functional flexibility, and cutting fixed overheads. Line managers are evenly divided between external and in-house provision. But this catch-all category includes disparate groups such as unions and parent firms whose orientations are diverse. Line supervisors, with goals of control over staff members, are likely to prefer internal provision, while trade unions' strong desires for independence of advice and total detachment from corporate processes are likely to predispose them towards external provision.

In spite of these distinct tendencies for initiating functions to diverge in a major way in their preferences between the type of EAP or counselling to be chosen, a general feeling was expressed by all groups that counselling is not well defined or understood in Britain. The lack of objective information about EAPs, including their potential benefits and shortcomings, was widely expressed. It may, however, weaken the validity of the rationales and preferences expressed by firms. This topic was developed further in Chapter 5.

## THE FINAL DECISION TO INTRODUCE
## A COUNSELLING SERVICE

Important though the initiation or sponsorship of a counselling service proposal may be, the ownership of the final decision demonstrates the real locus of information and power (see Figure 7.3). This figure shows, first, the extent to which the managing director (or equivalent) plays a key role in an expenditure item that may well not be particularly large in relative corporate terms. The need for the managing director to make the final decision rests, however, in the central cultural effect that an EAP or counselling provision can have on the political and social structure of the enterprise. Secondly, the largest single category is that of 'not sure' or a 'combination' of postholders, which reflects another characteristic of the introduction of counselling to an organization. An EAP or counselling service has a wide-ranging and pervasive impact on the organization, and requires extensive consideration, consultation and preparation for its introduction: it is far from being 'social tinkering', of which it is sometimes accused.

A revealing point is a comparison between the initiating or sponsoring departments or functions for counselling, and the final decision-makers (see Table 7.3). It is evident that initiation or sponsorship on counselling may originate from the specialist functions (personnel or human resources, occupational health, and welfare) in a total of 60% of EAP and counselling only instances combined. But a total of 47% of the final decisions are made at senior or top management level. By comparison, only a total of 16% of final decisions are made by specialists in personnel or human relations and occupational health combined. This lack of a final decisional role may reflect the lack of

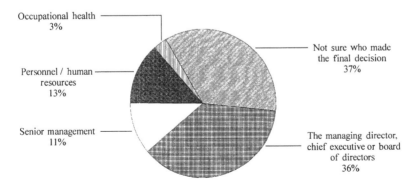

**Figure 7.3** *Who made the final decision to introduce a counselling service?*
*Source:* Highley & Cooper (1995)

organizational power on the part of personnel or human resources directors, or their budgetary penury. But when this evidence is related to the generally felt lack of definition and understanding of EAPs and counselling in Britain (see earlier in this chapter), it may be asked on what criteria are the 47% of decisions taken by senior or top management really based? Do counselling and EAPs give the impression of being 'championed' by middle and upper-middle people-specialist functional managers for valid technical, social and organizational reasons, but approved by top management on far less explicit criteria? A relatively conspiratorial motive is ventured by two of the present authors:

> One would expect that senior people in today's cost-conscious organisations would want some proof of the benefits of introducing a service, unless it is the case that the service is really being introduced to salve the conscience of the organisation which is undoubtedly putting excess strain on its staff, but is not prepared to do anything to change it (adapted from Highley & Cooper, 1995: 165–166).

**Table 7.3**   *Initiators and decision-makers on counselling introduction*

| | Counselling or EAP provision introduction | |
| --- | --- | --- |
| Department or function | Sponsorship or initiation % | Final decision-making |
| *Social science or medical professions* | | |
| Personnel or human resources | 48 | 13 |
| Occupational health | 8 | 3 |
| Welfare | 4 | – |
| Sub-total | 60 | 16 |
| *Senior or line management* | | |
| Managing director (or equivalent) | 11 | 36 |
| Other departments (e.g. line managers, unions, parent firms) | 29 | – |
| Senior management | – | 11 |
| Not sure/combination | – | 37 |
| Sub-total | 40 | 84 |
| Total | 100 | 100 |

*Source:* Highley & Cooper (1995).

But in the absence of detailed information on firms' business strategy in individual cases, such a contention is not capable of being proved.

## WHY DO FIRMS INTRODUCE COUNSELLING?

Firms have a wide variety of motives for introducing counselling, each organization responding to a perception of its internal and external environments, and how well it is adapting to them.

An analysis may be carried out formally via an attitude survey, indirectly through a study of indicators such as accidents, absenteeism, staff turnover or retirement statistics, informally through impressions of behaviour and morale, or intermittently through critical incidents coming to the attention of key opinion-shapers or central decision-makers. The organization's corporate strategy towards its environment will influence the relative importance of the factors in making that analysis and subsequent choice. The matrix of Miles & Snow (1978), incorporating the strategic roles of defender, prospector, analyser and reactor could predispose the organization to re-state these values in its rationale for adopting an EAP. The point here to be underlined is that consistency is required between the organization's strategic type, internal characteristics, formal and informal culture, procedures and perceptions — and the counselling provision adopted. For instance, a defender role (characterized by stability and retrenchment) could encourage the adoption of an in-house EAP in which the control element was dominant. A prospector role (opportunistic, flexible) could match up with an externally sourced EAP in which the developmental elements were emphasized. An analyser type (both protective and innovative at the same time) would require a counselling provision where counsellors possessed a discriminating knowledge of the organization. A reactor strategy (passive, minimalist) would predicate (if at all) in-house provision, for reasons of damage limitation and concealment of problems.

It is against this strategic background that employers' motives for introducing counselling and EAPs can be analysed. The six-fold categorization of employers' rationales for EAPs developed in Chapter 5 (humanist, efficiency, political, excellence, HRM and industrial relations) also will be used to illuminate the pattern of employers' motives.

Figure 7.4 depicts the motives cited for employers for introducing counselling in their organizations. Respondents were able to list six reasons and the 'total' figure indicates the percentage of employers who mentioned each factor among any of their motives. The lower section of each column indicates the percentage of times that each motive (when cited) was listed as the 'primary' reason for the introduction of counselling.

The two most frequently found reasons were those of 'generally to support staff members' (92%) and 'giving the impression of being a caring company' (76%). While accepting that both reasons are relatively qualitative and diffuse, they both fall within the category of 'humanistic', as mentioned in Chapter 5. They are difficult to define or to evaluate, but both relate to the creation of an appropriate corporate culture, with its potent influence upon attitudes, behaviour, and quality, particularly in the services and intangibles sector of employment. These two reasons probably equate most closely to the 'analyser' strategy, with its goal of tracking environmental changes, and compensating for or adapting to them. The high incidence of citation of both reasons highlights the near-ubiquitous nature of these motives — and their causal origins.

The third reason cited is 'help in adapting to organizational changes', an ever-present condition in contemporaneous companies as they seek competitive advantage ('prospector' strategy) or, indeed, survival ('reactor' strategy). Mentioned by 70% of respondents, this organizational and political motive points up the ever-present restructuring and re-engineering process that is essential for competitive organizations, as well as the de-layering and cost-cutting response of firms in economic troubles.

The stress ensuing from such processes and activities represents the fourth factor, affecting more than half of organizations (57%). This issue of stress in organizations was explored in detail in Chapter 1. A notable characteristic of job-related stress is its echoing effect on the workgroup and (more relevantly) on people's out-of-work context of social and personal life. A further remarkable feature of this category is

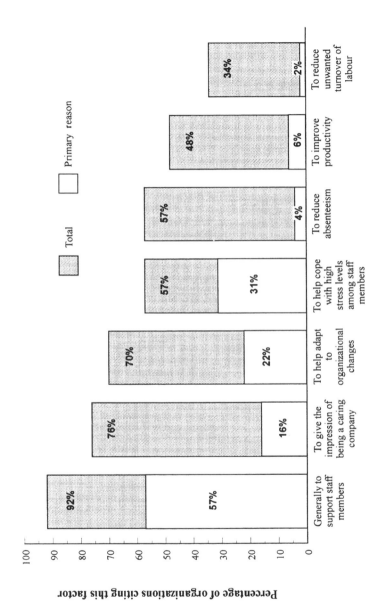

*Figure 7.4* Principal factors cited for the introduction of counselling. *Source:* Highley & Cooper (1995)

that 31% of respondents on this issue defined it as the 'primary' cause of the institution of counselling in their organization. This category of motives spans both management's humanistic concerns for stressed employees, and the economic sub-set of motives expressed by employers who wish to ensure full utilization of the labour factor — a condition that would not apply so acutely under a solely humanistic mind-set. While this category of motives contains several strategic-type roles, it coincides closely with the 'defender' role, and perhaps also with the 'reactor' role.

Factors, 5, 6, and 7 in rank of citation are:

- to reduce absenteeism (57%)
- to improve productivity (48%)
- to reduce unwanted staff member turnover (34%)

all of which contain elements of the economic and industrial relations rationales. As primary reasons for adopting counselling, they were mentioned only very infrequently, ranging between 2% and 6% of motives; this marked lack of concern for them as part of counselling undermines the suggestion sometimes made that counselling is a disguised form of industrial relations disciplinary tool.

The seven reasons cited demonstrate that humanistic–developmental reasons remain clearly the main focus for the adoption of counselling — despite the well-chronicled difficulties of evaluation of counselling or EAPs on such criteria. The third reason (adapting to organizational changes) illustrates how organizational and internal political issues are rising up the corporate agenda, and are increasing stress levels. The three least-cited motives (absenteeism, productivity loss, turnover reduction) are at the heart of traditional personnel management, and latter-day HRM. But the fact that all three reasons are lowly placed indicates the need for the revised HR function to move out of its traditional individual interventions at the foot of the organizational hierarchy and to transform itself into dealing competently with more conceptual, more intangible and strategic questions where higher-order qualitative skills will be in demand.

As a concluding study to this section, it is instructive to compare the raw scores of motives cited by employers with the weighted scores, when the degree of importance to them of each factor is taken into account. Table 7.4 illustrates this comparison.

Important differences are revealed by this table by comparison with Figure 7.4. The generalized humanistic factors ('general support' and 'impression of a caring company') both remain major reasons for the adoption of counselling, but both factors showed reduced weighted importance, and 'caring impression' falls considerably as a ranked factor from second to fourth. By contrast, 'coping with high stress levels', which is a more concrete performance-related factor, shows a much higher weighted score, rising from fourth to second, reflecting the depth of management's concern for this aspect. It is only one of two factors (the other being 'improve productivity') to display an enhanced score on the weighted basis: these two augmented factors demonstrate a definite heavier emphasis on the economic rationale on a weighted basis. The unchanged third factor ('adapt to organizational changes') with a near-unchanged weighted score underlines the continuing salience of organizational–political issues as an indication of the need for counselling support.

The remaining two factors ('reduce absenteeism' and 'reduce unwanted labour turnover') both remain secondary factors in

**Table 7.4** *Raw and weighted scores and rankings of employers' factors for the introduction of counselling*

| Factor | Raw percent- age of frequency of citation | Weighted percent- age of frequency of citation | Raw ranking among motives | Weighted ranking among motives |
|---|---|---|---|---|
| General support for staff members | 92 | 87.5 | 1 | 1 |
| Help in coping with high stress levels | 57 | 81.0 | 4 | 2 |
| Help in adapting to organizational changes | 70 | 68.8 | 3 | 3 |
| Giving the impression of a caring company | 76 | 63.2 | 2 | 4 |
| To improve productivity | 48 | 62.8 | 6 | 5 |
| To reduce absenteeism | 57 | 48.8 | 5 | 6 |
| Reduce unwanted labour turnover | 34 | 28.0 | 7 | 7 |

*Source:* Computed from Highley & Cooper (1995).

employers' motives for adopting counselling. This de-emphasis on industrial relations issues again highlights the view of decision-makers and sponsors of counselling that it is less an economic tool, but more a high-level cultural and organizational intervention—even if conducted more at the level of individual coping rather than at that of corporate strategic advice.


## ANALYSIS OF FIRMS' REASONS FOR THE CONTINUATION OF COUNSELLING

It has to be recognized that firms' reasons for continuing with counselling may differ from their motives for introducing it. Highley and Cooper (1995) did not explore such reasons explicitly, but indirect evidence is provided by data on the age of counselling service provisions in organizations. The assumption can be made broadly that employers who continue to finance counselling must, however, be deriving some satisfactions and benefits from their investment.

Figure 7.5 illustrates the length of duration of counselling provisions in organizations. The fact that 30% of services had only been in place up to one year demonstrates both the upsurge in interest that has grown throughout the 1990s, and the rapid expansion of the EAP and counselling industry.

In-house services tend to be longer established than external provisions, resulting from their occupational health origins. In-house services have, however, undergone major changes in 40% of cases, compared with 18% that have done so across the whole sample of companies. Most in-house services have moved on dramatically from

> providing basic information, advice and guidance to now providing professional counselling through a well-structured, sophisticated and often separate counselling service (Highley and Cooper, 1995: 172).

By contrast, external services tend to be more recently established, often stemming from the relatively recent phenomenon of provider firms' highly refined and targeted marketing of a relatively standardized product. Such external services have experienced little change, once installed, and modifications tend

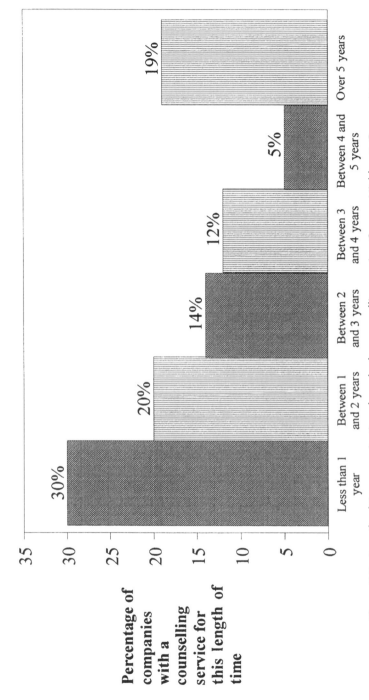

***Figure 7.5*** *Length of time organizations have had a counselling service. Source:* Highley & Cooper (1995)

to be evolutionary, minor or presentational: EAP and counselling contractors experience commercial pressures to routinize their product and its applications in the light of economic business logic over the past few years. On the basis of experience in other areas of business consultancy relating to the installation of administrative and procedural systems, it may, however, be expected that major revisions may be required to EAPs in the six- to eight-year points in their operation. Hence, the substantial modifications to many EAP external provisions may well be expected quite shortly.

## ASSOCIATION OF COUNSELLING SERVICES WITH COGNATE DEPARTMENTS

The extent of undue or inappropriate influence or control over counselling services is crucial to their effective and confidential operation, and to their perception by employee clients. A linkage between a newly adopted counselling service and long-established functions, such as personnel/HRM or occupational health, might be of great organizational assistance to the counselling function, because of the latters' superior organizational knowledge and greater political power. Professional values and practice standards, however, argue for as much independence as possible for counselling, in a privileged relationship with other centres of organizational authority.

Figures 7.6 and 7.7 illustrate the association between counselling and these cognate functions, for in-house and externally sourced counselling, respectively. The personnel/HRM function overshadows the external counselling provision with up to 69% of the interface with the provider. For internal services, the personnel/HR function still plays a role in 52% of instances, but significant influences are occupational health (up to 38%) and a completely separate welfare function (10%). Internally, however, a substantial 21% of services are operating independently of functional oversight, reporting directly to the board of directors or the top management tier. For the vast majority of counselling, the question must be raised whether the counsellors themselves are professionally content with lay influence, if not *de facto* indirect control of their activities and

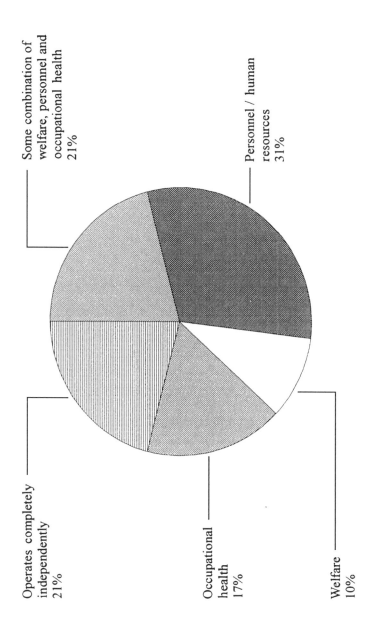

Some combination of
welfare, personnel and
occupational health
21%

Personnel / human
resources
31%

Operates completely
independently
21%

Occupational
health
17%

Welfare
10%

**Figure 7.6** Departments with which internal counselling services are most closely associated. Source: Highley & Cooper (1995)

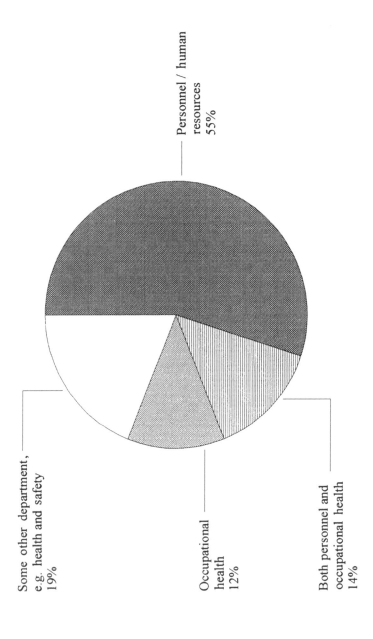

**Figure 7.7** *Departments with which the external counselling services are most closely associated. Source:* Highley & Cooper (1995)

their outcomes, being exercised by other professional or expert functions within the organization.

## CONCLUSIONS

The HSE Report survey of counselling and employers' motives for its adoption has shown considerable replication of the practice criteria set out in Chapter 5 (Highley & Cooper, 1995). External, contractor-provided services predominate, and the 'champions' of counselling are the personnel and HRM function. For new counselling service installations, a decision by top management is most often the key factor, since this introduction marks a step-change in the organizational culture — a fact that is shown again in the cultural–organizational orientations that are most cited in management's expectations of the EAP or counselling outcomes. The long-run form and future of counselling remains unclear in a context of expansion of coverage across many sectors of British business, industry and commerce. If counselling is to follow HRM's dictum of ensuring its future by acquiring organizational centrality, it will have to move its present principal focus on the employee client to wider and more prestigious goals, such as integration with quality initiatives, and inclusion in corporate plans and strategy.

# 8

# EAP Counsellors: Their Views, Qualifications, Training and Experience

## INTRODUCTION

As more and more organizations see the benefit of counselling, so the need for well-qualified professionals has increased and will continue to do so. The irony is that there are few professionals available who have the wide range of skills necessary to help organizations. What is needed is an individual who has professional counselling training and experience as well as an experience and understanding of organizations. Stress acting on a particular individual at work can stem from a number of organizational sources. Whilst it is important to help and counsel a troubled person on a one-to-one basis, it is also crucial to get at the root of the problem. In some cases, the sources of difficulties are internal or rooted in the client's past. But in many others, they are linked to the way in which a job is organized or a work group is structured, or to the way in which managers or supervisors treat their subordinates. Thus, we need a new breed of professional who can utilize not only counselling skills but also understand organizational behaviour (Cooper, 1986). In addition, counsellors must be able to appreciate the pressures that both employees and organizations are under, and not lose sight of the distinctive workplace counselling perspective. An individual's personal difficulties are more likely than not to impact on work performance, and a workplace counsellor is asked to address these, even if they are secondary issues (Galliano, 1994).

So, the work of an Employee Assistance Programme (EAP) or workplace counsellor is very different from any other form of counselling, requiring not only that the individual has recognized qualifications, but also ideally possesses experience of the world of work and workplace counselling. In addition, workplace counsellors need to be well qualified in short-term counselling, which is the dominant therapeutic model of EAPs, ranging from as little as three to a maximum of eight sessions: many British EAP providers use a five- or six-session model. The same counsellor, in many instances, is called upon to make an initial assessment of the client and to make a decision about the type of therapy that the client needs. The counsellor then has to decide whether or not she or he has the ability to work with the client, or whether to refer the client on for some alternative therapy (Highley & Cooper, 1994).

## WHAT IS COUNSELLING?

In times when the word 'counselling' is used freely and loosely by many occupations (especially in selling jobs), clients are understandably unclear, if not wary, about its practice. Orlans (1986) distinguishes between 'psychotherapy', 'counselling', and the use of 'counselling skills'. Whilst all three may be potentially helpful to organizational members and clients, there is often considerable confusion as to what is on offer and the relevance of different approaches to different problems. The popular view, however, appears to regard counselling as 'less serious' than psychotherapy, in terms of presenting problems. Counselling skills are seen as the stock-in-trade of lay, if not untrained, advisers — often their only skill or practice model.

The definition of counselling proposed by the British Association for Counselling (BAC) is:

Counselling occurs when a counsellor meets the client, in a private and confidential setting, to explore a difficulty the client is having, distress he may be in, or perhaps the vague dissatisfaction with life and loss of a sense of direction or purpose. It is always at the request of the client and no one can be properly 'sent' for counselling (BAC, 1988).

This definition predates the major growth of EAPs in its final caveat: while independent professionals may well subscribe to this restriction, many experienced EAP counsellors may feel that they have little choice other than to accept the limitation. According to Orlans (1986)

the overall objective of counselling is to help individuals live more effective and fulfilled lives. Whilst this general goal is part of all counselling, the extent to which general or specific goals are emphasised will depend on the orientation of the particular counsellor.

An emphatic rejection of the organization's goals and culture is unlikely, however, to bode well for a contractor hoping for a renewal of the service contract.

## COUNSELLING IN THE WORK SETTING

The Institute of Personnel Management's (IPM, now Institute of Personnel Development, IPD) *Statement on Counselling in the Workplace* (1992) does not make a clear distinction between the activity of counselling and the activity of counselling skills, but uses the concept of a continuum. The statement recognizes that 'almost all personnel specialists and managers are engaged in some kind of activity which could be termed counselling'. The continuum ranges from advanced psychotherapy at one end, to, at the other, line managers or supervisors, who have no structured training, but who possess an intuitive conviction that their experience and their natural talent will suffice. The current (1996) professional education programme of the IPD recognizes that interpersonal skills and organizational knowledge, including issues of stress, are important aspects of the personnel manager's intellectual and practical toolkit. An optional module, entitled *Employee Counselling, Support and Welfare*, provides a credible introduction to the counselling role, including EAPs. Its assessment includes an element of basic practical skills. But, overall, its aim is realistically limited to an appreciation of counselling and its role within welfare, occupational health and Human Resources Management (HRM) services.

However, according to Berridge (1993b):

> Professional counselling requires far more than personnel management training, particularly that which handles the personal non-work related problems, calling for cognitive, analytic and affective skills of a relatively high order. These are usually developed through training within a socio-psychological discipline and the sensitivity required normally is developed through directed practice.

It is commonly recognized that any categorization of presenting 'troubles' within an EAP brings definitional problems, as has been discussed in Chapters 2 and 6. Complex problems of troubled employees are many-faceted, requiring multiple categorization. In Britain, the most common categories of 'problem areas' in workplace counselling are debt, health, relationships, general emotional disturbance and, especially, anxiety. Alcohol and drug dependency account for only 5% of presenting problems, though the proportion rises when underlying issues are also assessed. General personal distress, plus marriage and family conflict, account for 50% of the counsellor's daily task. Job pressures are the primary source of stress in 22% of cases, and are probably implicated in many more (see Figure 6.3). Financial and legal worries account for 18% of problems being dealt with by EAPs (Highley & Cooper, 1994). This categorical confusion serves to reinforce the role of the skilled counsellor in the referral stage as much as in the therapeutic process.

Only a tiny proportion of those who use counselling services would be diagnosed in clinical terms as mentally ill. Instead, they are often self-reliant and capable individuals, troubled by conditions of overload, overstretch and underopportunity for analysis. One commentator puts it vividly:

> What most counsellors are dealing with are 'excesses' in one of a number of key areas. In one or the other — often in two or three at the same time — people have overspent their 'capital', their credit, their resources and are, so to speak, temporarily running in the red. This is most obvious in the case of financial resources. It is, however, just as tempting for many to 'overspend' in other areas, e.g. physical resources, social resources, psychological resources, skills resources (Reddy, 1991: 51–52).

Thus, today, many clients of workplace counsellors are receiving help for problems that do not reflect the degree of severity that many counsellors are used to dealing with. The problems confronting counsellors are likely to be universal problems of living, which call for different techniques and models of assistance. Counsellors must have a 'person-in-situation' perspective that emphasizes the need to understand the situational contexts of the problems that people experience (Cunningham, 1994).

This chapter will focus on the views of counsellors working for EAP providers. Little, if any, independent work has been carried out in Britain to assess the qualifications, training, experience, theoretical orientations and attitudes to the EAP work of EAP counsellors. To gain this information, in-depth interviews were conducted and a questionnaire was devised as part of an independent study of EAPs and workplace counselling, carried out for the Health and Safety Executive by Manchester School of Management (UMIST), during 1993–1995, and reported in the HSE Report (Highley & Cooper, 1995), see Introduction.

## NUMBERS AND BACKGROUND
## OF COUNSELLORS

The labour market for workplace counsellors demonstrates an immature state in Britain, typical of an embryonic industrial sector. Few counsellors are employed full-time by a single provider company, or obtain their sole professional activity from EAP or workplace counselling activities.

Only a minority of counsellors work for only one EAP provider, with the vast majority (62%) working for at least two providers. Many counsellors work in general or specialist private practice as well as doing EAP work. The survey showed first that 34% of counsellors report working for between 10 and 40 hours per week for EAP providers, whole 65% do EAP counselling for less than 10 hours per week. A positive view of this ratio is that EAP practice is hence receiving considerable input from other counselling areas and from a variety of therapeutic models, thereby encouraging a professional richness of perspectives.

Secondly, the previous employment background of counsellors is extremely varied. Some counsellors have been in managerial positions within industry, and have entered counselling at a later stage in their career. Those counsellors who have been qualified for some time have worked in a variety of professional roles, including: careers guidance; alcohol and drug abuse; the NHS; outplacement; industry; education; and the police service. This variety may give rise to some concern that workplace counselling is a minority and undervalued activity, especially if the concern is linked to the activity levels mentioned in the preceding paragraph.

The number of clients seen by counsellors varies considerably. One counsellor explained that she had received very little work over the period of two years that she had been working for a provider, which was in contrast to another counsellor who lived in the same area and was having to turn away work from that provider because of other commitments. Counsellors were generally in agreement that the amount of work is variable, and it depends upon where the counsellor is located geographically in relation to a provider's contracts. In some cases, the work is seasonal, with spring and summer being the busiest periods. Counsellors with specialist skills in post-traumatic stress find themselves carrying out block contracts for particular companies; in some cases, this comprises the bulk of their EAP work. The consensus is that counselling in itself accounts for about 10% of a professional counsellor's work, and as one counsellor stated: 'You couldn't make a living from it'. Counsellors who are registered for more than three EAP providers state that they rarely work for more than two with whom they are registered at any one time. In some instances, counsellors had been registered with five providers, but only ever received referrals from two of them.

The 'Balkanized' labour markets for workplace counsellors, as depicted by the survey findings, indicates a fragmented labour supply, and a fluctuating demand pattern, characterized by only occasional gluts. A lack of clear definition of workplace counselling, combined with a high substitutability of labour amongst counsellors, seems to suggest a relatively chaotic market in which employers can exercise considerable economic dominance, but in which they also experience problems of quality assurance. The counsellors themselves have yet to move toward any qualitative or quantitative control of the counselling labour market. Such a situation parallels to some extent the professional EAP counsellors' market in the United States, with labour market deregulation and the employer's 'right to hire'. But in the American context, counsellors have professionalized counselling training to a high level, with the Master in Social Work (MSW) degree becoming almost obligatory for occupational entry (Cunningham 1994; Berridge 1996a).

## COUNSELLORS' QUALIFICATIONS AND TRAINING

The test of workplace counselling is at the point of face-to-face contact between counsellor and client. However well designed or monitored the programme, the client's needs are satisfied according to the capability and professional expertise of the counsellor. Many early counsellors (especially those in industrial alcoholism) and many early welfare officers, possessed high talents for personal persuasion and empathy. But with increasing professional responsibility for the outcomes of counselling, the demand rose for quality and consistency: as in other professions, training and recognized qualifications were seen as the solution.

The research suggested that the quality of counsellors' training and qualifications is generally satisfactory, but that some 22% of counsellors involved in workplace counselling and EAPs are not properly qualified. The findings do not support the recommendations put forward by the EAPA Standards document with regard to the minimum levels of qualifications and experience that an EAP counsellor should have. The result revealed that between 10% and 20% of counsellors are currently being recruited without formal counselling qualifications and/or appropriate experience. There was a general concern amongst counsellors about this proportion of people who are not qualified and lack experience of EAP counselling. Most counsellors were aware of people working for providers without appropriate qualifications and experience, but they did not have the capability to change this state.

The EAPA Standards document states that:

> Each EAP shall retain counsellors qualified to perform their duties. The quality of provision depends on the professional qualifications, training and experience of its counsellors (EAPA, 1994: 18).

The Standards go on to explain that staff competence is critical to programme success and that, depending upon the type of services provided, various levels of experience, professional training, and supervision may be required. However, basically the work of an EAP counsellor is that of crisis intervention, assessment and short-term counselling, and a high level of generalized and specialized professional training is required. The EAPA also states that:

> The minimum professional Standards for EAP counsellors are: training and experience to a level required by the registration and accreditation systems of the different professional bodies, e.g. BAC, BPS (EAPA, 1994:18)

Among those counsellors surveyed, nearly 80% held a fully recognized qualification in counselling, such as a Postgraduate Diploma in Counselling. However, 11% held no formal counselling qualifications, and a further 11% held only a basic Certificate in Counselling. A number of these counsellors were working for between 10 and 40 hours per week, carrying out EAP counselling, despite having no formal counselling qualifications. In addition, a number of counsellors said that they were concerned about the levels of qualifications and experience of some counsellors, and, consequently, about the dangers for the client when faced with an inexperienced counsellor; they felt that clients should be made aware that they can complain if they are not satisfied with the standard of counselling they receive.

One counsellor explained how he had only been qualified as a counsellor for one year and had been working for three providers for this same length of time. This counsellor recognized that he did not have the experience of some counsellors and genuinely expressed surprise that he had been recruited. Another counsellor held only a basic Certificate in Counselling, yet felt that his experience outweighed the need to undertake further qualifications. One counsellor was concerned about counselling standards and qualifications *per se*, in that a growth industry in counselling courses has existed over the last five to ten years, from basic level upwards to intermediate. His concern was that people consider that the completion of basic courses enables them to call themselves counsellors. On the other hand, colleagues were aware of counsellors who were working for EAP providers, having completed in-depth counselling courses, but who were totally unsuitable to carry out counselling. In one instance, a counsellor explained how he had been a professional supervisor for an individual who was ill-equipped to counsel, and yet who had been recruited nevertheless by an EAP provider without taking up his professional reference.

Counsellors who lacked counselling qualifications were quite open about this absence, tending to justify it by stating that they had experience of counselling within the workplace; for instance, personnel or welfare. The basis of their expertise was the simple use of practical counselling skills without any wider formal training. By contrast, professionally qualified counsellors revealed widely that they are often faced with an individual who had been referred with a fairly minor problem that was not the underlying issue. It was only through extensive training and experience that the counsellor was able effectively to assess and deal with the client's problems. Thus, a 'counsellor' who has no formal counselling training is unlikely to be appropriate for EAP work. It is extremely disturbing that some providers are recruiting unqualified individuals on the strength of their practical workplace experience only.

There was concern amongst counsellors about BAC accreditation and whether or not this is an appropriate mechanism for judging the standard of counsellors, especially as anyone can become a member of BAC. Some counsellors had abstained from BAC accreditation for this reason. Certain EAP counsellors with backgrounds in psychology (enabling them to become members of the Division of Counselling Psychology) raised concerns about the way counsellors are accredited with the BAC, which bases accreditation on the number of hours' training and supervised practice counsellors have received. One psychologist stated his view that 'the BAC is trying to turn counselling into a profession': in his opinion 'stand-alone counselling is not appropriate as a profession'.

Another Standard relates to the fact that:

> EAP counsellors should have training and experience in work-related and organisational issues, and EAP practice (EAPA, 1994: 18).

This has to be an essential component, along with recognized training in brief counselling and experience over a certain period of time.

> An EAP counsellor must be trained in short-term counselling and problem management (EAPA, 1994: 31).

Whilst providers report that counsellors need to be experienced in short-term counselling, they also feel that experience of workplace counselling is not essential. The survey showed that 18% of counsellors said that they did not have any previous experience of short-term counselling prior to working for EAP providers. The majority of counsellors qualified to practise in EAP work use a brief-therapy approach. There are theoretical and practical variations between these counsellors, but in the main they subscribe to the view that they actually prefer brief counselling as opposed to long-term counselling, and had backgrounds in brief therapy. These counsellors stated clearly that it is important to use the approach best suited to the client. It was felt that counsellors with no previous experience in brief therapy would find EAP work quite difficult to adapt to and perhaps quite frustrating. It is felt essential that counsellors have sufficient training and experience to carry out an appropriate assessment at the first session. One of the areas that caused these counsellors the most dissatisfaction was resolving work-related problems. It was found that counsellors with only basic training and experience in workplace counselling were somewhat out of their depth, and had genuine difficulty in defining what approach they used when carrying out their counselling. EAP providers who are recruiting unqualified counsellors are, to a certain extent, undervaluing the training and experience of 'good' counsellors who have undertaken extensive training, and they are also potentially endangering clients.

Whilst the prime responsibility for counsellor qualifications and training must lie with the EAP provider, it is also the individual counsellor's responsibility to ensure that she or he has the relevant skills to do the job:

EAP counsellors have to show that they have a level of training and competencies equivalent to that recommended by the EAPA in the UK (EAPA, 1994).

Furthermore, according to the EAPA Standards:

> Individual EAP counsellors are responsible for recognising the limitations of their competencies and making certain that all work is performed within those limitations (EAPA, 1994: 18).

The variability between counsellors' training, qualifications and experience must give rise to disquiet in the provision of a sensitive, qualitative personal service. It must be problematic whether the EAPA, the BAC and the workplace counselling industry can regulate their own occupational qualifying association in the classic professional pattern (Millerson, 1964). The alternative is to institute statutory licensing for the protection and information of clients.

## SELECTION OF COUNSELLORS AND THEIR FACILITIES

The methods used by provider firms for selecting counsellors were extremely varied, and gave rise to considerable concern among counsellors themselves. Where counsellors worked for more than one provider (a common occurrence), the variability caused counsellors to comment adversely about the inconsistency and inadequacy of the general selection process, and on the methods used to evaluate assessment and diagnostic skills. According to providers, the general method of selection for network counsellors is the interview (63% of cases), although in many instances this is conducted over the telephone. The extent of the formality and structure of interviews varied greatly, with some 50% of counsellors feeling it was informal. It is surprising to find that 18% of counsellors selected had no interview at all, and a small number were hired solely on the recommendation of a third party. It was also a matter for concern that references were not taken up in a number of cases, the counsellor's suitability for short-term therapy was not always checked, nor was the candidate's professional supervisor always consulted. In the interests of the protection of clients, these omissions are imprudent (to say the least) on the part of the provider organization.

The evaluation of applicants' assessment and diagnostic skills equally presents an inconsistent picture, as shown in Figure 8.1.

Applicants reported that the largest proportion of providers (30%) use comprehensive written procedures, including case studies and in-depth interviews. The 4% of providers who interview and require BAC accreditation also approach this desirable criterion. The lack of any personal evaluation of the individual's counselling skills on the part of those providers who select only on qualifications (13%) or a directory entry (4%) must represent a potential gap in providers' quality assurance procedures. The lack of clarity in evaluation perceived by 27% of counsellors represents a disturbing opacity of professional relationships, which again must impinge on the quality of service given to clients. Finally, the reliance on previous experience and training (18%) or previous voluntary experience (4%) raises issues of the quality and level of such training and of the professional supervision associated with it. Certainly, workplace counsellors are an experienced group in terms of personal counselling, as depicted in Figure 8.2, but not necessarily in workplace counselling.

The many years of experience also reflect counselling in areas other than workplace-based counselling, as well as untrained or voluntary experience. Such length of practice may serve to some extent as an assurance of quality.

The location of the counselling activity can have a significant influence on the perception of the EAP, as held by the individual client or the employing organization. Only a few providers, as part of a comprehensive selection and evaluation procedure, included a formal inspection of the counsellor's premises. The locations used are shown in Figure 8.3.

Some counsellors' reported that the selection process used by at least one of their provider employers had included an informal interview in their own homes, in anticipation of their counselling work being carried out there.

As mentioned earlier, counsellors were often dissatisfied with the lack of rigour and comprehensiveness in the selection and initial professional evaluation process of provider organizations. One counsellor (who was registered with five providers) was generally unimpressed with the selection processes and standards of EAP providers. Concern was also expressed about

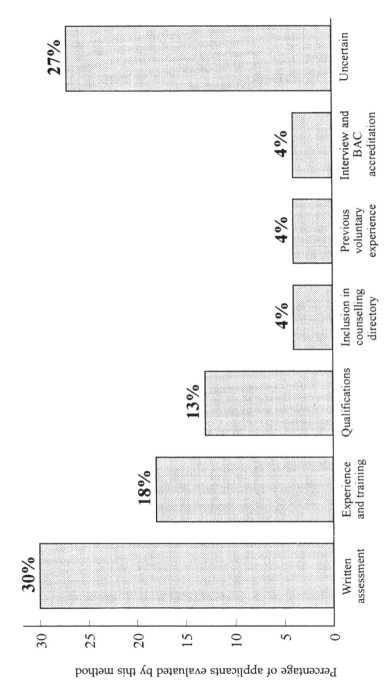

*Figure 8.1* Selection methods: evaluation of assessment and diagnostic skills. *Source:* Highley & Cooper (1995)

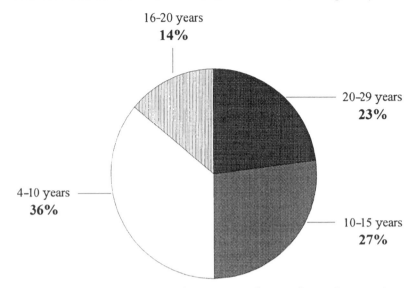

**Figure 8.2**   *Counsellors' years of experience of counselling (all types). Source: Highley & Cooper (1995)*

EAP providers who were willing to accept as counsellors persons with qualifications as diverse as clinical psychology, social work and nursing: it was felt that such people were selected on the basis of having a general professional background, and not on their tested counselling abilities and qualifications. If individuals are trained in a cognate but different profession, it does not bestow on them the necessary expertise to practise counselling with professional integrity.

In summary, the selection process of counsellors presents a somewhat disturbing picture. The geographical spread of EAP provider organizations poses undoubted problems of standard-ization, as do unanticipated levels and types of service demand. The standards and procedures of the most demanding providers ensure a consistent and high-quality standard of counselling for clients, and justify the fees paid by employers with contracted-out EAPs. Yet too many procedures are informal, and in too many instances standards and facilities are evaluated informally, implicitly and taken for granted. It could well be that some of the problems associated with counsellors' qualifications and training (mentioned in earlier parts of this chapter) are a reflection of the inconsistent and unsatisfactory selection practices used by some providers.

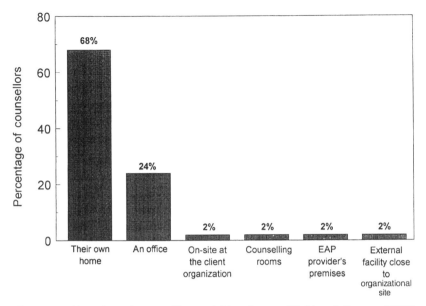

***Figure 8.3*** *Location of counselling activities. Source:* Highley & Cooper (1995)

## COUNSELLORS' VIEW
## OF PROBLEMS ENCOUNTERED

The essence of British employee counselling practice is that of short-term therapy and brief therapy, centred around practice models using a restricted number of counselling sessions to assist the client in the resolution of a problem. In terms of a classification of EAPs (Jones et al., 1988), it is a 'limited utilization' programme that aims at assisting a relatively 'functioning' employee to cope with and resolve limited and short-term non-acute issues. By contrast, a 'full service' programme would aim to tackle any kind of problem, however severe, and would provide unlimited access in terms of time and cost.

Many counsellors said that they had been able to cope with the problems that clients were reporting: anxiety, depression, and mental ill-health are considered fairly routine by counsellors. But there was some concern about receiving some particularly difficult cases, including attempted and potential suicides, major family traumas, and sexual abuse. In the majority of such cases, the 'real' problem had not been the presenting problem.

Counsellors reported finding it generally difficult to work within the allocated sessions and either tended to negotiate extra sessions, or referred clients back to the provider immediately. Some counsellors explained that what they undertake in EAP counselling, in many cases, is to reach a satisfactory diagnosis and assessment and often some motivational work in order to enable the client to recognize her or his problem. It can often take four sessions to achieve this limited objective. One counsellor stated that she was not prepared to deal with psychiatric cases, as she is not paid enough. Counsellors expressed concern that clients had been referred to them with severe problems that counsellors were not trained to cope with, and, consequently, they had to refer the client back to the provider. Furthermore, counsellors said they were not aware of what happened to individual clients when they were referred back to the provider.

The actual number of sessions provided varies according to EAP providers' practice and the contracts negotiated with their client companies. While counsellors, in general, report being able to negotiate extra sessions, some counsellors felt that it was important to work within the session limit. One counsellor argued: 'Three sessions, to a person who is in need, are better than no sessions at all'. Counsellors are not necessarily satisfied with the session limits but accept such constraints since 'that is the nature of the beast'. One particular counsellor had succeeded in helping a client with severe depression in only three sessions, managing the case by giving the client 'homework' and by spacing the sessions over a period of a year. The counsellor explained that she feels that anything is possible if one is prepared to be flexible. However, the consensus amongst counsellors was that a three-session limit is extremely difficult to work within, particularly when the problem first has to be assessed. The referring problem is invariably not the 'real' problem and it can take up to three sessions to find this out. However, one counsellor states: 'I am convinced that short-term counselling (six to eight one hour sessions) is extremely beneficial to most employees who are reasonably "functioning" individuals: but counsellors need to be alert to cases where short-term work could be an abuse of therapy'.

# SUPERVISION

In a geographically dispersed service like that of employee counselling, and in the context of some 90% of counsellors being affiliates working part-time, perhaps for several provider companies, ensuring professional supervision for counsellors is a key operational activity.

Whether in-house or external, counsellors themselves recognize and accept the need for regular supervision. According to the BAC, supervision is necessary in order to:

> enhance the therapeutic effectiveness of the relationship between counsellor and client; enable the counsellor to develop his/her professional identity through reflection on their work; clarify the relationship between counsellor, client, supervisor, and organization; and ensure that ethical Standards are maintained throughout . . . (BAC *Code of Ethics*, 1989).

With a similar philosophy, the EAPA Standards state that:

> Every EAP counsellor must receive regular professional supervision from a senior counsellor trained in supervision (EAPA, 1994: 20).

Professional counsellor supervision serves to protect the clients' interests, to assure the quality of client services, and responds to the EAP counsellor's skills and effectiveness. The EAP provider must ensure that each EAP counsellor receives professional supervision that is equivalent to that recommended by the BAC.

The quality and nature of individual professional supervision by EAP providers to their counsellors varies considerably. Some providers give in-depth supervision, whilst others offer none and rely on counsellors having their own supervision. The general view is that EAP providers expect their counsellors to provide their own suitable private supervision at least once a month and to subscribe to the BAC *Code of Ethics*: whilst this may be a reasonable request, providers should check its existence and relevance. It is an aspect of the counsellors' role that provokes criticism in cases where the provider organization undertakes the delivery of professional supervision. Counsellors are most dissatisfied over providers' supervision, with about one-fifth rating it as almost non-existent and another fifth rating it as no more than average. The provider organization is in a dilemma over supervision. The demands of internal quality control and assurance militate for employing organizations carrying out supervision. Yet such provisions have considerable disadvantages in terms of cost, practicality, effectiveness and acceptability.

# CASE MANAGEMENT

Within an employee counselling programme, case management performs a triple function. Primarily, its purpose is to provide the counsellor with support and guidance from a senior professional colleague. The second purpose is that of ensuring conformity to the design, philosophy and contractual terms of the EAP. A third purpose (the primary reason in the view of many providers) is the control and maintenance of quality standards for the client, and costs for the provider company.

The EAPA Standards address case management:

> Case management is distinct from counselling supervision, in that it focuses principally on the role the EAP plays in supporting individual clients. Case management is essential where clients are seen by freelance affiliates contracted by the EAP provider (EAPA, 1994: 21).

After initial assessment, the EAP counsellor and the case manager need to consider whether or not the individual can benefit from short-term counselling, or whether referral is more appropriate.

This clearly does not happen in some cases, because counsellors say that they only have to report back to the provider after counselling has ended, not after initial assessment. However, some providers have very detailed, clear and systematic case management procedures, whereby the counsellor is required to feed back to the case manager after every counselling session. Thus, variations exist amongst providers with regard to the levels of expected feedback. In some cases, providers require detailed reports on individual clients and 'masses of information' (to quote one counsellor respondent), which is sent to their supervisor. In contrast, other providers only require a telephone call after referral and a 'one-liner' after the first session. In one case, a counsellor claimed to have never submitted any feedback on any of the cases she had seen.

A minority view was voiced by one counsellor (who did not do EAP work, but *did* provide workplace counselling) who was adamant that no counsellor ethically would agree to any feedback about the client—'the organization must trust the counsellor's judgement'. However, the majority of workplace counsellors (not EAP counsellors) *do* report having links with personnel or occupational health, whereby they can give confidential feedback to the company.

## CLIENT COMPANY INFORMATION

The extent of integration of employee counselling into the organization's administrative and managerial process, as well as into its corporate culture, is a key issue in the design of any such programme. At one end of the continuum, programmes offering information and referral only (Jones et al., 1988) need little, if any, organizational integration or knowledge. Full-service, in-house programmes inevitably are closely meshed into the corporate polity, with a large amount of exchange of organizational information. The externally contracted, limited-utilization programme represented by most EAP and workplace counselling services is in an intermediate position.

Although most EAP clients refer themselves for non-work-related problems, the work environment may be having a major impact on clients in ways that are significant. EAP and workplace counsellors cannot ignore issues of work. For counsellors to remain alert to potential work factors in their clients' problems, it is necessary for them to have a dynamic understanding of the employing organization—its structure, policies, personnel, and current stresses, and how these fit into some historical perspective. Importantly, in-house workplace counsellors were believed to have a better appreciation of the organization's procedures, policies, and culture, than EAP counsellors (Highley & Cooper, 1995).

Few companies are altruistic enough to adopt employee counselling without expecting an organizational impact and (hopefully) payoff. Few provider contractors, however, will wish to offer a full organizational assistance programme (OAP), as described in Chapter 4, where internal interventions are made by counsellors in a consultancy manner in order to modify or remove stressors. Equally, many counsellors do not see such an organizational role as the logical end point of EAP and similar interventions—although it is argued to be so in some US literature (Cunningham, 1994).

From the survey (Highley & Cooper, 1995), the majority of counsellors felt that there is no need for them to have any information about the client company, as they see their role as being to work with the individual, and any external information may hinder this process. Some counsellors said that they do not need such background information because they go by what the client tells them about the organization. They feel that if they have information about the organization, then they may have a prejudice or perception about the client. Many counsellors exclude any information from third parties because it enables the client to go through a therapeutic process in relieving themselves of their problems. It is the client's interpretation of the problem that is important, according to most counsellors. In practice, they felt the issue was hypothetical since most EAP counsellors had not been involved with client organizations as part of their EAP work. Nevertheless, one counsellor who carries out private workplace counselling usually insists on receiving support from a board member within the client company and complete autonomy within the organization.

Most providers, on the contrary, do not give counsellors information about client companies as a matter of course, but only if it is felt necessary for some cogent reason. Only a minority of counsellors expressed any concern about such lack of information, stating that they are not prepared to work with a provider unless thorough information about the client company is provided. They also often insist upon a contact name within the company, so that if faced with a potential work problem they know to whom to speak.

Information, of necessity, is a two-way process if change is to ensue. If the counsellor feels a responsibility to feed back information to the organization, then issues of confidentiality arise (see Chapter 11). The moral issues apart, since they are treated elsewhere, the survey examined the possibility of feedback of information from the counsellor to the employing organization. The opinions expressed by counsellors are given in Figure 8.4.

These views can be aggregated into four categories approving feedback totalling 58%, one category (9%) of conditional approval, and a final category (33%) rejecting feedback of information. The fact that a total of 67% was found supporting feedback by counsellors contrasts with a relatively small minority who would be willing to make organizational interventions. These two sets of attitudes appear contradictory, given that feedback of information is rarely neutral in organizational terms. Any modifications of structures, processes and practices that are stressors will probably be assisted by feedback from counsellors: opposition to feedback by counsellors could, therefore, be counter-productive in terms of the total system.

A unique feature of workplace counselling is the dual responsibility that counsellors should have towards both the companies they work for, either as paid employees or contractors, and the individual employees who become their clients. A contingent responsibility to the organization with whom the provider is contracted is not a burden that counsellors feel often in the British context. At times, the counselling service may suggest interventions in the organization to bring in practices or structures (e.g. supervisory styles, job re-design) in order to modify negative attitudes that are undermining the welfare of both the company and its employees. But such primary interventions are rare in British circles, where counsellors seldom have the skills or the wish to make primary interventions—at least among external contracted providers, although in-house programmes may differ.

Many counsellors will not have worked in a private-employment context, and should be aware that every counsellor–client contact is likely to have organizational implications (Megranahan, 1994). It is argued, hence, that the counsellor who is accustomed to seeing a client on a one-to-one basis needs to understand the client in an organizational context, and anticipate any problems others may have with the counsellor's assessment and recommendations for treatment. Counsellors need to be familiar with organizational structures and channels

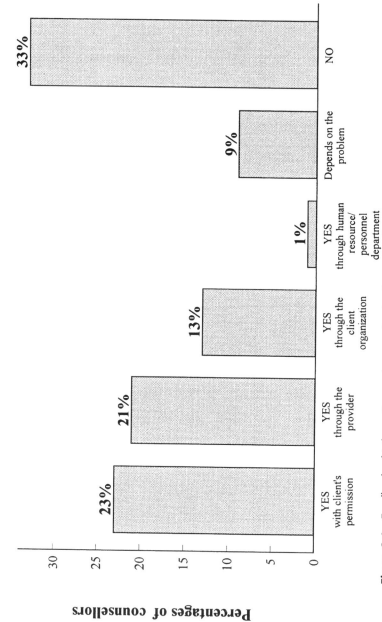

**Figure 8.4** *Feedback of information to the organization by counsellors. Source:* Highley & Cooper (1995)

of communication if they are to be able to influence management to make changes that could contribute to less stress and greater well-being.

The steps between passive possession of company information, active use of such knowledge to assist a client, and direct interventions to change the internalities of the company, are few indeed. Counsellors can be criticized for excessive professional detachment in working solely with clients, while the causal dysfunctions of the employing organization are ignored in spite of being widely evident. The alternative course of action (close proactive involvement) runs so many political risks and threats to professional credibility that it is not surprising that many counsellors choose not to be even tainted by access to organizational information.

## COUNSELLORS' GENERAL VIEWS ABOUT EAP COUNSELLING

Counsellors are relatively satisfied, on the whole, with carrying out EAP work. When counsellors had agreed to register with one or more provider organization, they had few complaints about them. Similarly, counsellors felt positively that EAP work serves a useful function in respect of employment problems, that their own role was a source of much satisfaction, and their perception was that clients showed positive approval of the employee counselling process.

Nevertheless, considerable variations between contractors were reported, with dissatisfaction voiced (in order of importance) on issues such as selection procedures, level and amount of feedback, quality of supervision, and the limitation in the number of sessions authorized in short-term counselling. The amount and quality of professional training received from the provider organization was judged very poor by 45% of counsellors. A number of provider organizations were rated as good on these questions, often by counsellors with several registrations with different providers. One provider organization was widely criticized for its standards and service, and 60% of counsellors surveyed had been approached, but refused to work for it. Positive opinions on providers showed particularly on the topics of confidentiality policies and the support of senior colleagues in the face of difficulties.

The interface between treatment of a client within an EAP and treatment on a private basis causes some tensions, since providers' practices vary greatly. Certain providers will not allow counsellors to continue on a private basis with an EAP client: if more counselling is needed after the set number of sessions, then the client is referred back to the provider. Counsellors felt that once a relationship of trust is built up between counsellor and client it is difficult, if not unethical, for the provider to direct the client to another counsellor. Others felt it was unethical to continue seeing a client on a private basis, because of the need to protect the client from possible professional abuse or exploitation by the counsellor.

But, overall, the majority of counsellors stated that they would not carry out their work if they did not feel that they were providing a useful role in benefiting individuals. Additional concerns included the level of professional competence of the people setting up clinical services within certain EAP providers. There was also some concern that individual employees 'are on the receiving end' of the counselling process and not the client organizations that often caused or contributed  to the client's troubles. To adapt an ecological maxim: 'let the stress producer pay, but it is the stressed-out employee who suffers most!' In normal circumstances an individual can choose a counsellor, but with EAP work the individual is presented with a counsellor. There was some worry, therefore, about the 'dangers' involved, in particular, when a client is faced with a counsellor who has no formal training or experience.

## CONCLUSION

In Britain opportunities are increasing all the time for counsellors to work in a variety of workplace and employee assistance settings. However, in the future these may well be open only to individuals who can satisfy the training, professional and business requirements that will be demanded by counsellors themselves and their professional bodies, the workplace counselling and EAP providers, and the client organizations.

Assistance offered by EAPs (and most other work-based programmes) will, by its very nature, be short-term (eight sessions maximum), so counsellors need to demonstrate the skills of focused short-term (problem-solving) approaches. Counsellors also need to be comfortable with assessment techniques that are designed to elicit information about issues as diverse as alcohol and drugs, mental health and suicide risk, and, equally so, familiar and comfortable with referring clients to specialist services (Galliano, 1994). Counsellors, together with client organizations and providers, face the challenge of helping to raise further the standard of all workplace counselling to a level at which there is ubiquitous recognition of its help to organizations, as well as to individuals.

# 9
# The Impact of Workplace Counselling: Methodology and Results

## INTRODUCTION

There have been very few evaluations of the impact of workplace counselling conducted in Britain. One early example was the Post Office study (Cooper et al., 1990), which evaluated an internal workplace counselling service. Because of this paucity of evaluation research, an evaluation of British workplace counselling programmes was commissioned by the Health and Safety Executive (HSE), carried out independently by the Manchester School of Management, and reported to the HSE (Highley & Cooper, 1995). Numerous references have been made to this study in earlier chapters of this book. This study offers major insights into understanding the effects of these programmes in Britain—see Chapter 1. The primary aim of this research was to evaluate a sample of British EAPs and workplace counselling programmes on a nationwide basis, at both the individual and organizational levels, involving a self-report questionnaire and also the collection of company data on absence, sickness and other indicators of stress. The measures used, the methodology, and the principal thrust of the results will be presented here, and a discussion of the possible explanations for the findings will follow.

# METHOD

## Methodological Considerations

It was essential that the research evaluated the benefits of counselling at both the individual and organizational levels, since such services operate at the interface between the two, and for their mutual benefit. At the individual level, a questionnaire-based study of stress and employee well-being was used. Mental well-being, physical well-being, job satisfaction, interpersonal relations at work, home/work relationship, self-reported absence and attitudinal factors were assessed. These subjective measures required self-report, and details of the measurement instrument are given later. At the organizational level, objective data were collected from company records, such as attendance and sick leave.

One of the common criticisms of research evaluating the effectiveness of programmes aimed at enhancing well-being is that many factors other than the treatment programme itself can influence the results. The criticism is particularly valid when no comparison group is used, and when measurement is taken only at the point of entry into a programme and at a single point in time immediately after completion.

There are several problems with such a 'before and after' design when evaluating the effectiveness of counselling programmes:

1 Without comparative data from individuals who have not used the programme, it is extremely difficult to differentiate effects owing to the counselling process from those owing to external factors related to the individual being counselled, or to the organization itself.

2 Because an individual is likely to be in a high stress state at the time of entry into the counselling process, regression to the mean effects may influence findings (since, statistically, there will always be spontaneous movement towards the mean and away from the extreme).

3 The evaluation of benefits is limited to immediate impact when, in fact, the time lag between the application of the counselling process and the manifestation of its effects is not known.

Indeed, the 'effectiveness' of a counselling programme, from an employer's (and individual's) point of view, is likely to be defined, in part, by its ability to have a positive impact beyond the time of contact. Given that the manifestation of effects is likely to vary between individuals, problem types and over time, it would have been unjustifiable to restrict the assessment of benefits to those of immediate impact only, and possibly unfair in making judgement on those providing counselling services. For these reasons it was decided that a control group was desirable, as was the need to follow up clients some months after counselling had been completed.

One of the positive aspects of this research was the opportunity to work with a number of counselling providers, enabling an assessment to be made of the benefits of counselling to employees across a variety of occupations and locations (provided sufficient sample sizes were available). The overall external validity of the research and, consequently, its ultimate practical value to all parties is thereby enhanced. It was recognized, however, that 'treatment effects' might influence the results, because even though the overall goals of different counselling programmes may be the same (at least compatible), the way in which these goals are met differs — as a function of the structure, implementation and operation of programmes. Confidence in the overall results, and in the evaluations for each individual EAP/counselling provider, is, therefore, greatly increased if data collection is not set within the context of a single organization. It was planned, therefore, to collect data from at least two client organizations for each provider, in order to enhance validity and make the evaluation more meaningful, to increase sample sizes, and to minimize the risk of any possible influence of potentially unique organizational factors.

Linked closely to these design considerations, several potential sources of variance intrinsic to this study may potentially have confounded the results and these must be considered. As stated earlier, the benefits derived from counselling (outcomes) will vary between individuals, problem types and over time. 'Treatment' is also variable, since short-term, focused counselling is necessarily eclectic in its techniques and responsive to the needs of the individual client. Furthermore, observed effects may be influenced not only by the experiences and personal qualities of the individual being counselled, but also by the experience, personal qualities, techniques and qualifications of the counsellor. Since the researcher has no control over these factors, they can at best be measured, and at least acknowledged as potential sources of variance. In recognition of these complexities, our study included a short questionnaire to be completed by counsellors themselves (after the final session with each client), in addition to a section for the clients' evaluation of the counselling process. Finally, as with all assessments of treatment programmes, an individual's willingness to opt for counselling and her or his expectations for therapeutic gain can influence results. Since the majority of employees using such services will have referred themselves voluntarily (and not everyone who may benefit from counselling will elect to participate), self-selection into groups cannot be avoided. However, some measure of employees' attitudes towards the provision of counselling was included on the questionnaire. Although this will not have eliminated selection effects, it will provide data on the perceived value of counselling, and ties in with the suggestion that such programmes can serve an internal public relations function simply by being in place.

## SELECTION OF CRITERIA AND MEASURES

It is true to say that regardless of however creatively designed, well controlled and smoothly executed a research design is, its ultimate value is largely determined by the measures from which data are derived. The choice of what to measure and which measures to use must be guided by the relevance of the variables selected to the goals and objectives of the research; standardization of the measurement instrument; technical features of the measurement instrument (reliability and internal validity); and feasibility in terms of access, time and cost constraints.

Given the multiple outcomes that counselling can produce, the definition of which criteria should determine success demanded careful consideration. Take-up/usage rates are sometimes put forward as a measure of success, but these rates are more accurately interpreted as an index of the demand/need for services than as an index of the success of programmes in gaining employees' confidence. Take-up rates are, therefore, a powerful statement in themselves: if 10% to 15% of the working population feel that professional assistance will be of value in dealing with difficulties, it has to be a serious option for employers. But, on their own, take-up rates say nothing about the benefits derived from having been through the counselling process.

As stated earlier, the potential value of EAPs/counselling programmes to industry is that they offer benefits to both individuals and employing organizations. Outcome measures must, therefore, tap both these levels and reflect the interaction of the individual with the organization. As Roman, Blum & Bennett (1987) state, '. . . exclusive attention to individual employee outcomes can lead to neglect of EAPs' potential as a humane and reasonable mechanism for trying to stabilise both individual and organisational performance'. To be of practical value, measures should also have implications for organizational policies and procedures.

The function of any evaluation is to assess effectiveness in achieving predetermined objectives. One of the main purposes of the researchers' preliminary discussions with providers and organizations with EAPs was to gain a deeper understanding of the issues involved and to avoid the omission of important areas of concern for providers and their clients. A starting point in deciding what to measure was therefore gained from those individual and organizational factors upon which EAPs/ counselling programmes are said to impact. Potential benefits to the individual include: improved mental well-being, coping ability and interpersonal relations; and increased job/life satisfaction. Potential benefits to the organization include: increased morale and improved interpersonal relations; decreased rates of absence/sickness and employee turnover; fewer accidents and formal grievances; and increased performance in terms of both quality and quantity.

## Organizational-level Measures

For evaluation at the organizational level, access was ideally required to individual absenteeism/sickness absence rates. Such rates are, first, of serious concern to employers, and, secondly, they are a relevant indicator of a programme's effectiveness. Previous research has found a significant relationship between subjective and objective measures of stress and absenteeism, suggesting that any significant decrease in stress should, in turn, result in a decrease in absenteeism (Cole et al., 1982). Finally, objective measures will enhance the rigour of the evaluation by minimizing the dangers inherent in relying on subjective, self-reported data.

It was recognized, however, that many British organizations do not monitor absenteeism: a 1991 survey by accountants Arthur Andersen estimated that 40% of British businesses fall into this category (Arthur Andersen, 1991). It was also realized that access to individual employee records may not be acceptable on ethical grounds, but organizational data — even in summary form — was still deemed useful. Existing performance indicators (productivity, for instance) could also have formed outcome measures at the organizational level, and required detailed discussion with client organizations.

### Individual-level Measures

When evaluating programmes that can produce multiple outcomes for the individual, we cannot possibly include all potentially relevant variables in a single study. This would be far too demanding on respondents — even if identification of the relevant variables was possible. Individual outcome measures considered for inclusion in this study were: coping ability; job satisfaction; and mental/physical well-being. Of those, job satisfaction and mental/physical well-being were selected as outcome measures. These were selected for two important reasons:

1 They are the most common individual benefits said to be derived from the provision of EAPs/counselling services in industry.
2 There is extensive research evidence indicating their relationship with individual turnover, absenteeism and job performance — all of which are of obvious relevance for effective organizational functioning.

As stated earlier, it is imperative that measures specifically reflect the interaction of the individual with the organization and assess the stated goals of EAPs/counselling. It is also true to say, however, that the experience of negative stress — its causes and consequences — is unique to the individual. Personal characteristics and circumstances will influence whether and how distress is experienced. The benefits derived from counselling are, therefore, also likely to be influenced by these factors.

The personality characteristics implicated as having an important influence on stress include: type A/B; locus of control; hardiness; coping ability; and trait anxiety. Again, we cannot assess all these potential influences within the context of a single study. Furthermore, reliable existing measures designed to tap such characteristics tend to be lengthy. While it is undoubtedly important to endeavour to discover what makes one person more susceptible and/or able to cope with stress than another, it was not the purpose of this study. To minimize the time taken to complete the proposed questionnaire, none of the above characteristics was included in the current study.

The personal characteristics selected for this study were: age; sex; educational achievement; and marital and parental status. Job characteristics and health habits were also included. In recognition of the subjective nature of stress, all respondents were also asked whether they were experiencing stress in particular spheres of their lives at the time of completing the questionnaire and, if so, to give these experiences a subjective stress rating. The selection of which life spheres to include was based on problem categories commonly addressed by EAPs/counselling services. This was viewed as more meaningful, and less time consuming, than including a standard life events scale that is both lengthy and not directly relevant to those problem areas addressed by counselling services.

A major strength of EAPs/counselling services lies in their holistic approach to well-being and their recognition of the fact that a clear distinction between personal and work-related problems is not possible: distress in one area is likely to adversely affect the other unless dealt with effectively. Individual functioning at the interface of home and work domains is desirable because it is realistic: people will bring their personal worries to work at times, just as they will take work problems home with them. It was imperative, therefore, that this research included some measure of the home/work interface.

It was equally imperative that work-based pressures were assessed, because of the potential of EAPs/counselling to perform a proactive role in organizational well-being. It was recognized that it is not within counsellors' power to change an employee's job, rate of pay, or how the organization is structured. Nonetheless, EAPs/counselling services do have a potentially important role to play in alerting organizations to internal factors that may be inhibiting performance in groups of employees. These are the factors over which employers have the most control and can change. Unless these factors are examined, important implications for effective organizational functioning will be overlooked. A concentration in the research solely on personal stressors would not do justice to the potential that counselling services have for facilitating action that can enhance both individual and organizational well-being.

# THE MEASURES USED

## The Questionnaire

The self-completion questionnaire designed for this research consisted of a biographical section and three sub-scales. The questionnaire measured:

- individual variables that may influence the experience of stress
- major consequences of distress for the individual
- major sources of pressure (at the interface of the individual with the organization)

The decision on which measures to use was dictated by the standardization of the measurement instrument, reliability and internal consistency of the instrument and time/cost constraints. Access to a large normative database is particularly important when research is being conducted with diverse groups of people in diverse settings. The measures selected for use in this study are outlined below.

*Current state of health: mental and physical well-being.* The GHQ-12 (Goldberg, 1972) and mental/physical health sub-scales of the Occupational Stress Indicator (OSI) (Cooper, Sloan & Williams, 1988) were selected for use in this research. Used in conjunction, they respectively provide both a context-specific (work-related) and global measure of mental health. The work-related nature of the mental health scale of the OSI is obviously of value given the objectives of this research. It was felt, however, that a more global measure of mental well-being, which can identify minor psychiatric disorders, was also needed.

*Job satisfaction.* The job satisfaction scale of the OSI (Cooper, Sloan & Williams, 1988) was selected for use in this study.

*Demographic variables.* Personal and job demographic variables included: age; sex; marital and parental status; education; job grade and tenure. Questions relating to life style/health habits (alcohol and nicotine consumption) were also included. This section also included a question about stressful situations currently being experienced in seven different life spheres, and asked for a subjective stress rating of those situations (where appropriate). Respondents were also asked if any changes/ events were currently occurring within their organization that they perceived as affecting their job — either directly or indirectly. The purpose of this question was to identify whether any factors unique to that organization were exerting an influence on findings.

*Sources of pressure.* Four of the six sub-scales of the OSI (Cooper, Sloan & Williams, 1988) sources of pressure scale are highly relevant to the nature of this research, since they tap the interface of the individual with the organization and allow the identification of perceived organizational sources of pressure. The Likert-type response options for these sub-scales allowed the identification of the extent to which each potential source of pressure is perceived by individuals.

The four sub-scales are:

1 *Home and work relationship.* Addresses whether home problems are brought to work and whether work is perceived as having a negative impact on home life. It does not address specific home or work-based problems, but assesses the extent to which the individual experiences conflict between the two.
2 *Relationships with others.* Considers perceived pressures arising from personal contacts at work. The sub-scale taps the issue of interpersonal relations and allows an assessment of changes along this dimension over the course of time.
3 *Organizational structure and climate.* Addresses problems that commonly arise from bureaucracy, communication problems and morale in organizations. The sub-scale is focused at the level of the organization.
4 *Factors intrinsic to the job.* This sub-scale looks at workload, variety of tasks and rates of pay. It is focused at the level of the job itself.

It was important to identify organizational and job sources of pressure in this research, since whether individuals perceive their main sources of pressure as coming from within the organization, or outside it, is likely to be a source of variance influencing findings.

*Other information.* In addition to the scales outlined above, opinions regarding the provision of a counselling service were sought. The questionnaire included a short section on employees' attitudes towards the provision of counselling, in terms of perceived values of such a service for both individuals and the organization as a whole. Individuals were also asked whether they had been absent from work in the last six months and, if so, on how many occasions and for how long. An additional counselling evaluation section was including for those individuals who had been through the counselling process, so that their views of the service could be assessed in terms of their perceptions of the helpfulness of counsellors, quality of service provision, and positive benefits both at home and at work.

### Objective Sickness Absence Data

In addition to collecting self-report questionnaire data, consideration was given to whether individuals' attendance at counselling had any impact on the organization. It was decided that sickness absence data may be one of the organizational statistics affected by the provision of counselling, and hence such data were collected.

# METHODOLOGY

### Evaluation at the Individual Level

The original methodology comprised a retrospective design consisting of an experimental (counselled) group and a control (non-counselled) group. In the event, it proved to be impractical to select a control group, but the data collected from the experimental (counselled) group were nevertheless found to be valuable and usable.

Pre- and post-counselling measures were taken for the experimental group over a period of eight to twelve months. Pre-counselling measures were taken at the first counselling session and post-counselling measures were taken after the last session, as agreed between the individual client and counsellor. A control group (equal in size to the experimental group) was to have been selected at random from a list of all appropriate employees, and would have been given the same questionnaire. A follow-up measure was then given to the experimental group (and would have been given to the control group) after an interval of three months. Time restraints meant that follow-up measures could not be taken after a longer time interval; ideally, more than one follow-up measure, over a greater time interval — even several years — would have been desirable. While restricted, the follow-up period was sufficient to stabilize the effects of regression to the mean and to identify the benefits of counselling to the individual, beyond immediate impact.

The research design allowed the benefits of counselling for the individual employee to be effectively evaluated since it enabled the assessment of:

- the immediate impact of counselling on individual well-being for those employees who chose to use the service
- the longer-term impact of counselling on individual well-being for those who had used the service, compared with their personal pre- and post-counselling levels

Because of the lack of a control group it was not possible to assess whether the changes seen in the experimental group were more marked than those seen in the control group.

### Evaluation at the Organizational Level

Access to hard organizational data was desirable in order to assess the benefits of counselling at a company level. Ideally, individual sickness/absence records of the experimental group collected retrospectively for the six months prior to counselling and six months after completion of counselling would have served this purpose. In practice, any individual sickness absence data could only be collected with the informed consent of the individuals concerned. The data were collected in two forms—first, the total number of days of absence in the six-month period, and, secondly, the number of absence events in the six-month period.

## ADMINISTRATION AND DISTRIBUTION OF QUESTIONNAIRES

The questionnaires took no longer than 30 minutes to complete. The way in which the questionnaires were administered to the experimental group was closely linked to the need to maintain the assurance of confidentiality given by counselling providers to their clients. The importance of keeping disruption to the counselling process itself to a minimum was also recognized.

It was decided, therefore, that for the experimental group (i.e. employees who presented for counselling) questionnaires would be distributed by the counsellors themselves. The pre-counselling measure was distributed at the first session and the post-counselling measure at the end of the final session. It was also essential, however, that it was possible to match measures taken at pre-counselling, post-counselling and follow-up for each individual counselled. Each individual was, therefore, allocated a number by the counsellor at the beginning of the first session. The resultant list of identifiers was held in strictest confidence by the counselling providers, and each number was written on the first questionnaire by the counsellor and on questionnaires handed out at the end of the last session. Measures taken at follow-up were also distributed via the counselling provider, using the same identifier. A covering letter explaining the purpose of the numbering system, as well as outlining the research, was given out with each questionnaire. By adopting this approach, the individual's right to confidentiality and anonymity was protected; only the counselling providers know the identity of employees presenting for counselling. However, this arrangement required a great deal of commitment and co-operation from individual counsellors. In general, the counselling providers fully appreciated the reasons for this approach. To maintain confidentiality and to encourage individual employees to respond, freepost reply envelopes addressed directly to the researchers were provided.

## RESULTS

Questionnaire data were collected from the clients of nine separate company counselling services and EAPs, at three different time points (pre-counselling, post-counselling, and three to six months after counselling). Absence data were available from a further four companies. In addition, it was possible to collect questionnaire data from a sample of all staff in two of the nine companies, both of which had EAPs. The data were collected at two time points — the first, just as the EAP was introduced or re-launched, and the second, between eighteen months and two years after implementation.

The following findings are formulated in general terms, and apply to an overall assessment of employee counselling provisions. Their focus is in terms of a technical evaluation of broad aims for such counselling at individual and organizational levels. Certain data have been used in earlier chapters in more specific contexts, and sometimes in different formats.

## Individual Questionnaire Data

The key findings in relation to the pre-counselling, post-counselling and follow-up psychological measures were:

### Individual Finding No. 1

*After receiving counselling (and at follow-up), clients reported significantly improved mental well-being and physical well-being compared with before counselling. However, there were no reported changes for job satisfaction levels or on any of the sources of pressure scales.*

To a great extent, this finding is not surprising. Counselling, whether internal or external to the organization, is aimed at helping the individual to cope better with her or his personal and work lives. As such, we would hope to find some change in a client's mental and physical health (coping skills) after receiving counselling. However, job satisfaction is concerned with an individual's positive or negative perceptions of, and adjustment to, various aspects of the job; the sources of pressure scales measure employees' perceptions of the origins of perceived stress within the organization. None of these aspects is likely to change as a result of opting for counselling, because counselling services are not organizational interventions. It is, therefore, unlikely that any organizational changes are addressed; it is the organization that stays the same, and the individual who adapts. Hence, we cannot expect to see an impact on levels of job satisfaction or sources of pressure. In effect, the individual still views the workplace in the same way as she or he did before (because it *is* the same as it was before). Consequently, no changes result for job satisfaction levels or perceived sources of pressure. Individuals may well be able to cope better, and therefore should be more mentally (and probably physically) healthy.

Similar findings were obtained when comparing pre-counselling and follow-up scores, suggesting that any psychological changes resulting from counselling are likely to be sustained over a period of at least three to six months after counselling. The effects of counselling may, then, continue well after counselling ends, and therefore greater effects may be seen at some later stage. This possibility will be addressed further in Finding No. 4.

Individuals were asked at the pre- and post-counselling stages to rate the severity of the problems they may or may not have been experiencing at that time. Responses revealed that after counselling the clients reported having fewer family, health, job and colleague problems, and that where problems continued to exist they were rated as less severe. Individuals reported having more marital and financial problems at the post-counselling stage and also rated them as being more severe, particularly marital problems.

Clients were also asked whether or not they had been absent from work in the last six months, and, if so, how many days of absence they had taken. The results showed that after counselling fewer people had been absent from work in the last six months, and that those who had been absent had had fewer days of absence.

At the pre-counselling stage clients were asked who had suggested that they should use the service. The results were: 24%—their manager; 21%—Occupational Health; 14%—a friend; 5%—Personnel; and 3%—the union. However, the majority (33%) reported that they referred themselves.

Clients were also asked whether or not they thought that the provision of a counselling service was valued by staff: 88% said it was definitely valued; 10% believed that it was possibly valued; and 2% said that it was not valued.

Clients reported their initial problems as falling into the following categories: 38%—marital; 29%—work; 26%—health; 24%—family; 18%—colleagues; 11%—legal; and 10%—financial. Obviously, some clients reported that their problems fell into more than one category.

The speed of response by counselling providers revealed that 44% of clients were seen by a counsellor within one week of contacting the service and 86% felt that this was quickly enough. The average number of sessions was seven, over an average of 11 weeks. Some 74% of clients felt that the number of sessions they had was enough to help them, and 89% reported seeing the same counsellor throughout.

In general, the counsellors were rated very highly (5.5 on a 6-point scale) in terms of being friendly, honest and open, concerned to help the client, and trustworthy. Slightly lower (5 on a 6-point scale) but still high scores were given for the counsellors' ability to help the client; overall satisfaction with the service received; counselling having helped the client to understand the problem better; and enabling the client to handle difficulties better. In terms of the effects of counselling on the clients' work and non-work life (i.e. ability to concentrate on tasks; relationships with colleagues, family and friends; self-confidence; job performance; overall enjoyment of life; and decision-making ability) all areas were rated highly (around 4 out of 5). A majority of clients (74%) believed that counselling had not resolved the problem but had enabled them to handle it better, and 85% of clients would use the service again if the need arose.

## Finding No. 2

*Differences were detected in the results for internal and external services, suggesting that the internal counselling services were having greater individual effects in terms of mental and physical health than were the EAPs.*

The hypothesis has been raised earlier of the greater ability of internal services to deal with workplace issues (Highley & Cooper, 1994). If an individual is counselled as a person within the workplace context, and if the culture, policies and procedures of the organization are known to the counsellor, we would expect the counsellor to be more effective at helping the person to cope with both their work and home life. This more effective coping can be expected to have an effect on the person's mental and physical health, as may well be the case with internal counselling services.

In contrast, externally-contracted EAPs are less able to deal with organizational issues, primarily because the counsellors do not know enough about the organizations involved. Thus, clients seeing an EAP counsellor are likely to be counselled as individuals, but not within the context of the workplace. Therefore, the whole of the person's life is not being addressed. If the individual's personal problems only are being dealt with, and she or he is not better able to cope with work-related issues, then a significant effect on mental and physical health is unlikely.

If an internal counselling service does have the ability to feed back organizational issues to the company, we would expect there to be an effect also on the other variables contained in the questionnaire (i.e. job satisfaction and sources of pressure). A somewhat surprising finding is that respondents did not report improved scores on these two aspects. This finding may be explained in at least three ways:

1 The pre- and post-counselling questionnaires were completed by individuals at the start and finish of counselling. The time period between completion of the two questionnaires is, therefore, quite short, averaging about 10 weeks, according to clients. Even if an organizational problem were recorded by a counsellor and relayed back to the company, it is unlikely that any changes at the organizational level would be instituted and have had an effect before the client finished counselling. Therefore, we would not expect to see an impact on the job satisfaction and sources of pressure scales within this time period.

2 Although internal counsellors do indeed have the opportunity to feed back issues of employee concern to the organization, it may well be that they do not always do so in practice. It is quite possible that they use their knowledge of the company to help individual clients (hence the effect on individual well-being scores), but do not then feed back issues to the organization for reasons of protecting the client's identity. If such is the case, then no impact on job satisfaction or sources of pressure can necessarily be expected.

3 It may be the case that even if the counsellor does feed back problems and organizational issues to the company, these may not be addressed by the organization, or, for a variety of reasons, it may choose not to do anything about them. If this is the case, then again there would be no impact on an individual's job satisfaction or sources of pressure.

A further, more technical, explanation for the differences found between the internal and external services may relate to the sample sizes. Much more data were collected from the internal services than from the EAPs, so the sample sizes, and hence the likelihood of significant findings, are much greater for the internal services.

## Finding No. 3

*Where positive changes were detected for counselling employees on the mental and physical health scales, an unmatched control group of a sample of all employees within two companies showed no changes.*

Whilst these two groups of employees were not ideal as controls, they were considered to be suitable for this use, given the fact that it was not possible to collect data from matched controls from within the same organizations. The non-counselled individuals showed no changes in the scores for the scales on which the client (counselled) group *did* show changes, suggesting that the effects found for counselled employees are likely to be the result, to some extent at least, of the counselling process.

## Finding No. 4

*There were no significant differences among the counselled group from the immediate post-counselling stage to the follow-up stage (three to six months after counselling) on any of the mental and physical health measures. Clients did report, however, significantly more stress as coming from the organizational structure and climate factors.*

As mentioned earlier in Finding No. 1, there is a belief that counselling may well continue to have an effect for some time after counselling itself has ended. This suggestion is not borne out by the results of this research, because no improvement in mental or physical health was found from post-counselling to follow-up. By contrast, at the follow-up stage clients did report significantly more stress coming from the organizational structure and climate. The longer-term impact of counselling may have been obscured by an increased perception of more stress. Indeed, if employees are reporting more stress from work, but their psychological health is unaffected, then this is positive in itself as a coping capacity, since we would expect to see a reduction in mental health when more stress is being experienced.

## Sickness Absence Data

### *Finding No. 5*

*There was a significant reduction from pre- to post-counselling, in both the total number of days of absence, and the number of absence events, but there was no such reduction for the matched control group.*

The findings from the objective sickness absence data are in line with the self-reported sickness absence given by clients on the questionnaires. The self-report absence statistics reveal that after counselling fewer people have been absent from work in the last six months, and those who have been absent have had fewer days off.

### *Finding No. 6*

*The absence statistics (days and events) for the control group and client group were identical at the pre-counselling stage, but differed significantly at the post-counselling stage, when the client group showed significantly less absence compared with the matched control group.*

These sickness absence results can be considered in conjunction with the questionnaire results on psychological health, suggesting that opting for counselling has a positive effect on the individual's health (mental and physical well-being) and health behaviours (i.e. sickness absence). Both these factors appear to be influenced by counselling, but not so the organizational indicators (i.e. job satisfaction and sources of pressure). An explanation may be that counselling is essentially an intervention that focuses on the individual (not the organization), and in which the emphasis is on changing the individual's response to stress rather than changing the organizational sources of stress. It is, therefore, understandable that the greatest effect will be shown for individual outcomes, such as absence, mental well-being and physical well-being.

## Company-wide Questionnaire Data

The results from the company-wide questionnaires were:

*Finding No. 7*

*The introduction of an EAP does affect the individual being counselled, but not the whole employee population, in terms of mental and physical health, job satisfaction and sources of pressure.*

This finding is not surprising since an EAP is an *individual*, not an organizational, intervention; hence, no organizational impact can necessarily be expected. To have an organizational effect, an intervention at that level would need to be introduced in addition to the counselling. An organizational-level intervention would enable the organization to identify its sources of stress and, where possible, to address them appropriately. Simply introducing an EAP in an attempt to affect organizational indicators is unlikely to work, since an EAP does not have any global effect on the organization, although it does help individuals psychologically and reduce their absence.

Such a finding challenges the argument sometimes made that an EAP is a positive functional intervention in an organization's culture or is a step towards the creation of a learning organization. The organizational development approach attempts to mould culture, and the organizational assistance programme has such objectives (Cunningham, 1994) as an extension of the EAP. It could be argued that an internal counselling programme has more potential for gaining such influence if its counsellors so wished. Additionally, as EAPs mature and operate over many years, key opinion-formers in the organization may be more likely to have been clients, or used the EAP managerially by recommending their staff to do so. As a consequence, some of the values underpinning the counselling process may come to be more accepted in the organization, especially in a stressful context. But the survey of EAPs did not reveal that this had been the effect, although this lack may be due to their relative youth in organizational terms.

Whilst this research offers support to the argument that a healthier workforce is likely to lead to a healthier organization (if sickness absence is an indicator), the company-wide data does not suggest that an EAP has any effect on the organization other than reducing absence in those who use the service. This is not surprising, since if an organization is to manage stress effectively, then it is essential to intervene at both the individual and organizational levels.

*Finding No. 8*

*Individuals who have access to, but do not use, an EAP do not benefit psychologically, or in terms of their job satisfaction or perceived sources of pressure, from knowing that it is available.*

This finding is in direct opposition to some organizations' and/or providers' claim that the knowledge that EAP help is available (should it be needed) can reduce stress overall among employees. This contention is not supported by these data, which show no effect on individuals who have not had counselling. In fact, the employees in one of the companies surveyed reported being less job-satisfied, and experiencing more stress coming from the organizational structure and climate, following the implementation of the EAP.

## CONCLUSION

Workplace stress interventions may be classified into three levels, focusing respectively on the individual, the individual/ organization interface, and the organization (DeFrank & Cooper, 1987). At the moment, British EAPs and workplace counselling programmes are focused largely at the individual level, although there is no particular reason why they should not target the organization. Indeed, a comprehensive stress management programme attempts to identify and reduce (or eliminate) stressors at each of the three levels (Cooper et al., 1990). To employ interventions that focus purely on the individual, which most EAPs do, is to make the individual responsible for problems, even if they are work-related. Arguably, this is an abdication of the responsibility of the employer who, by funding an EAP, places the employees' problems back on themselves rather than tackling root causes.

However, individual-level interventions do have an important organizational role to play, because individuals may suffer stress from both their personal and work life and this will impact upon an employee's performance at work and psychological well-being.

A key finding is that whilst the introduction of a counselling service may well be of benefit to individuals psychologically, there is unlikely to be any impact at the organizational level unless a consonant and related intervention targeted at changing the organization is also in place. Employers who institute an EAP in the hope of also gaining unspecified secondary organizational benefits are likely to act in vain. There is a need for British companies to look much more closely at their reasons for buying counselling services. If their aim is altruistically to support staff, then the service is probably useful, but not universally so in this respect. However, if employers are hoping positively to influence bottom-line indicators at the organizational level, then they are likely to be disappointed. The survey evidence suggests little hard organizational impact beyond the reduction of sickness absence in those employees who use the service.

# 10

# Selecting an Employee Assistance Programme

## THE SELECTION PROCESS

Before deciding upon the need for a counselling service, hopefully you have conducted some form of stress audit. This will not only help you to decide whether there is a need for a counselling service, but the data collected can act as a baseline for any future evaluation of the counselling service.

Once you have decided that there is a need for a counselling service within your organization, and if you have also established that an externally provided Employee Assistance Programme (EAP) is your preferred option, then it is important to ensure that you purchase the right service for your organization. The key to a successful EAP lies in selecting the most appropriate service for your organization. You may choose to consult an independent specialist to help make this decision. Most organizations want to provide a quality EAP for their staff, but, given the general lack of knowledge about counselling and counselling qualifications, it may be difficult for you to make a clear assessment as to the quality of each provider. This is why so many organizations now seek independent advice before starting the tender process.

Before going ahead with introducing an EAP, it is paramount that you are clear about your reasons for wanting a service, as this will have an impact on the most suitable provider for your organization. Once you are clear about your reasons for having the service, it is crucial to think carefully about every aspect of the EAP and what characteristics you do and do not want. Most providers offer standard packages, but it is important, however, that your EAP is tailored to your organization, so you need to be sure of what you want. The discussion of issues that follows should enable you to consider most of the important aspects of service provision.

Once you have decided upon the characteristics of your EAP then you need to compile a service specification that details your requirements. This specification should then be sent to all identified EAP providers, and they should be asked to tender against this specification and return their tender by a set date. In this way, the tender documents and associated costings that you receive from the providers should all be based at the same time-frame, and on the same service and, therefore, comparisons can be made between providers. Some providers, however, will still quote for their own standard EAP or merely make such additions to the in-service as you have specified.

It is sometimes difficult to identify all the providers of EAPs in Britain. The UK Employee Assistance Professionals Association (EAPA) holds a list of EAP providers who are members of the EAPA, although there are certain major providers who choose not to join the EAPA, but do provide EAPs. It is worthwhile finding out about as many providers as possible, from as many different sources as possible, before sending out the service specification.

When the various EAP tenders have been submitted, a shortlist needs to be drawn up. This is best carried out by comparing each aspect of the tenders against the service specification. Any provider who has disregarded your requirements should be rejected at this point, as should any other providers you feel unhappy with for whatever reason. The assessment of tenders should be done in detail, comparing each aspect of the service with what the provider is suggesting and has quoted for. It is important to note any shortfalls or any areas where there is added value (i.e. where a provider is offering more than you have asked for, but without additional cost). A shortlist of three to four providers should work well in this situation.

When you have your shortlist of providers you need to invite them for an interview. At this time you need to confirm your requirements and raise any queries you may have with their tender. It is also important to clarify exactly what the cost will be and what is covered. The provider may be suggesting additions to the service that, if removed, will reduce the cost. You need to select a preferred EAP provider from the shortlist, or begin the tender process again if all those providers you shortlisted are unsuitable.

Once you have carefully selected your preferred EAP provider you need to negotiate the contract and the price you will pay. When the contract is drawn up, both the service specification and tender document should be incorporated. The contract should be detailed and specify exactly what will be each part of the service and how it will operate (i.e. what the benchmarks are). In addition, it is crucial that you build in to the contract the fact that you will be independently auditing the service at regular intervals. This ensures that the provider is happy to allow an independent auditor to assess the EAP and also means that standards can be set against which the service will be audited. These standards are usually those laid down in the service specification and tender document.

When all aspects of the service have been agreed and the contract has been signed, the EAP can be introduced to your staff. It is important not to rush the selection stage, as it can make the difference between having the service that is right for you or just one that will do. It is tempting to rush ahead with introducing an EAP once it has been agreed to do so, but time and care at this stage will reap rewards in the future.

To help you to select an EAP provider, we have devised a 10-stage model for selecting an EAP (see Table 10.1). If you follow the stages in the 10-stage model, and, if possible, involve an independent consultant throughout, you should select the right EAP for your organization.

## CHARACTERISTICS OF EAPS

The following information should help you to consider various aspects of the EAP and decide which ones you require before compiling your service specification.

**Table 10.1** *The 10-stage model for selecting an EAP*

| | |
|---|---|
| 1 | Be clear about why you want an EAP. |
| 2 | Carefully consider all possible aspects of the service and decide on the characteristics you want your EAP to have. |
| 3 | Compile a service specification of your requirements. |
| 4 | Identify as many EAP providers as possible. |
| 5 | Send the service specification to the providers and ask them to tender against the specification. |
| 6 | Compare each returned tender document with the specification to assess the degree to which the proposed service meets your requirements. |
| 7 | Draw up a shortlist of three or four providers. |
| 8 | Interview the shortlisted providers to ask any questions you may have and to confirm your service requirements. |
| 9 | Decide upon a preferred provider and negotiate in terms of the exact specification and the cost. |
| 10 | Draw up a detailed contract, which should incorporate the service specification and tender documents. |

*Source:* Authors' research.

## The Provider's Professional History in the EAP Business

Most providers will have been established relatively recently, probably at some point since 1979. They will all have a number of client organizations and it is important to find out which clients are on their list in terms of their size, geographic locations, and business sector. You need to ensure that the provider has experience of providing an EAP in an organization similar to your own, or to satisfy yourself that the provider has the ability and resources to do so. It is always helpful to seek references from a number of the EAP provider's client companies, preferably ones you track down through some means other than the provider.

## Relevant Professional Bodies

The EAPA is the main body concerned with workplace counselling programmes of all types, and particularly EAPs. The UK EAPA was established in 1991 and provides a forum for anyone involved in counselling in the workplace to discuss a wide range of issues concerning this specialized type of counselling. The UK EAPA has developed UK Standards of

Practice and Professional Guidelines for Employee Assistance Professionals and a Code of Ethics (EAPA, 1994). Currently, a set of guidelines for the audit and evaluation of EAPs is being compiled (EAPA, 1997). All EAPA members subscribe to the standards as set out in these documents, so the quality of the service can be assessed against these standards.

The British Association for Counselling (BAC) is one of the key counselling-related professional bodies and aims to raise the standards of counsellor training and practice in Britain. Many EAP providers subscribe to the BAC's Standards, and Codes of Ethics and Practice when selecting counsellors (BAC, 1989). The BAC has a sub-division, the Association for Counselling at Work (ACW), that is concerned particularly with workplace counselling.

Another relevant professional body is the British Psychological Society (BPS), which regulates the actions of psychologists, whom EAP providers employ.

## The Type of EAP Required

It is necessary to consider whether you want a full EAP, or a limited-scope provision. Most EAP providers offer a range of services in addition to the full EAP. Most providers can tailor the design of the EAP to the specific needs of your organization. The types of counselling service currently available from external providers are:

- telephone-only counselling
- telephone counselling with additional information-based services such as welfare, legal and financial advice
- face-to-face counselling only
- telephone counselling and the associated information-based services, with referral on to face-to-face counselling. This is often described as a full EAP

Your specification and not the provider's preference should determine the type of counselling service that you offer to your employees. Some providers emphasize the telephone approach, whilst others favour face-to-face counselling. You need to select a provider who has similar thoughts to yourself in this respect.

Telephone-based services are usually cheaper than services that also make face-to-face counselling available. However, telephone counselling only may limit the range of issues that the service is able to deal with. Whichever type of service is in operation, individual clients can usually make unlimited calls to the service.

Almost without exception, the initial contact with the service will be via the telephone. However, this aspect of the EAP can vary in terms of hours of access of the service and the rate at which clients are charged for the calls, as well as the way in which the calls are answered.

A twenty-four-hour, 365 days a year service is offered by most providers, although it is rare that such hours of access are necessary. It is important for you to be clear about whether you need to provide access to the EAP 24 hours a day or if more restricted access is sufficient. However, limiting the hours of access may not bring a reduction in the cost of the service if 24-hour cover is a standard part of the provider's EAP, so you will need to query this with individual providers.

When the charge to clients for making the call is relatively low, then this is likely to encourage use. The charge to callers can be free by using a freephone number or can be kept low by using a local call rate for all calls. However, either of these options will increase the cost of the EAP. Some providers can set up dedicated lines for each purchaser so that when clients call the EAP the telephone is answered as being their particular organization's service. Again some providers will charge extra for this.

Some providers have dedicated telephone counsellors who are always available to answer the calls for a specific organization. This means that the purchasing organization is guaranteed that all calls from their employees will be answered by one of a discrete set of counsellors. However, this is very rare and again is likely to incur additional expense.

There are undoubtedly times when all lines into the EAP will be busy and it is important to consider what happens in such an instance. Some providers have a call waiting facility, whereas others have an answer machine for the client to leave their name and number.

If the service is a telephone-counselling-only service, then callers are likely to be diverted to a counsellor with whom they can have on-going support and counselling. However, if the service is face-to-face based, then after the initial call, a face-to-face referral will be made. Providers usually guarantee that individuals who require face-to-face counselling will be seen at a convenient location within a set period of time. Each client will be allocated a maximum number of sessions depending upon the contract with their employer. Some providers offer this number of sessions per individual per year, whereas others offer this number of sessions per problem per individual per year. So, if an employee received the maximum number of face-to-face sessions for one issue and then re-contacted the service at a later date for help regarding a different issue, then that number of sessions would be made available again. The maximum number of counselling sessions offered is usually eight, but this will depend upon how much you want to spend on the EAP. However, if possible, you should make a maximum of eight sessions available to employees as this number of sessions appears to be the optimum in terms of being able to help as many employees as possible. Even with an eight-session model there will still be clients who need more help, but eight sessions should ensure that the number of employees needing onward referral is kept to a minimum. Where it is felt that the short-term counselling available via an EAP is not likely to be sufficient for the client, an onward referral is made to an outside specialist resource (e.g. a psychiatrist or clinical psychologist).

## Launching the Service

When the EAP is originally launched, most providers run promotional events within the client organization. These detail the types of problems the service can deal with and reassure individuals of confidentiality. It is essential that employees know about the service and what it is for if they are to feel happy about using it in the future. Posters, videos, leaflets and wallet cards usually accompany these promotional events. Laminated wallet cards help employees to have access to the EAP telephone number at any time.

Training for managers is also offered by most EAP providers. This accompanies the introduction of the EAP and explains to managers how the counselling service operates and how they can encourage individuals to contact the service. Such training for managers can also be on-going in order to ensure that new managers receive the same information as was originally disseminated and to help to keep the EAP profile high in the minds of managers.

All written information about the EAP can be tailored totally to your requirements in terms of content and also your company logo. Some purchasers create a name especially for their EAP and this appears on all promotional literature for the EAP. However, customized literature usually involves extra cost, so it is essential to state your requirements at the time of drawing up the specification.

### The Cost of an EAP

EAPs tend to be charged on a per capita basis, which involves paying a fixed fee per employee per year. The average cost is £20–£25, although there is a huge range in prices, from as little as £10 to as much as £57. The per capita fee charged is contingent upon a number of factors, including: the number of employees; the geographic location of employees; whether the service is telephone or face-to-face counselling based; the number of face-to-face sessions available per employee per year; whether family members are covered; whether legal and financial advice are required; and whether other services are to be provided to the organization. This is why it is so important to consider carefully which aspects of the service you want and which are unnecessary. The cost is also usually based on average usage and if usage is very high, then additional payment may be due to the provider. You need to clarify whether or not this is the case when you interview providers. In addition, you need to ensure that if usage is very low you can negotiate a refund.

Some EAPs are paid for on an as-used basis, whereby a management fee is payable annually and then individual sessions are charged on an as-used basis, termed 'fee for service' in US usage. Some providers include the telephone aspect of the service in the management fee and only charge separately for face-to-face sessions, whereas others charge separately for telephone counselling and face-to-face sessions.

Whichever payment system you opt for it is crucial that you are aware of any additional costs. For example, initial set-up and launch costs may be charged separately, as a one-off payment.

The per capita system has been the most popular way of paying for an EAP in Britain, because it allows for easier allocation of funds and budgeting, by making the fee clear from the onset. However, paying on an as-used basis can be beneficial, particularly in the early stages of the introduction of the service when usage may be very low. In addition, if payment is made only for face-to-face counselling, the benefit in the early stages may be even greater as only a proportion of those who contact the service will actually be referred on for face-to-face counselling. Paying on an as-used basis allows organizations to determine the initial uptake and, if it is of a satisfactory level, then conversion to the per capita payment system should not be a problem. When organizations are paying on an as-used basis, then it is obviously paramount to be aware of the number of sessions that have been paid for and to speak with the provider if the figure appears to be particularly high.

With regard to family members, in general EAP providers encourage organizations to include family members in the service. However, this can affect the cost, so it is necessary to consider carefully whether or not you want employees only to be covered, or family members as well. It is possible to be flexible here; for example, it should be possible to allow family members access to telephone help, but to offer face-to-face counselling to employees only, unless the problem is marital in nature.

## Quality Control Issues

Most providers have their own telephone counsellors who are centrally based. It is essential that their qualifications and training (including an understanding of the workplace) are of a suitable level for this type of work. Initial assessment is a key aspect of a telephone counsellor's work and the ability to elicit exactly the nature of the problem (which may not be the problem the client initially telephones about) is crucial. Assessment is so important, because the client needs to be referred to an appropriate counsellor with the skills needed to help the client, or to be referred on to an outside agency where longer-term work with the client is more appropriate.

Providers vary greatly in what they ask clients on the telephone. Some providers have a standard set of questions that all callers are asked, and a proforma on which to write the callers' responses. This type of questioning is important because it allows the provider to give the organization more detailed feedback on the issues affecting their staff, although obviously not on an individual employee basis. It also allows the case management of telephone counsellors to be performed in a professional manner.

Where a client is to be referred for face-to-face counselling, again the procedure used differs. Sometimes the telephone counsellor is able to arrange the face-to-face counselling appointment on the client's behalf, whilst others encourage callers to telephone the face-to-face counsellor themselves.

All EAP providers do not offer a nationwide service and those who do offer it do so in one of two ways: either via regional offices with full-time and affiliate counsellors; or, more probably, via a network of freelance affiliate counsellors. It is essential that all counsellors are of a high quality in terms of their training and qualifications. They should have a minimum of a Diploma in Counselling and also be experienced in short-term counselling. In addition, all EAP counsellors need a thorough understanding of work issues, so that they can deal effectively with work-related problems.

Affiliate counsellors often conduct the counselling sessions at their own premises, although some EAP providers have local offices that counsellors are expected to use when seeing EAP clients. You need to ensure that the provider has inspected the premises of all affiliate counsellors who are likely to be engaged on your contract.

When a referral is made to a counsellor the provider usually sends a written indication of the maximum number of sessions the particular client involved is entitled to under the company's EAP. Some providers also issue other information about the company and any special aspects of the service at this time. For the quality of the face-to-face counselling to be high, it is essential that procedures are in place to manage the delivery and reporting of the counselling that is undertaken. This is often referred to as case management and is crucial to the success of an EAP.

All counsellors need to be trained in the particular provider's referral procedures and also need to be briefed about individual client companies. Case management procedures and supervision requirements, as well as the feedback required from counsellors, should all be discussed before a counsellor is given any EAP clients. You need to verify that this has, in fact, been the case.

The internal management practices of an EAP provider are another crucially important aspect of the service. Case management involves the monitoring of a case from start to finish. It is there to ensure that clients receive a quality service from the provider and that reports are given to the provider at the end of each case. Case management ensures that clients are referred correctly to an appropriate counsellor and that this happens within the specified time-frame. The individual's progress through counselling should also be monitored as part of the case management procedure, although this does not take place with all providers.

Counsellor supervision is very important and appropriate and regular professional supervision is a requirement of BAC membership. Professional supervision allows counsellors to discuss individual cases with their selected supervisor, within the bounds of confidentiality. Supervisors need specialized training, which is available through the BAC. Good supervision is part of the quality control process, just the same as case management.

Most affiliate counsellors have their own supervision arrangements, but these must be verified and approved by providers at the time of selection. Although counsellors may already have chosen their own supervisory arrangement for their own private work, it is essential that such supervision is extended to cover their EAP work also. To ensure that this is, indeed, the case some providers expect counsellors to undertake extra supervision provided by the EAP provider. For telephone counsellors (and sometimes face-to-face counsellors) this may take the form of group supervision, which is generally viewed as being acceptable.

## Statistical Reports

Regular reports on the usage of the service should be supplied by all providers. This is usually in the form of a statistical report and some qualitative comment by the provider. No information regarding individuals is ever reported. The usage of the service is broken down into a number of areas including sex, age, job status, and problem type. It is essential that you state what type of breakdown of the statistics you require, in order for them to be meaningful to you. It is also possible for providers to indicate organizational problems that have been raised by employees. However, very few providers feed such information back to companies, so it is essential to state that this is required from the outset.

## Customer Feedback

Most EAP providers have customer feedback questionnaires that are given to clients at the end of their counselling. This allows users of the service to feed back comments anonymously to the provider. Sometimes these forms are passed directly to the organization and sometimes they are compiled into report form by the provider. However, it is possible for the forms to be sent directly to someone in the organization, or, better still, for an independent customer feedback form, designed particularly for the organization involved, to be administered and collected independently.

## Independent Audit

After the EAP has been in place for about nine months you should initiate an independent audit of the service. No EAP should simply be put in place and then left to run. All EAPs need careful monitoring to ensure value for money and a quality service. An audit will consider whether the EAP operates in accordance with what is stated in the contract. This is why it is so important to have a detailed contract that specifies exactly how the service will operate and what are the benchmarks. If a detailed contract is not available, it is still possible to conduct an audit, but the purchaser, provider and auditor have to agree the standards before the audit can take place. Audit assesses the efficiency and quality of the EAP as a whole, in terms of both its design and operation. There is more information about the audit and evaluation of EAPs in earlier chapters of this book, and particularly in Chapter 11.

Hopefully the previous discussion has raised most of the issues you need to consider when you are drawing up a service specification. A summary follows this information, which should help you to ensure that you set out your requirements accurately in your specification for the EAP.

## ISSUES TO CONSIDER WHEN WRITING A SERVICE SPECIFICATION

### Operation

1  The EAP should operate according to the UK EAPA Standards of Practice and Professional Guidelines for Employee Assistance Professionals (EAPA, 1994).
2  Is the service to be local or nationwide? If it is to be nationwide, some indication of the geographical locations of employees is helpful. How confidential is the information about the employing organization? Can it be preserved?
3  Are all employees to be covered? If so, state how many employees you have. If only a section of the workforce or a specific site are to have the EAP, you need to detail this and, again, give the approximate number of employees to be covered.
4  Are family members to be included? You need to make the extent of this coverage explicit.
5  You need to state what hours of access you require for the service. If it is to be 24-hour then you need to detail whether answerphones, etc. are acceptable out of normal working hours.
6  What type of service do you require? You need to state whether you want telephone-only counselling or face-to-face counselling as well, and whether you want legal and financial

advice to be available. If you want all employees who contact the service to be offered face-to-face counselling, then make this explicit.

7 If you want a dedicated telephone number for your EAP, then you need to state this. You also need to inform the provider if you want freephone or local call rates to operate.

8 Any benchmarks regarding the operation of the telephone aspect of the EAP need to be specified. This could include: the time taken to answer the telephone; and whether an engaged tone is acceptable.

9 The session limit for the face-to-face counselling also needs to be stated. The first counselling session is usually an assessment of the problem, but it is usual to state a session limit including this assessment (e.g. if you state that the session limit is to be six, then this will actually be one assessment session plus five counselling sessions). Again, you need to state benchmarks that you require to be adhered to, including: how quickly referral for face-to-face counselling should happen; how quickly the first face-to-face counselling session should take place; and the maximum distance an employee can be expected to travel for face-to-face counselling.

### The Counsellors

1 Some organizations ask for dedicated counsellors to work on their EAP. This means that there is a pool of counsellors who have been briefed about your organization, and all employees who contact the service will be counselled by one of this pool. If you require this, then you need to ask for dedicated counsellors. You also need to make it clear that it is the provider's responsibility to ensure that all information regarding your organization is passed on to the dedicated counsellors.

2 You need to state the qualifications and training you expect the counsellors to have. This should be a minimum of a Diploma in Counselling, together with experience of short-term counselling and dealing with workplace issues. You

should also insist that all counsellors' CVs be made available for inspection should you ask for them.

3 Specialists, such as legal and financial advisors, require different training and you need, therefore, to state that they should be qualified in their profession, in addition to being trained in counselling skills.

4 Where providers are using affiliates to provide the face-to-face counselling from their own premises, you should require them to have inspected the premises of all counsellors who are likely to be engaged on your contract.

5 The counsellors should all be expected to adhere to the BAC *Code of Ethics* (BAC, 1989), with psychologists adhering to the BPS *Code of Ethics*.

## Launch of the Service

1 You need to state whether you require customized literature and what sort of promotional events you require (e.g. briefings only for managers; briefings and training in problem recognition for managers; awareness sessions for all staff; awareness sessions for a sample of staff; etc.)

## Monitoring and Evaluation

1 You should ask for a named Account Manager to be assigned to your EAP with whom you will have regular meetings and raise any problems.

2 The provider should have adequate case management and supervision arrangements in place to ensure the high quality of the EAP.

3 The frequency of statistical reports needs to be stated, as does the breakdown you require. If you require regular meetings with the provider, then the frequency of these also needs to be stated.

4 You should ask what sort of customer feedback is sought and think about having your own questionnaire designed, and possibly administered, independently.

5 You should state clearly that an independent audit of the EAP will take place within 12 months and that the provider must agree to this before the contract is finalized.
6 Professional indemnity insurance of at least £1 000 000 needs to be held by the provider, and individual counsellors also need to be insured to this level.

# 11
# How to Audit and Evaluate Workplace Counselling

## INTRODUCTION

An Employee Assistance Programme (EAP) is one human resource strategy that may help to combat the now well-recognized human and organizational costs of workplace stress. With the growing acceptability and use of counselling in British organizations, there is an increasing demand for information on the effectiveness of EAPs. The potential benefits of counselling for the individual in distress include improved mental well-being, better functioning at work, and enhanced job and life satisfaction. For the organization, the benefits potentially include reductions in sickness absence, unwanted turnover and accident rates, and improvements in internal communication, health and safety performance, and external public relations (in being perceived as 'caring employers').

In the United States the financial and other benefits of stress-care are widely recognized and most of the *Fortune 500* companies have employee counselling services in place. British companies are now also recognizing that by helping employees to cope with stress, they may be able to reduce absenteeism, improve morale, and ultimately boost profitability. Most larger companies in Britain are, therefore, beginning to see EAPs not as an additional cost, but as a possible investment. This is almost certainly true in the medium- to long-term, although conclusive measures of the benefit are not yet available relating to Britain. For that reason, some British employers are sceptical about the benefits, particularly financial, of stress counselling schemes.

In Britain, evaluations tend to be almost exclusively qualitative in nature, other than basic statistical reports on usage rates and similar measures. However, in the United States there has been a move away from such anecdotal evidence of EAP effectiveness towards insisting upon hard data, such as cost–benefit ratios.

> Almost every company with an EAP in the US is subjecting it to close scrutiny in terms of cost–benefit, utilisation and success rate. All sorts of bottom line quotations are being asked (Bickerton, 1990).

In the future, this type of hard data is likely to be demanded by British companies as well.

Since most US and British EAPs were created in an era of increased accountability, and because of their relationship to cost-conscious, profit-directed organizations, we would expect EAPs to have generated many evaluation studies. In fact, researchers (Knott, 1986) in this field seem to be still searching for identity, direction, methodologies and information. Most EAPs attempt to assist employees in a variety of ways; with a mixture of 'hard' and 'soft' benefits. Their simultaneous provision to the same employees makes the identification of a clear 'outcome-orientated by intervention' model difficult, if not impossible. As a consequence, the greater the vagueness of interventions and services provided to employees, the greater the vagueness of defining the impact and outcome of such interventions.

## US STUDIES

A number of evaluations have been conducted in the United States, with varying degrees of scientific rigour (US Department of Labor, 1990). The McDonnell Douglas Company commissioned a financial impact study that was an independently conducted, scientifically valid cost–benefit analysis. It involved the longitudinal analysis of the costs associated with health care claims and absenteeism for a four-year period (1985–1988), before and after an EAP intervention. Each client was matched to

10 other employees on six demographic variables, thus establishing an appropriate control group. The research did not try to measure the financial impact of factors that could not be objectively and concretely measured — 'soft' dollar items such as productivity, job performance level, replacement labour costs and other subjective data were ignored. The result was, therefore, the most conservative possible study on outcome. The overall saving for the EAP population (compared with control) was $5.1 million and the dollar return on investment was 4:1.

One of the most ambitious and sophisticated cost–benefit evaluations was undertaken by the US Department of Health and Human Services Employee Counselling Service (ECS) Program. It required the co-operation of ECS programs in 16 operating units throughout the United States, which provided services to the Department's 150 000 staff. ECS counsellors saw in excess of 2500 troubled employees during the 30-month period of evaluation. The evaluation had a number of important aspects: confidentiality of clients was guaranteed; the evaluation was compatible with existing policies and procedures; the minimum burden was placed on EAP staff; feedback was given to management to aid decision-making; the design was rigorous so that results were credible (this was achieved by collecting individual-level data); and the emphasis was on outcome (i.e. cost–benefit). Employees who had not used the EAP were the control group and were selected in terms of unit, sex, age and salary level. Cost–benefit analyses revealed that the estimated cost per client was $991; the estimated benefit in six months was $1274 saved per employee, and for every dollar spent the return in six months was $1.29. Ultimately, the program should realize a return of $7.01 per dollar invested (Maiden, 1988).

Nadolski and Sandonato (1987) examined the work performance of employees referred to the EAP for counselling over a six-month period at the Detroit Edison Company. The measures used were lost time (instances and number of days), health insurance claims, discipline warnings and accidents — all of which are generally accepted as valid measures of work performance. A measure of work productivity was also developed for use with those clients referred by their supervisor.

A longitudinal, comparative study was used and data were collected for employees at initial entry to the EAP (for six months up to that point) and for six months following treatment. A sample of 67 employees was used — 31 supervisory referrals and 36 self-referrals. Instances of lost time reduced by 18% and the number of lost days reduced by 29%. There was a reduction in health insurance claims of 26% and written warnings diminished by 13%. There was also a 40% decrease in suspensions and a 41% reduction in the number of job-related accidents. In addition, the quality of work improved by 14%, the quantity of work by 7%, peer relationships by 7% and relationship with supervisor by 13%. Unfortunately, no control group was used with this piece of research.

McClellan (1989) reports on the cost–benefit study carried out as part of an overall evaluation of the Ohio State EAP. No evidence of reduced health insurance costs was found and no reduction in sick time or employer turnover was cited. Again, no control group was employed. All in all, the direct financial savings of the Ohio State EAP probably did not off-set its cost to the state government. The employees, however, were very satisfied with the service, and so, as an employee benefit, it had some value.

The General Motors Corporation reported a payoff of 2:1 for its EAP and HARTline (Florida), comparing pre-EAP figures with post-EAP figures, and found that accidents had declined by 50%. The time an employee had taken off work (a week or two) was counteracted by the counselling time at the EAP. Workers' compensation claims dropped from 60 to 49 and liability expenses, such as bodily injury and property damage, shrank from $1 million to $29 951. Chicago Bell credits its EAP for slashing its poor customer performance ratings from 28% to 12%. In 1984, the EAP saved the company almost $500 000 in reduced sickness and disability absences (Pope, 1990). Masi (1984) summarizes that overall 'EAPs average a 3:1 return on the dollar'.

## BRITISH STUDIES

Even though findings from US studies have indicated generally positive outcomes, calls for good quality, independent evaluative research of EAPs are increasing. Despite the wide-scale potential benefits of services, there is still a paucity of information about these services in Britain, and an even greater lack of robust research substantiating their effectiveness.

## Independent Evaluation of British EAPs for the Health and Safety Executive

The first nationwide independent evaluation of British EAPs and workplace counselling programmes, completed at the Manchester School of Management (Highley & Cooper, 1995), was commissioned by the Health and Safety Executive in order to evaluate the effects of counselling at both the individual and organizational levels. Details of research methods are given in Chapter 10. The research tools included provider and client questionnaires, scrutiny of employers' records, especially sickness absence records. Control groups were established on a matched basis.

The mental and physical health of clients was found to have improved significantly from pre- to post-counselling. However, there were no effects on job satisfaction or the perception of stress as originating from relationships at work, the home/work interface, organizational structure and climate, or factors intrinsic to the job. The unmatched control group showed no significant differences for mental or physical health. Thus, whilst the mental and physical health of clients improved after counselling, no improvement was detected for the control group. There were some differences in terms of the results for internal and external services. The data from this research suggest that it is mainly the internal counselling services that have the effects described above. There was a significant reduction in both the number of absence events, and the total number of days of absence, from pre- to post-counselling, but there was no such reduction for the control group. The absence levels of clients and controls were identical at the pre-counselling stage, but whilst the clients had less absence at the post-counselling stage, the controls showed no reduction.

One of the only other evaluations to take place in Britain was carried out in the Post Office (Cooper & Sadri, 1991). The study systematically assessed the impact of stress counselling among postal workers, from shop-floor level to senior management. The research found that there were significant declines, from pre- to post-counselling, in sickness absence days and events, clinical anxiety levels, somatic anxiety and depression, and increases in self-esteem. The sample was 250 employees who had counselling over a one-year period. A control group was used and showed no changes over the study period.

Intuitively, we would expect that if a significant proportion of employees are reporting the early resolution of potentially serious problems and returning to work, then this must show up on the bottom line. It is a virtual impossibility to obtain purely quantitative proof, and so the decision to institute an EAP is still more often a leap of faith than a measured decision. Given that many employers in Britain are not just concerned with showing a return on investment, this is likely to remain the case. Many British companies are, quite rightly, primarily concerned about the human factor, rather than a simplistic pay-off decision.

## EVALUATION ISSUES

Reddy (1993) believes that the way in which organizations evaluate their EAP, and what they call success, will be related to their reasons for embarking on it in the first place. They also come up against the classic problem with outcome studies, namely the near-impossibility of controlling or eliminating all other variables that might influence the results. From a research point of view, one of the most fluctuating aspects of EAP evaluation is the measurement of indirect results. It must be true that a person who has been relieved of a considerable psychological burden must be returning to work with a degree of constructive energy and commitment. But how is this uplift translated into productivity, and subsequently to be measured quantitatively and qualitatively? What of the intangible, but potentially no less real, benefits of improved company morale and added value to the product or service?

However, the importance of evaluating an EAP cannot be overestimated. Many programmes must be assessed to justify their existence to some external authority. Even if this is not the case, an EAP should be evaluated to ascertain the extent to which it is reaching its objectives, and to find ways to improve its effectiveness. The goals of an EAP service should be built in from the beginning, and it is essential for organizations to be able to evaluate whether or not those goals are being met.

## Process Evaluation/Audit

In the first place, companies need to know that the EAP is running smoothly and that the efficiency and quality of the service is high. Whilst such *process evaluation* or *audit* is an essential basis for continued improvement and development of the service, it does not measure 'value for money', or whether the EAP is effective.

Audit is concerned with critically examining the running of the service, and includes scrutinizing procedures, checking that counsellors are sufficiently well trained, and ensuring that the organization is getting what it is paying for. Such audits are invaluable, but must be carried out independently of the provider and the organization. Audit allows the quality of the EAP to be monitored and changes made where appropriate. EAPs need to be audited/assessed in terms of the appropriateness, effectiveness and efficiency of internal operations. In the United States, all EAPs are regularly audited and some organizations in Britain have also conducted them.

In the Employee Assistance Professionals Association (EAPA) *Standards of Practice and Professional Guidelines for Employee Assistance Programmes* there is a recommendation that

> EAPs should be audited by external, independent, professionals to agreed British standards, as laid down in the standards document (EAPA, 1994).

In addition, the EAPA is to publish a set of guidelines specifically relating to audit (EAPA, 1997).

The EAP audit is based on the premise that a quality EAP that has a consistent and effective service delivery also needs to have a co-ordinated and standardized set of policies, procedures and services for both the administration and operation of the EAP. These need to be developed in response to programme objectives and organizational needs. A programme designed in such a way should prove both viable and effective for customer organizations and their employees. Audit is concerned with verifying that this is the case. The auditing of policies and procedures serves to improve the quality and effectiveness of EAPs.

The numbers and qualifications of staff must match the needs of the programme and all staff must be qualified to perform their duties, having clearly defined descriptions of their roles and responsibilities. The quality of provision of an EAP depends on the professional qualifications, training and experience of its practitioners and counsellors. Staff competence is critical to programme success. To maintain quality standards of service, all EAP counsellors also need to have their work monitored and evaluated appropriately by qualified senior counselling staff. Professional counselling supervision serves to protect the clients' interest, to assure the quality of client services and to improve the EAP counsellor's skills and effectiveness. The EAP audit should also address these key issues.

There is a need to match the client who has an identified problem with the appropriate level of support. Accurate assessment, intervention or referral will increase the likelihood of employee well-being and improved job performance. Verifying case management and follow-up procedures, via an audit, again enhances the programme's quality and effectiveness.

EAPs need to be positioned in order to maximize the value of their benefits in the human resource and organizational areas. There is a need to ensure that the EAP functions as an integral yet independent part of the organization and that it offers support to all involved in change and other company developments. The EAP needs to be positioned at an organizational level where it can be most effective and where it can gain support and endorsement from all levels of management. EAPs operate at their optimum when they are fully integrated with organizational internal structures. Linkages within the organization should maximize programme effectiveness. This is one of the key areas in which audit is involved.

## Outcome Evaluation/Effectiveness

Many organizations validly conduct process evaluations, but on its own this type of evaluation is not enough. EAPs rely on the premise that well-run EAPs do help staff in distress, and, as a consequence, help the organization, and pay for themselves in the long run. However, this assumption should not be made automatically, as every organizational context is different. It is essential to evaluate the 'whole service' in order to show that this assumption is, indeed, valid in the particular organization involved. Thus, in addition to audit (process evaluation), *outcome evaluation* is needed to ensure that the EAP is correctly designed for the organization in which it is operating, and that it is meeting the needs of that organization and its employees. Encompassed within this should be an analysis of the organizational bottom line personnel data, such as sickness absence, and unwanted turnover, because it is necessary to be able to establish a link between counselling employees and personnel performance criteria (Reddy, 1993). Outcome evaluation can encompass a whole range of activities that include evaluating effectiveness, cost–benefits, cost-efficiency and cost-effectiveness. Each of these is treated in the following discussion.

*Effectiveness*. This usually addresses the issue of whether those who receive treatment actually improve. Pre- and post-counselling comparison is one way of evaluating effectiveness, the aim being to show that a change has occurred following counselling. However, difficulties arise in attributing change solely to counselling, because counselling is not the only activity that is taking place — other major influences may account for the change. To help address this, a proper control group is needed (Barkham, 1991).

Maiden (1988) believes that one of the critical aspects of a growing concern about effectiveness is the need for comprehensive programme evaluations to demonstrate the cost-effectiveness and cost–benefits of EAPs. Indeed, there is increasing pressure, both political and economic, to evaluate the cost of interventions. As EAPs become more of an everyday occurrence in Britain, organizations will increasingly be expected to justify their spending on an EAP, and evaluation is essential for this.

*Cost–benefit analysis*. This aims to evaluate costs and benefits solely in monetary terms. However, there are doubts about the validity of converting psychological outcomes into monetary terms (Barkham, 1991). It is useful to distinguish between 'hard' and 'soft' data. Hard data (e.g. absence and performance) tend to be quantifiable, whereas soft data (e.g. client self-report measures—both quantitative and qualitative) are less easy to verify independently. However, verification is possible using third party sources, so that reliance is not being placed solely on the client's perspective.

*Cost-efficiency.* This involves comparing quantitatively and qualitatively two or more interventions in terms of the cost of achieving a specific outcome (e.g. getting an individual back to work).

*Cost-effectiveness.* This looks at more unspecified outcomes (e.g. psychological well-being). The aim is to establish which intervention achieves the best therapeutic results in relation to the cost of implementation. In light of the evidence of diminishing returns as the counselling sessions continue (Howard & Szczerbacki, 1988), decisions have to be made as to how limited resources are best utilized to achieve the maximum therapeutic effect for people at work (Barkham, 1991).

The evaluation of counselling services and EAPs is a goal of both academics and business alike (Megranahan, 1993). Academics attempt to measure scientifically the counselling process and to give insight into the value of counselling by showing a tangible outcome from an activity that is intangible. However, counselling providers simply want to prove that counselling works and has some quantifiable benefit, so that organizations will buy counselling services. Such a motivation gave rise to many of the US studies cited earlier, and, as a consequence, many of the studies are methodologically weak and somewhat biased, having been undertaken by organizations wanting to show particular results (Megranahan, 1993).

## PROBLEMS WITH EVALUATION

Clearly, once the decision has been made to go ahead with an evaluation there are many obstacles to be overcome. Evaluations that are not rigorously designed are difficult to compare with other findings for a number of reasons: problems exist in defining what constitutes a problem; the nature of the counselling process varies; there are inherent differences both between and within EAPs; there is no universally accepted definition of success; and the way in which an EAP is costed varies.

Sonnenstuhl & Trice (1986) expand upon the possible reasons for the paucity of counselling evaluation research. They believe that this dearth is understandable for a variety of reasons. Evaluation research is both time-consuming and expensive; EAP counsellors are generally more oriented to treatment than to research, and the issue of confidentiality has made it difficult for outside researchers to evaluate programmes. The relative lack of evaluation is also the result of the difficulty that researchers have in gaining access to programmes. EAPs are particularly sensitive research sites because programme staff, management, union representatives and clients are all likely to resist the encroach-ment of outside evaluators. Those who attempt to conduct research in occupational contexts are often put off by the relatively complex relationships that must be negotiated. Coupled with the problem of access is the practical impossibility of sustained randomized research design within work settings. Evaluation studies require effort and co-operation among researchers, work organizations and EAP providers. They also require the recognition that they have a common obligation (moral and legal) to protect the employees' rights to privacy and the anonymity of the programmes studied. However, without access to the everyday experiences of managers, employees and counsellors, researchers are not able to understand what happens in EAPs and cannot develop concepts reflective of reality or useful to practitioners. Researchers also stress that although EAP providers do often attempt to evaluate their own programmes, this is a practice fraught with the irresistible temptation to make their programmes look good.

Holosko (1988) closely examined the EAP literature and found that the lack of attention directed towards why EAPs work or do not work is conspicuous. More specifically, there is a distinct void in the literature related to scientifically-based evaluations of EAPs. He too cites the possible reasons as being: lack of resources for evaluation; lack of scientific instruments for evaluation; organizations' reluctance to evaluate EAPs; and lack of attention towards planning EAP evaluation.

## Practical Problems with Evaluation

The major problems with carrying out counselling evaluation research in organizations are: questionnaire administration; selection of a comparison group; confidentiality; extraction of 'hard' data from company records; and access to providers and organizations. Each of these is now discussed.

*The questionnaire.* A questionnaire-based study of stress and employee well-being can be used to investigate the effects of counselling on individuals. When designing questionnaires for this purpose there is a need to balance the length of the questionnaire against the depth of information to be gleaned from it. If the questionnaire is seen as too lengthy by providers, organizations and/or counsellors, it is likely to affect the response rate adversely. It is worth considering using shorter questionnaires, which although providing less detailed information, are likely to lead to a higher response rate and, hence, a larger sample size. The effective use of multivariate, inferential statistics requires large sample sizes. So for findings to be of value, it is essential that a sufficient number of individuals who have been through the counselling process are assessed, in order to enable meaningful statistical analyses to be carried out.

A counselling evaluation section for those individuals who have gone through the counselling process is also essential, so that their views of the service (in terms of perceived helpfulness of counsellors; perceived quality of service provision; and perceived positive benefits both at home and at work) can be assessed. This section can be viewed quite sceptically by some counsellors, who believe that this may be used to monitor their individual performance. A further problem concerning questionnaire use is that many organizations, providers and counsellors feel that it is too much to expect a troubled or distressed person to fill in a questionnaire, and that asking them to do so will somehow reflect badly on the service and affect the client–counsellor relationship. (This argument can sometimes be used by threatened counsellors.)

Self-report measures are a useful means of determining the level of effectiveness of counselling. If many different measures are used, then it is difficult to compare different services. It is better to use a core battery (e.g. OSI (see Chapter 9) or General Health Questionnaire (GHQ)) for which normative data are available (Barkham, 1991). Work productivity measures that are objective, reliable and valid also need to be developed.

*The control group.* One of the common criticisms of research evaluating the effectiveness of programmes aimed at enhancing well-being is that many factors other than the treatment programme itself can influence the results. This criticism is particularly valid when no comparison group is used. For an evaluation to be strong methodologically, the research therefore needs to demonstrate not only that benefits exist, but that these benefits can be attributed to the provision of counselling. Without comparative data from individuals who have not used the programme, it is extremely difficult to disentangle effects resulting from the counselling process from those resulting from other factors related to the individual being counselled.

However, the controlled experimental approach is comparable with the clinical trial in medical research. The use of this approach requires a situation in which it is possible to deny the programme to some individuals (control group), while the researcher randomly assigns individuals to each group. We clearly cannot withhold treatment from a group of potentially stressed people, particularly when the basis of an EAP largely is voluntary self-referral.

Even in situations where controls do exist, they may not be comparable. There is a need for longitudinal research that incorporates time and repeated measurement, both of which are necessary if we are to learn whether or not positive results are maintained. Shapiro, Cheesman & Wall (1993) believe that EAP evaluation research is promising, but not conclusive. They see the main problem as being the absence or inadequacy of control groups. Those individuals who seek psychological help have massive fluctuations over time, and also tend to seek help when they feel at their worst. As such, improvement over time is somewhat inevitable, whether counselling occurs or not. A comparison group over a similar period is needed to demonstrate the effectiveness of the help received. However, these authors are unhappy about using a comparison group of people not seeking help, because such people are likely to be much more psychologically healthy to begin with, so improvement over time is less likely. They assert that control groups of this type therefore tell us very little about the effectiveness of the treatment.

According to Shapiro, Cheesman & Wall (1993) more studies are needed that randomly allocate those seeking help to one of two groups, providing either immediate or delayed help. However, it is difficult to see how this is possible within the British EAP model.

However, this point is disputed by Swanson & Murphy (1991), who believe that, in reality, every member of an organization where an EAP is present is a waiting list control, since they may at any time refer themselves to the EAP. It is their belief that there is no reason to assume that those who do not refer themselves are less stressed, because in a free choice situation not everyone who may benefit from counselling will opt to use the services. Ideally though, we need more than one control group, perhaps from another site of similar size, engaged in a similar activity, from the same organization, where the service is not available. In the absence of this possibility, normative data bases are an appropriate comparison group for some outcome measures, but the organizational factors specific to each case will be ignored by this.

Barkham (1991) suggests that each client can be used as her or his own control if at least one baseline measure is established for each client at some time prior to counselling. He goes on to discuss the relative merits of having different numbers of pre-counselling measures. With only one pre-counselling measure, it is not possible to determine how stable the measure is, whereas two pre-counselling measures give a summary about change, so that it is possible to gauge whether or not improvement is occurring because of the client's expectation of counselling. However, three pre-counselling measures are ideal, according to

Barkham, in order to give a much more robust measure of stability.

The use and selection of the comparison group, therefore, is a major problem. In addition, providers are generally unwilling or unable to select these individuals from company records, because the employer then has access to the names and addresses of people not using the service. When a comparison group is being used, the questionnaires should be sent to the employees' homes. This procedure ensures that individuals are not wrongly assumed to be using the EAP by other staff members, who may catch sight of the questionnaire and jump to a wrong conclusion.

*Confidentiality.* A longitudinal research design can present problems on ethical grounds. This relates especially to the issue of confidentiality, the main barrier to rigorous evaluation design. It has been suggested that trust in confidentiality and the perception of a service being truly confidential is the cornerstone of a successful EAP (Feldman, 1991). Employees have a right to confidentiality, where any data originating from them is protected from others.

Balgopal & Patchner (1988) believe that there are a number of obstructions that a researcher will encounter in conducting an EAP evaluation, and perhaps the most difficult issue is that of confidentiality and employee privacy. Because of societal values about many problems, employees are reluctant to seek assistance from EAPs. This reluctance is further compounded if they are not guaranteed that the data shared by them will be kept in complete confidence.

Since the assurance of confidentiality is crucial to the success of the service, many providers are understandably wary about releasing sensitive employee data to researchers. Masi (1984) reinforces the fact that the reputation of the programme could be destroyed if employees perceive the evaluation negatively. Strict adherence to the principle of confidentiality, in some way, limits the amount of data an evaluator can obtain, but preserves the integrity of employees, the programme and the researcher.

While preserving confidentiality and respecting the privacy of employees, the evaluation process should be conducted openly, with the purpose of the research being fully explained. There is a need to clarify to all concerned that evaluation results will not reveal the personal identity of any employee. Having a comparison group of individuals not using the EAP can create problems because the individual may accidentally be perceived as a client by others. It is thus essential to protect all individuals taking part in the study. Unfortunately, these procedures are often perceived as additional chores by providers/counsellors, who therefore resist finding a rationale for participation in evaluation research involving rigorous methodology. There is no easy solution except that the benefit of such research has to be portrayed as a payoff for all.

*Organizational-level data.* It is essential that research evaluates the benefits of counselling at both the individual and organizational level, since such services operate at the interface between the two, and for the mutual benefit of both. For evaluation at the organizational level, access to individual absenteeism/sickness absence rates is desirable, because such measures enhance the rigour of the evaluation by minimizing the dangers inherent in relying on subjective, self-reported data. However, many British organizations do not monitor absenteeism. A 1991 survey by accountants Arthur Andersen estimated that 40% of British business falls into this category, despite an estimated annual cost of absenteeism to British industry of £6 billion (Arthur Andersen, 1991). Adequate evaluations cannot be conducted objectively unless adequate data are recorded by companies to make the evaluation of 'hard' data possible. However, 'soft' organizational data, even in summary form, is still useful.

Even if records are available, access to individual employee records is not always seen as acceptable by organizations on ethical grounds. There are severe problems, therefore, in gaining access to records. Even if access is granted there is always some debate about exactly who should extract the data. The extraction of such data is very difficult and requires detailed discussions with providers, the organization, the union and any other relevant parties, in order to come up with an acceptable formula. Internal counselling services tend to have an advantage in this respect. Internal counsellors, employed by the organization, have access to personnel records and can therefore extract the necessary data on their clients. They are also in a very good position to select comparisons, because they know upon which characteristics to match individuals. They are also bound by an implicit code of ethics, so confidentiality is ensured.

*Access to providers.* Traditionally, EAP providers in the United States, and in Britain, have resisted any form of evaluation by stating that EAP benefits cannot be quantified. The McDonnell Douglas Company believes that 'this myth is perpetuated because providers are fearful that results may not be favourable' (US Department of Labor, 1990). An experienced US evaluator of EAPs says that she hits 'a wall of resistance' when she talks to EAP providers, probably because evaluation is inherently threatening (Knott, 1986). Providers and counsellors may be hesitant about the evaluation outcome and concerned that the results may not positively reflect their programmes. Balgopal & Patchner (1988) suggest that 'these dynamics may not only bias the research, but also impede the endeavour'. Swanson & Murphy (1991) have also suggested that EAP providers are unwilling to be evaluated by independent researchers because it is threatening to their business interests. Sonnenstuhl & Trice (1986) believe that EAP providers often assume the effectiveness of their EAPs automatically, and EAP personnel are therefore apt to put a rather low priority on programme evaluation.

Kurtz, Googins & Howard (1984) believe that providers and counsellors often fail to see evaluation as part of their mission. By virtue of their professional training and commitment, they have confidence in the efficacy of their work and place low priority on the need to confirm the validity of their services. As Kurtz, Googins & Howard suggest,

> if the evaluation is in the hands of independent outsiders who may not understand or be sensitive to the intentions of their profession, their enthusiasm is even more diminished.

If a provider does not really want to participate and hence lacks commitment to the research, there is no guarantee that the providers or counsellors will fully co-operate in facilitating the provision of data collection.

Orlans (1991) points out that while the overall goals of different programmes may be the same (or at least compatible), the way in which the goal is met—staffing, basis for referral, assessment, implementation—might differ. Indeed, in a competitive market it is necessary for providers to be able to differentiate themselves from one another and, therefore, no two programmes are ever the same. For competitive survival reasons and to be effective, the EAP must tailor its services to the requirements of the organization in which it operates and be responsive to the needs of the individuals within the organization. All these factors make any uniform evaluation of their effectiveness complex and open to the influence of confounding factors that we cannot control. It also means that some providers are reluctant to allow an independent researcher into their organization, for fear that information may be passed on to others. It is thus important that independent researchers can demonstrate credibility, particularly in terms of confidentiality.

*Access to organizations.* Client organizations can also be very reluctant to participate in research. Their reluctance stems from a number of different concerns. Some organizations implement an EAP as a public relations exercise to 'show they care'; they may not, therefore, be particularly interested in its effectiveness. In some organizations, the usefulness of the EAP has been heavily advocated by a particular individual, who has fought hard to get the EAP implemented. This person potentially has a lot to lose, therefore, if the EAP is shown to be either ineffective or not worth the cost. As discussed earlier, 'confidentiality' can be a problem. Apart from the issue of client confidentiality, some organizations are keen that their name should not be associated with the research, because they do not want to be perceived by the outside world as a 'stressed organization'. Also, most organizations take it for granted that programmes are effective. They are assured by providers that EAPs are effective, and because other organizations have them they do not perceive a need to invest in their own evaluation.

Masi (1984) develops the point made earlier that confidentiality can be used as a defence against having an evaluation. People can be threatened by the thought of being evaluated, and will try to think of reasons why an evaluation of the EAP cannot be done. According to her, 'a major battle emerges between those who apply pressure for the programme to demonstrate its effectiveness and those who claim that documentation is impossible'. Unfortunately providers rarely realize that evaluation can help them 'sell' their programmes. In most cases, they are providing valuable, needed services, and evaluations can help them to demonstrate this.

# QUALITATIVE VS. QUANTITATIVE DATA

Because of the possible inappropriateness and problems inherent in trying to evaluate scientifically counselling at work, some authors are now calling for a more qualitative approach to be adopted, in conjunction with more quantitative approaches. Orlans (1991) believes that the evaluation literature provides insufficient data to assess the differences between schemes, and to relate these to research outcomes in any systematic way. Many aspects of human existence and experience are not objective, or easily quantifiable, and EAPs or counselling services are operating at precisely this level. In her opinion, increasing attention should therefore be given to qualitative research methods for gaining insight. She believes that it is pointless solely to concentrate on those factors that can be easily identified, when less tangible factors are certainly involved. By ignoring these less tangible factors, we are not fully evaluating the effectiveness of EAPs. Certainly, soft factors are problematic to measure, but that does not make them invalid or outside the scope of any research that claims to be evaluating the effectiveness of an EAP. One commonly accepted view of stress is that it is in the eye of the beholder, so, according to Orlans, we should be talking to the people involved, getting their views and, having gained this insight, we should not call it unreliable and put it to one side. Teram (1988) also calls for a greater emphasis on qualitative research methods and points to the value of such data in evaluations, precisely because EAPs usually have multiple interventions coupled with poorly defined success criteria.

## THE ORGANIZATIONAL FRAMEWORK OF EVALUATION

Some researchers have pointed towards the need for more research *before* a service is introduced. Kim (1988) says that most evaluation reports are so much concerned with the specific aspects of internal components of EAPs that they tend to lose sight of the totality, context or external framework of the evaluation. Utilization analysis is more informative and useful as an evaluative tool if utilization rates can be compared with some predetermined measure of 'need' (i.e. prevalence of problems prior to the introduction of the service). We can only sensibly ask whether a programme is being successful in meeting the needs of a particular organization's employees if information is available about how many distressed employees are within the organization and what their needs are.

Outcome evaluation can thus make a significant contribution to the further development of good quality and 'value-for-money' EAPs in Britain. However, to what extent complete evaluations are demanded by organizations will depend largely on the organization's reasons for initially implementing an EAP. For some organizations, an EAP is seen as a 'company benefit' that should also help the corporate image. In such cases, organizations are unlikely to feel the need for outcome research or the need to justify the EAP's cost. Nevertheless, whatever the reason for EAP implementation, companies should ensure that they receive value for money, that the service is being run efficiently and to a high standard, and that the EAP is designed in a way that best meets the need of the organization and its employees.

## CONCLUSION

Myers (1984) believes that in the haste and enthusiasm that often accompany the development and implementation of an EAP, evaluation planning is either ignored or assigned a low priority on the 'things-to-do' list. It appears that the importance of investing in evaluations has been temporarily obscured by the unprecedented growth and popularity of the programmes.

However, as the novelty and excitement of the initial growth of the movement subsides, there will be an increased demand for documentation of the benefits of EAPs.

Research could help to spur the growth of EAPs if the result is that management see financial benefits. Kurtz, Googins & Howard (1984) summarize by stating that,

> In the end, quality evaluations will develop only to the extent that researchers are willing to adapt their approach to occupational contexts, programme staff take the lead in assisting researchers to navigate the politically treacherous current of the workplace and that organisational leaders accept such assessments as routine responsibility.

# 12
# Future Roles and Challenges for EAPs

## INTRODUCTION

Any judgement or prognosis for Employee Assistance Programmes (EAPs) in Britain must be as problematic, if not downright risky, at the time of writing (1996) as it has been at any time over the past fifteen years back to 1981 when the first EAPs were instituted (Woollcott, 1991: 14). There is wide acceptance of their functional role, in respect of individuals and organizations, especially in helping to cope with negative stress (distress). This is felt by some to be a particular characteristic of British programmes that emphasize reactive coping rather than dynamic homeostasis (Clarkson, 1990). Positive stress, advocated by macho managers (Edwardes, 1983) and international eclectics alike (Semler, 1993), can be seen as positive also by professional commentators (Selye, 1975; Geare, 1990) as good stress in suitable forms, proportions and places. So even the issue of stress itself can be seen as contentious, and, likewise, the role and function of EAPs in Britain are far from universally agreed.

This chapter will bring together the future of British EAPs under seven themes:

1  the accepted present form and role of the EAP;
2  the developmental path along which EAPs are proceeding;

3  the future forms of EAP provision;
4  the threat to EAP (or opportunity) represented by managed health care;
5  EAPs and the counselling profession;
6  the evolving statutory, legal and official situation of the EAP;
7  Human Resources Management (HRM)'s relationship with EAPs.

Such a survey will draw on our personal contacts in the professional and academic world of counselling, as well as on the Health and Safety Executive Report (Highley & Cooper, 1995). As previously expressed by the authors (Berridge & Cooper, 1994b: 79–80) we shall adopt a position of 'qualified optimism', but, nevertheless, put forward clearly the uncertainties and potential dangers facing employee counselling in Britain at present.

## EMPLOYEE COUNSELLING—ITS STATUS

As the authors have put it, employee assistance has 'a vigorous and growing . . . presence in Britain' (Berridge & Cooper, 1994b: 79), evidenced by two active professional associations (British Association for Counselling, BAC, and Employee Assistance Professional Association, EAPA), a growing research tradition, and a rapidly increasing volume of professional practice (Highley & Cooper, 1995; Reddy, 1994: 60–61). Counselling generally in Britain has a position that is uniquely configured— uniting in the BAC both professionals in guidance (coming from a wide spectrum of orientations, therapeutic models and practice, and levels of qualification) and counselling psychologists. Equally, counselling in employment is widely accepted in Britain by employers and employees in defined circumstances, such as careers and vocational guidance, outplacement, pre-retirement, or post-traumatic shock. Such recognition aids the acceptance of EAPs covering a broad range of other issues that trouble employees.

But the British experience of EAPs shows that there are many routes along which an organization may travel in the process of developing an EAP (Hoskinson & Reddy, 1989: 75). It may develop from a US parent firm's programme, although few such in Britain have had specific origins in a narrowly defined occupational alcoholism scheme. It may stem from long-established and traditional welfare or occupational health provisions. Under conditions of individualized HRM, its creation may be because of the need to create a comprehensive range of employee and family benefits, which are also tax-efficient for the firm. Productivity and quality considerations may be the drivers of an EAP, while limited-scope counselling programmes may develop into full EAPs; for example, in cases of company reorganization, stress, physical health, wellness or financial advice.

Nevertheless, not all British commentators have been enthusiastic about the adoption of EAPs, especially 'broad-brush' programmes. In the later 1980s, the decision-makers in one major British firm described those available at the time as 'clearly incomplete, overpriced or unethical—sometimes all three' (Teasdale & McKeown, 1994: 136). Another critic, writing from a medical viewpoint, accepts the value of the EAP in cases of acute behavioural or conformity issues, but feels that 'there may be sufficient [help] within the human resources management and the occupational health teams' and that 'its cost may not be justified for average need when there is a reasonable level of expertise in house' (Fingret, 1994: 111). Other alternatives to the EAP that are suggested include industrial chaplaincy services (Elkin, 1992) or a return to the lay origins of counselling through the creation of workplace mutual aid and self-help groups, for reasons of cost and ease of access (van den Berg, 1991).

The clarity of the EAP as practised in Britain is often clouded by the intensity with which competing contractor providers promote their various services with their differing modes of delivery. In reality, the clash and clangour of the market-place often conceal the relative similarity of the product. As demonstrated by the over-arching existence of British professional associations for counselling, there is considerable consensus that:

> employee assistance is more about a concept than a programme . . . more a philosophy about how employees can be supported in the interests of health and performance, . . . more a philosophy about how their needs can be identified and met, than it is any particular *device* to meet them (Reddy, 1994: 64)

## TRENDS IN THE EAP MODEL IN BRITAIN

The once-popular belief among employers and employees that EAPs were little more than an American transplant into Britain (with connotations of non-adaptation and risk of rejection) has been almost entirely dispelled (Hunt, 1989). Thanks to the professional-accrediting work of the BAC and the industry-regulatory work of the UK EAPA, the credentials, practice and functionality of employee counselling have been established in Britain on a distinctive basis from North American activities.

The British EAP has evolved in a distinctive pattern, through the stages shown in Table 12.1, into a highly professional service, to very differing extents in differing instances of implementation. In British practice, few instances of stages 1 or 2 are found, although many EAPs that have evolved from more restricted welfare and occupational health origins may have passed through them. Stage 3 is probably that most favoured by individual professional counsellors, especially those working on an affiliate or network basis, and who have a general counselling background. To some extent, this relatively 'hands-off' stance represents an easy option for external contractor providers, who do not need to

**Table 12.1**  *Evolution of stages of counselling models*

| No. | Stage | Model | Counsellor and skills need |
|-----|-------|-------|----------------------------|
| 1 | Moral deficit problem | Prescriptive advice | Social superior or lay person: status; empathy: sympathy |
| 2 | Problem as 'disease' | Rescue and rehabilitation | Medical knowledge; lay empathy and group skills |
| 3 | Client-centred | Focused short-term therapy | Professional counsellor; training for lay workers |
| 4 | Employee at work | Broad-brush, high-context | Professional counsellors with organizational behaviour skills |
| 5 | Company as client | Individual and organizational learning | Policy-making and therapeutic skills combined |

*Source:* Various, including Bull (1992).

understand the client organization's structure, processes, culture, or conflicts, or train their affiliates in these aspects.

Increasingly, British EAP providers and in-house services are moving towards stage 4, which has an obvious marketing appeal to the employer, noted in the United States (Cunningham, 1994: 9), as well as offering holistic opportunities for insight and treatment on the part of the counsellor (Hoskinson & Reddy, 1989: 78). Stage 5 may be the ultimate rationale for management adopting an in-house EAP, although many such programmes have limited potential for such practice, being hedged about with guarantees of confidentiality, and independence of direction. Intellectually, its justification is that without organizational adaptation to the internal sources of stress and other troubles (tackling primary causes), all employee counselling tends to become tertiary-level intervention (see Chapter 1). Nevertheless, stage 5 interventions are problematic for many of the actors in the organizational scenario. Managers are uncomfortable with mental health professionals being involved in corporate policies and decisions. Professional counsellors (especially affiliates) are usually neither willing nor trained to be effective business consultants. Clients are uneasy about confidentiality in such circumstances, wherever guarantees are given or however non-judgemental the corporate climate. Hence, few British EAPs have realistically developed to this stage, regardless of the promotional claims made for them. Usage in the United States advocates the Organizational Assistance Programme (OAP) (see Chapter 4 for model), where the professional climate may encourage it, especially in instances of organizational trauma (Cunningham, 1994: 169–188). An extension of the EAP to a similar extent of intervention, but on an individual employee basis, is the Employee Enhancement Programme (EEP) (Dickman, 1985: 9–11): using a 'total person' approach without linkages with the employer, counsellors may feel that their independence is not impugned.

## PROVIDER DEVELOPMENTS FOR EAPs

In a market economy, the provision of a service, especially if intangible in nature, such as employee counselling, is always subject to economic pressures, redefinition—and, hence, growth or decline. In Britain during the 1990s, the market forces impinging on EAP providers have principally been:

- expansion of the total market for employee counselling
- entry of new firms to the counselling market
- some market concentration
- some reduction of referral facilities in the not-for-profit sector
- some increase in the ratio of employees using the service
- some increase in complexity and severity of presenting problems
- employers' increasing expectations of cost justification for EAPs
- some change in employers' emphasis from soft to hard criteria
- some pressure on fee structure and on operating costs

Accordingly, the categorization of trends in employee counselling service provision that was evident in the late 1980s was suggested by experienced commentators (Hoskinson & Reddy, 1989: 79), as seen in Table 12.2. It is evident that category 2 provision (conventional EAP, linked to employer's interests) was seen rationally to be likely to assume a dominant position. It was predicted that it would absorb the limited-scale employee counselling provision (e.g. alcohol, relationships, drug abuse) and the free-standing provision of access to an independent

**Table 12.2**  *Trends in EAP service provision: late 1980s*

| Category no. | Type of service | Trends |
|---|---|---|
| 1 | Direct access by client: independent relationship with counsellor | Movement towards category 2 by control of entry, and with more evaluation |
| 2 | Indirect access through employer's gatekeeper: counsellor has ongoing but confidential contact with employer | Enlargement towards 'broad-brush' by widening client and counsellor base |
| 3 | Specialized restricted area counselling: direct or controlled access | Movement towards category 2, with broadening scope |

*Source:* Based on Hoskinson & Reddy (1989).

counselling service funded by the employer, but without work-related feedback.

In the event, such an economistic outcome has been less clearly found, for a number of reasons. First, many external contractor providers (who came to represent the expansion of the EAP industry) were unready to become so integrated, or unwilling to bear the organizational and training cost of doing so. Secondly, affiliate counsellors were opposed to such a loss of their independent status (unlike their US counterparts), and perhaps also reluctant to invest in such alien organizational lore. So the organizationally integrated EAP has comparatively advanced its cause only slowly in Britain, in respect of the externally sourced provision. Instead, a different model of provision of EAPs illustrates current trends perceptively, using different parameters that interrelate the EAP process and key organizational characteristics.

With increasing economic pressures on client organizations, as well as within the EAP provision industry, the traditional loosely coupled welfare services (see Table 12.3), whether self-referred (type 1) or via managerial pressure (type 2) are tending to give way to more purposive and directed approaches. The trends to types 3 and 4 reflect major cultural changes in organizations, and incorporate changes in economic, social and political beliefs.

**Table 12.3** *Counselling and EAP service provisions*

| Counselling and EAP types | | Organizational ideology | |
|---|---|---|---|
| | | Person-centred | Organization-centred |
| Referral route and client's reluctance to participate in EAP | Self-referral (hence low reluctance) | 1  Full counselling service—totally confidential employee counselling service | 3  Full counselling service with preferred corporate emphases (e.g. careers, supervisory styles) |
| | Confrontational referral (hence increased reluctance) | 2  Paternalistic, tending to traditional welfare and performance improvement | 4  EAP linked to corporate goals and line management tasks with clear performance enhancement objectives |

*Source:* Drawn from elements in Shaw & Sugarman (1990).

Major differences exist between US and British EAPs, especially over the referral route, which is predominantly managerial in the United States and self-generated in Britain. But as British managers become more familiar with, and educated about, EAPs within corporate cultures that increasingly underline their productivity function, it looks likely that the proportion of managerial confrontational referrals will increase, in line with the US trend.

A final aspect that can be anticipated of the evolution of employee counselling is in the location of the provision of services. The original EAPs in the United States and Britain were located in-house (Dickman, 1985: 217; Trice & Schonbrunn, 1981; Woollcott, 1991) because other sources of suitable counselling were scarce. But the recent growth in Britain of EAP provision has come almost entirely from externally provided services emanating from commercial contractor providers (see Chapter 3). The reasons for this trend are fashionable corporate beliefs in external sourcing, downsizing, leanness, market-testing and other aspects of quasi-ideology. Yet the external provision of EAPs has other potential dysfunctions in practical terms, including lack of integration to corporate plans; lack of understanding of organizational cultures, procedures and tactical business objectives; incomplete identification with the needs of line management, HRM or total quality management (TQM); and lack of linkages with surviving occupational health and welfare activities. Consequently, a current discernible trend is toward the *hybrid EAP*, combining in-house provision, externally contracted supply and external resources in the state or not-for-profit sector. Issues raised by client employees that are central to oganizational goals, productivity or culture are counselled in-house either by dedicated counsellors or by trained staff; for instance, in occupational health or HRM. Other issues with a less direct impact, or with longer-term, more profound therapeutic implications, or needing specialist informational counselling, are referred to the external EAP contractor. The state or not-for-profit sector (where it still offers such services free at point of delivery or on a subsidized basis) deals with the most serious problems susceptible to psychoanalytic or similar approaches, as well as absorbing wider non-acute issues of a general social nature.

A hybrid EAP maximizes the potential of each area of resources to provide services, according to defined criteria. As such, it represents an application of contingency theory in organizational structuring and operation. It also optimizes expenditure where best results can be achieved for the employee-client and the employer. But the hybrid EAP presents problems in itself. Clients are less sure of consistency and quality of attention across a range of problems than would have been the case if provided by a sole, in-house service or a single EAP contractor. Very acute assessment and referral skills are required of the programme administrative staff, who may not be highly trained professional counsellors. Finally, there is always the potential for referral decisions to be made principally on economic or financial criteria. Such a trend may lead to criticisms that employee counselling is sliding into managed care, rather than concentrating on clients' best interests (Reddy, 1994: 66).

## THE CHALLENGE OF MANAGED CARE

This contentious concept relates to the notion that the provision of medical, psychiatric or personal/social services is subject to assessment and control on criteria that are also economic, financial, managerial or technological, rather than being judged solely on the professional criteria of those providing the services. In times of economic constraints, the provision of care solely on the criterion of need runs into financial, practical, ideological and even moral arguments. Advocates of managed care assert that provision that is universal, ever-expanding, open-ended in financial terms, and uncosted in the evaluation of opportunities lost or gained is impractical in current contexts. The solution proposed is a multiple assessment of expenditure, rather than the imposition of any one view held by a dominant group of stakeholders. In practice, this usually means a dilution of professional judgement by managerial control.

In the United States, the EAP is affected to a major extent by considerations of cost, since many programmes are financed through insurance companies, based on premiums paid by employers. It is clearly in the interests of insurers to supply employee counselling services in the most cost-effective manner.

Accordingly, they will press for service provision in an economical, focused and suitably brief pattern. The level of employee counselling paid by insurance premiums will reflect the cost-effectiveness of the provision of employee counselling, as well as the extent of take up, and the severity of troubles experienced by employees. The result is a double pressure on services delivered by contractor-providers—and similarly on in-house assistance.

These pressures have not yet been fully experienced in Britain, for a number of reasons. First, in an expanding British market for EAPs, the extent of downward pressure has not yet been evident on the level of capitation fees or on fees-for-service asked for by provider organizations. Hence, EAP contractors have delayed, or been reluctant to exert the pressure for, a fully-fledged managed care approach. Their professional orientations have predisposed them to be reluctant to engage in the ever-tightening helix of managed care. But they are well aware of the dangers, as evidenced by one contractor's comment that managed care can represent a trap if they:

> allow themselves to be seduced into directing their major efforts into managed care (Reddy, 1994: 66)

and as a consequence that:

> the very survival of the EAP movement in the United States [is] linked to its integration with performance management (Reddy, 1994: 66)

whether in the client companies, the EAP contractor provider companies, or in the health care insurer companies. The insidious implication of this mind-set is that managed care will mutate into managed cost and that this tendency will move back upstream to the supervisor. Instead of a relaxed hands-off attitude of 'benign neglect' on the part of supervisors (managers), the managed care concept will turn them to an attitude of 'constructive activism' (Schneider & Cohen, 1991), which predicates an 'outcomes' orientation right from the confrontation or self-referral stage onward.

Nevertheless, in the British context, the 'managed care' approach is a potentially dominant factor for the future. In the US scenario, the EAP administrator can be seen as the managerial gatekeeper and door-opener to a range of employee services not only in the funded sector, but also in the not-for-profit sector (Strauss et al., 1963; Reddy, 1994: 66). In Britain, it is not the EAP administrator who demonstrates her or himself to be both clinically and organizationally adept in structuring the provision of employee services such as employee assistance. Given the frequent non-judgemental nature of the assessment and referral process in Britain, and the prevalence of self-referral,

> the greater part of the central delivery mechanism . . . is in the hands of associate counsellors, rather than assessors or gatekeepers, as it is in the USA (Reddy, 1994: 67).

Perhaps this professionally regulated context of practice is unrealistic in the current economic conditions in Britain. New pressures are arising—NHS roll-back and commercialization, insurers' demands, increasing governmental agency (HSE) encouragement, and a new stimulus from large awards in civil cases. Many of these factors could indicate a move towards managed care.

A new future managed care partnership in EAP provision could well be as indicated in Figure 12.1.

The intended outcomes of a managed care approach are the more precise identification of:

- trends in health care costs, and hence introduction of new procedures or techniques—by health care professionals
- high-claiming companies and individuals, and hence adjustment of premiums—by insurers
- principal sources of primary stress, and hence changes in organizational structures and mechanisms—by employers

Such a programme gives an impression of being a positive stimulus towards improvement and unexceptionable in its goals. Providing it is not (in effect) a reduction of quality and benefit to employee clients, a justification can be made for managed care. Providers of EAPs in the United States have in the past expressed surprise that British EAPs have flourished in a context of National Health Service (NHS) health care delivery free at the point of delivery. A major explanation of this phenomenon has been the comparatively low level of demand on the state-funded

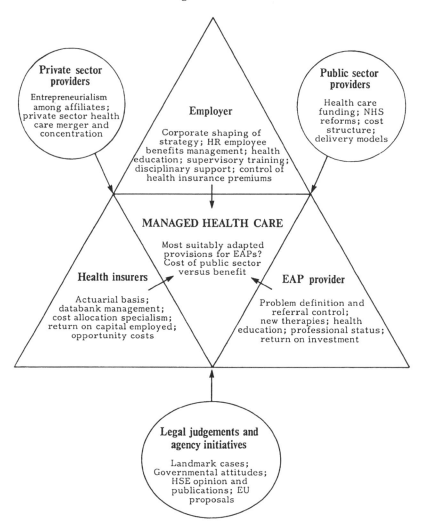

**Figure 12.1**  *Tendencies toward managed health care in EAPs. Source:*
authors' research

counselling or support services, and a concomitant meagre level of
provision. As managed care becomes part of the conventional
orthodoxy of the NHS, as well as of the private health care sector,
its invasion of EAP provision appears inescapable.

But a similarly logical conclusion would be for government to
allow tax breaks for employers in respect of expenditure on

employees' health care within EAPs and within other forms of occupational health, as well as on insurance premiums for delivery of similar sickness and wellness benefits in employment. Such concessions would relieve pressure on generally funded state health care provision, encourage employers to take a proactive approach to employees' physical and mental health, as well as promoting productivity.

## QUALITY IN COUNSELLING

As with any personal service, quality is the essential characteristic of EAPs, imbuing them with trust, uniqueness, psychological and social functionality, and reliability. Many aspects of quality can be adduced:

- codes of counselling practice (BAC, 1989)
- organizational criteria for provider firms (EAPA, 1994)
- accreditation standards for firms and individuals
- governmental sanctions and protection
- theoretical and professional corpus of knowledge
- process and skill criteria (especially for lay counsellors)
- control of relationships with contingent occupations (IPM, 1992)

A number of these issues have been addressed in Chapter 6, and it is outside the scope of this book to conduct a comprehensive survey of the occupational area of the counselling profession on the accepted criteria such as institutional structures (Millerson, 1964), exercise of power (Johnson, 1972) or medical problem definition and solution (Friedson, 1970).

The nub of quality in individual or personal services rests in the capabilities, knowledge, values, attitudes and skills of the practitioner—in the case of EAPs, the employee counselling professional. Various levels of counselling expertise are required in an organization, from appreciation of counselling (as required for the line manager or supervisor in many instances), to practical routine process skills (the manager, in some roles), to lay counsellor (often an informational role), to EAP functionary (whether receptionist or administrator), to professional employee counsellor (generally short-term or specialized) to psychoanalyst.

As with many evolving services and occupations at a formative stage, many accrediting, educational, official–governmental and regulatory bodies are seeking to establish authority in defining the employee counselling professional. The necessary elements for the professional counsellor need to be drawn broadly to allow for a wide role, but should include:

1  an undergraduate degree in a relevant social science, or a full professional qualification related to personal, social or medical services (e.g. social work, nursing, community services, etc.);
2  a recognized postgraduate-level diploma or degree in counselling or a closely cognate area;
3  specific and suitable training and practice in short-term therapy;
4  significant experience of work as a lay employee in an organization, whether in an entry-level job or in a position of responsibility, and an informed understanding of how organizations function;
5  registration and continuing professional training with a senior occupational body possessing statutory powers.

Such criteria for the full professional employee counsellor would lay a foundation for ensuring the quality of service for the employee client. It would also serve to establish public confidence and thereby create the perceived subjective status for the profession of employee counselling, as well as leading to objective status. For EAP contractor provider firms, it would be a demanding criterion, which would be achieved only over a period of time. If such steps are not taken, the many non-professional pressures on employee counselling (from the market forces in particular, as described earlier) will erode the uniqueness of the occupational domain.

## THE STATUTORY AND LEGAL DIMENSION OF EAPs

It is arguable that EAPs are in the national interest (see previous section of this chapter) and, as such, should be encouraged by government by statutory, official and agency methods. If health costs can be transferred, albeit in a partial way in respect of mental health aspects, from the Treasury to the employer or the insurer, then economies can be made in expenditure from the public purse. The economy is compounded if the employee client is referred to state provision, which is chargeable on a fee-for-service basis against the employer.

But a strong case can be made that the initial widespread growth of the EAP in the United States during the 1970s was the result of the encouragement given by the Hughes Act 1970 (see Chapter 3) for EAP provision in federal and state establishments, and the Drug Free Workplace Act 1985 (Murphy, 1988). Equally, governmental agencies have been prominent in using influence to promote EAPs in the United States (Masi, 1984), in Australia (Schmidenberg & Cordery, 1990:7) and in New Zealand (Chadderton & Milne, 1994: 3).

In Britain, such statutory backing has been lacking to date, and the encouragement for EAPs through governmental agencies has been generalized and non-specific. The Health, Safety and Welfare at Work Act 1974 (HASAWA) made no specific provision for employee counselling services, in spite of its title. The Act reiterated the traditional British emphasis on employees' physical health and on environmental initiatives—a trend continued by the more recent Control of Substances Hazardous to Health (COSHH) regulations.

The need for purposive action on mental health at work has risen only slowly up the agendas of employers and trade unions (Smith & Jacobson, 1988). A factor that may have inhibited official support for employee counselling or EAPs is that they lie in an indeterminate zone of departmental responsibility between the Department of Health and the Health and Safety Commission—which reports ministerially to the Department of Trade and Industry. In 1992, a joint Department of Health and CBI conference

> set out the agenda for raising the awareness of mental health at the workplace, and urged employers to change their attitudes . . . (Williams, 1994: 19).

The authors' HSE Report (Highley & Cooper, 1995) located employee counselling positively (but critically) in the range of philosophies and mechanisms of welfare and well-being at work.

The absence is conspicuous in Britain of any official and specific single agency promoting and campaigning for the provision of programmes in the area of employee counselling, help and treatment. Such an agency has proved to be central in developing EAPs and related services of employee help and protection in the United States, Australia, Canada and New Zealand. The form and powers of such a body are not fixed in any one model: it could well be oriented towards promotion, as the National Institute of Alcohol Abuse and Alcoholism (NIAAA) acted particularly effectively in the United States in the 1970s. It would need statutory support, but not enforcement powers; substantial and continuing financial resources would be required, as would an enthusiastic and robustly sophisticated promotional approach, and relative independence from the control of central governmental departments. Such an agency is not in the British tradition of public service, although it is so in the US federal mould. Nevertheless, the spirit of such an agency does exist, however, in the regulatory functions set up to monitor privatized public utility industries. But in an area like positive health, safety and welfare—in which all parties can be seen to win—such an agency could have a viable, attractive and effective role in Britain.

The legal support in Britain for EAPs and employee counselling is minimal, both in statutory obligations on employers, and as a result of landmark cases. A general duty of care exists on the part of the employer, but 'tertiary interventions . . . on their own . . . are unlikely to satisfy the duty of care', useful though they are in dealing with work-related problems where stressors cannot be eliminated (Earnshaw & Cooper, 1996: 111). In no way have British EAPs been incorporated into labour law, as had been done in New Zealand's Employment Contracts Act 1991, where EAP-style practices (or their absence) may be taken into consideration by the employment courts and tribunals (Chadderton & Milne, 1994). The Health and Safety at Work Act 1974 and subsequent codes of practice do not place specific obligations or make enforceable recommendations on employers to provide EAPs or employee counselling. Such a provision would be unlikely to represent a defence by an employer in a civil law action, although its absence would probably strengthen an applicant's case. The much-cited case of *Walker vs. Northumberland County Council* (1995) (see Chapter 1) may prove to be a turning point for claimants of compensation for work-induced stress problems, but it offers little guidance on the utility of an EAP or counselling provisions as a defence, or as a mitigating circumstance. Currently, British EAP provider contractors are hesitant to offer these supposed advantages in the US context as significant factors in the decision to institute an EAP in Britain.

In summary, official, legal, or statutory requirements do not play any substantial part in EAP provision in Britain at present. But while not a necessary condition, such requirements could enhance EAP acceptance, especially if reinforced by mechanisms to campaign for, and promote workplace counselling among, employers, trade unions and workpeople. Perhaps a useful framework is the New Zealand experience where an earlier narrowly focused Alcoholic Liquor Advisory Council (1976) founded under statute, led to the creation of EAP Services New Zealand (1991) as an independent promotional foundation with an operating grant. Both bodies are upheld statutorily by the Employment Contracts Act 1991, and the Health and Safety in Employment Act 1992. This self-supporting triangle of national expert council, proactive agency and legal requirement could well be a model of governmental encouragement but not intervention for other countries to adopt and adapt (Chadderton & Milne, 1994).

## EAPs, EMPLOYEE COUNSELLING AND THE PERSONNEL AND HRM FUNCTION

Employee counselling can be associated with both the traditional, impartial personnel management, and also with the new corporate, results-focused HRM. Since the inception of EAPs in the early 1980s, it can be argued that the emphasis of work-based counselling has tended to change away from the provision of a disinterested service, oriented externally from work, to an ethos of parallel benefit to the individual and the employing organization.

The network of affiliate professional counsellors used by most external provider contractors only has the loosest of links in almost all cases with the client organization; hence, counsellors' level of organizational knowledge and identification is low. Such counsellors have professional orientations primarily; their level of empathy with the aims of personnel or human resource managers is likely also to be low. Education of counsellors to appreciate the organizational contexts and the implications of counselling is costly, uncertain in its outcomes, and runs the risk of resistance on the part of counsellors who value highly their independent position. Even the 'old' even-handed personnel management was often mistrusted by professional counsellors because of its links with line management. Within the 'new' HRM, the EAP model is designed to intermesh with other organizational procedures more closely than former employee counselling provisions were usually intended to do (Orlans, 1989). Hence, the independence dilemma for professional counsellors was potentially more acute than with 'free-standing' employee counselling.

Yet perceptive commentators from a perspective of directors of contractor provider firms had no doubt that the development of EAPs lay in their integration with corporate objectives, which for counselling meant with those of line management as well as those of personnel and HRM (Megranahan, 1994). While considerations of marketing were no doubt present to some extent, providers saw companies adopting EAPs substantially for the achievement of corporate objectives, notably productivity (Sidney & Phillips, 1989). Yet such objectives were not necessarily those of productivity and performance in the narrow economic sense (Ahern, 1993: 44), and those concerned with EAPs in the future:

> will also be grappling with the perhaps unsuspected depths of the relationship between counselling and the core business of the organisation (Reddy, 1993: 99).

Nevertheless, a more direct and committed view of the links of employee counselling with personnel and HRM was provided by another experienced commentator:

> Organisations that have had the foresight to introduce an EAP are at the forefront of human resource management (Megranahan, 1990: 33).

and

> Employee assistance programmes are rapidly emerging as a significant human resource strategy . . . (Megranahan, 1991: 3).

Even if these claims are hard to substantiate objectively, there can be little doubt over the definite trend of convergence between EAPs and corporate objectives in the human resources field, as will be described in the next stage of the argument.

The linkages between traditional personnel management and employee counselling centre around the following points:

1 employee counselling is a linear descendant of the old welfare tradition, in a modern guise;
2 employee counselling is a civilized and worthwhile employment benefit for offer by a caring firm (Berridge & Cooper, 1993a);
3 employee counselling is a recognition that compassion (as well as competition) should be displayed by employers (Sonnenstuhl & Trice, 1986);
4 employee counselling, along with welfare and occupational health, can provide a wide protective panoply for the 'troubled' employee;
5 employee counselling represents a visible example of social responsibility on the part of the employer;
6 employee counselling is not intended to secure business advantage, but its provision will attract and retain a committed workforce;
7 employee counselling, by its independence from managerial control in respect of employees (especially those experiencing work-related problems) will complement the efforts of trade unions in looking after their members' interests, thereby helping to create a truly pluralistic climate in the organization.

The above range of rationales indicates that employee counselling is far from an altruistic or idiosyncratic intervention when used in conjunction with traditional personnel management. Employee counselling integrates well into personnel philosophies and policies, providing an additional confidential benefit for employees, and providing payoffs (albeit intangible) in terms of staff morale and retention.

From the mid-1980s onward, employee counselling and (increasingly) EAPs have been associated with HRM. This trend may have been associated with the more intensive marketing of EAPs than ever happened with the more professional and less organized world of employee counselling. Indeed, informed EAP commentators at that time found themselves unable to distinguish between personnel management and HRM (Orlans, 1989: 5). For a perceptive later essay on their differentiation, see Legge (1995b: 33–59), but it is worth making the observation that HRM is more closely identified with organizational interests and processes than is personnel management. Similarly, EAPs are more connected with other organizational mechanisms (discipline, training, culture) than is employee counselling.

The linkages between EAPs and HRM are considerable and indicate that it is likely 'that the EAP will enter into the mainstream of organisational intervention techniques and managerial thought . . .' (Berridge, 1992). They include:

1   to create a distinctive organizational culture in which individuals are valued, and their troubles are a sympathetic corporate concern as well (Berridge & Cooper, 1993a);

2   to encourage a developmental and learning culture, centred on problem-solving and personal growth (Peters & Smith, 1996);

3   to change an organizational culture, which is felt by management to be dysfunctional—for instance, in relation to issues of authority, control or dependence (Shaw & Sugarman, 1990: 10);

4   to disseminate and legitimize radical corporate strategies, especially at times of organizational crisis or major discontinuity, such as merger/takeover, closure, major downsizing or shift in business objectives (Reddy, 1994: 64);

5   to give coherence to top management's overall human resource strategy, which can become self-reinforcing in the achievement of corporate objectives (Berridge & Cooper, 1994b: 80);

6   to involve line management in the resolution of employees' problems at a more qualitative level than done by HR procedures, and to lead them to confront human problems as well as technical ones (Reddy, 1994: 65–66);

7   to promote enhanced product and service quality and added value by employees, through increased personal effectiveness and deepened commitment (Proctor & Ditton, 1989: 3–6);

8   to supplement other performance management and produc-
    tivity systems and initiatives by maximizing the contribution
    of the people factor (Reddy, 1994: 65);
9   to reinforce disciplinary procedures in a humane way,
    substituting rehabilitation for retribution, staff retention
    rather than punishment, as a more cost-effective tactic of
    behavioural modification (Berridge & Cooper, 1994a: 14);
10  to continue the trend of individualization of the employment
    relationship, weakening the collective identification with
    trade unions, and building a one-on-one with the employer
    (Bacon and Storey, 1993).

Any judgement on the extent of best fit between employee
counselling and personnel management, or between EAPs and
HRM must be relative. But these two pairings are self-reinforcing
conceptually. Factors (1) to (4) above also support the employee
counselling–personnel management logic, while factors (5) to
(10) are enhancing of the EAP–HRM case. Another way of
viewing the dichotomy posed is to see factors (1) to (4) as
supportive of 'soft' developmental–relational HRM, and the
second set of factors as compatible with 'hard', quantitative-
results-oriented HRM (Legge, 1995a; Beer & Spector, 1985). If this
analysis is to be adopted, the EAP is capable of satisfying both
HRM's criteria and those of personnel management, in its
cultural and developmental activities at least. This variant would
be likely also to accord with affiliate counsellors' preferences for
practice. If 'hard' HRM is the sole objective of a company client
for adopting an EAP, then the contract with the contractor
provider (whether external or in-house) will need to be very
explicit in its terms and expectations, especially in respect of the
roles of administrators, counsellors and line managers.

## CONCLUSION

We have tried to show that workplace counselling has a
significant role to play in managing the increasing pressures at
work, particularly in the future as we move toward less secure,
technology-driven, and more flexible working arrangements (a
euphemism for short-term contracts, part-time working and

other forms of less secure employment). It can also help individuals to cope with personal or family-related problems external to the organization, but which nevertheless tend to spill over into work life.

Organizations are more likely to be successful in their efforts to reduce workplace stress, however, if they combine counselling with stress audits and training, and prevention techniques. Stress management training, health promotion activities and counselling services are useful in extending the physical and psychological resources of the individual to modify their appraisal of a stressful situation and cope better with experienced stress. However, there are many potential and persistent sources of stress in the work environment that the individual is likely to perceive as outside her or his resource or positional power to change (e.g. the structure, management style or culture of the organization). Such stressors require organizational-level interventions if their dysfunctional impact on employee health is to be satisfactorily overcome. In some of these cases, this can only be done effectively if the organization is audited and a systematic intervention undertaken.

If organizations are to be successful in tackling the widespread problem of workplace stress, they need to create the kind of supportive organizational climate in which stress is recognized and accepted as a feature of modern industrial life and not interpreted as a sign of weakness or incompetence. This means that in order for organizational initiatives to succeed, be they EAPs or stress audits or stress management programmes, they need commitment from those at the very top. What organizations must begin to understand and internalize in their corporate cultures is what John Ruskin knew as long ago as 1871 when he commented on the nature of work:

> in order that people may be happy in their work, these three things are needed: they must be fit for it; they must not do too much of it; and they must have a sense of success in it.

# References

Ahern, G. (1993). Counselling provision in the UK. In M. Reddy (ed.), *EAPs and Counselling Provision in UK Organisations 1993*. Milton Keynes. 25–46.

Anthony, P. D. & Crighton, A. (1969). *Industrial Relations and the Personnel Specialists*. London: Batsford.

Arthur Andersen (1991). Absence rate is EC worst (Arthur Andersen Survey). *Independent on Sunday*, 20 October 1991.

Bacon, N. & Storey, J. (1993). Individualisation of the employment relationship and the implications for trade unions. *Employee Relations*, **15**, no. 1, 15–17.

Balgopal, P. R. & Patchner, M. A. (1988). Evaluating Employee Assistance Programs: Obstacles, issues and strategies. *Employee Assistance Quarterly*, **3**, nos. 3 & 4, 95–105.

Banking Insurance and Finance Union (BIFU) (1996). The best cure for stress is prevention. *BIFU Report*, April–May 1996, 9.

Barkham, M. (1991). Understanding, implementing and presenting counselling evaluation. In R. Bayne & P. Nicholson (eds), *Psychology and Counselling for Health Professionals*. London: Chapman and Hall.

Bean, R. (1995). *Comparative Industrial Relations*, 2nd edn. Beckenham: Croom-Helm.

Beer, M. & Spector, B. (1985). Corporate-wide transformations in human resource management. In R. E. Walton & P. R. Lawrence (eds), *Human Resource Management: Trends and Challenges*. Boston MA: Harvard Business School Press.

Benbow, N. (1995). *Survival of the Fittest*. London: Institute of Management.

Berridge, J. (1990a). The EAP employee counselling comes of age. *Employee Counselling Today*, **2**, no. 4, 14–17.

Berridge, J. (1990b). The EAP and employee counselling. *Employment Bulletin and Industrial Relations Digest*, **6**, no. 1, 4–7.

Berridge, J. (1992). Companies care—or do they? Paper presented to *IPM/EAR Conference*. Barbican, London, 8 October 1992.

Berridge, J. (1993). Human resource management and the EAP. *EAP International* **1**, no. 2, 6.

Berridge, J. R. (1996a). New roles for employee assistance programmes in the 1990s. *Personnel Review*, **25**, no. 1, 59–64.

Berridge, J. & Cooper, C. L. (1993a). Employee Assistance Programmes—a growing tradition. Occasional paper. London: Coutts Career Consultants.

Berridge, J. & Cooper, C. L. (1993b). Stress and coping in US organisations. *Work and Stress*, **7**, no. 1, 89–102.

Berridge, J. R. & Cooper, C. L. (1994a). The Employee Assistance Programme: Its role in organisational coping and excellence. *Personnel Review*, Special issue, **23**, no. 7, 4–80.

Berridge, J. R. & Cooper, C. L. (1994b). Qualified optimism: EAP prospects for the 1990s. *Personnel Review*. **23**, no. 7, 79–80.

Berridge, J. (1996b) Justifying an employee assistance programme. In A. McGoldrick (ed.), *Cases in Human Resource Management*. London: Pitman, 129–143.

von Bertalanffy, L. (1950). General systems theory. *General Systems*, **1**, 1–10.

Bickerton, R. (1990). In L. Stern, Why EAPs are worth the investment. *Business and Health*, May, 14–19.

Blau, P. M. & Scott, W. R. (1962). *Formal Organisation*. San Francisco CA: Chandler.

Blauner, R. (1964). *Alienation and Freedom: The Factory Worker and his Industry*. Chicago IL: University of Chicago Press.

Blum, T. C. & Roman, P. T. (1988). Purveyor organisations and the implementation of Employee Assistance Programs. *Journal of Applied Behavioural Science*, **24**, 397–411.

Braverman, H. (1974). *Labour and Monopoly Capitalism*. New York: Twentieth Century Publishing.

British Association for Counselling (BAC) (1988). *Counselling and Psychotherapy Resources Directory*. Rugby, Warwickshire: BAC.

British Association for Counselling (BAC) (1989). *Code of Ethics and Practice for Counsellors*. Rugby, Warwickshire: BAC.

Bull, A. D. (1992). Confidential counselling service—a new breed of EAP. *Employee Counselling Today*, **4**, no. 2, 25–28.

Cartwright, S. & Cooper, C. L. (1994). *No Hassle! Taking the Stress out of Work*. London: Century Books.

Chadderton, J. & Milne, R. (1994). The history of EAP development in New Zealand. *Employee Counselling Today*, **6**, no. 3, 3–6.

Clarkson, P. (1990). The scope of stress counselling in organisations. *Employee Counselling Today*, **2**, no. 4, 3–6.

Cole, G. E., Tucker, L. A. & Friendman, G. M. (1982). Absenteeism data as a measure of cost effectiveness of stress management programs. *American Journal of Health Promotion*. Spring, 12–15.

Cooper, C. L. (1986). Job distress: Recent research and the emerging role of the clinical occupational psychologist. *Bulletin of the British Psychological Society*, **39**, 325–331.

Cooper, C. L. (1996). *Handbook of Stress, Medicine and Health*. Florida, USA: CRC Press Inc.

Cooper, C. L. & Cartwright, S. (1996). *Mental Health and Stress in the Workplace. A Guide for Employers*. London: HMSO.

Cooper, C. L. & Payne, R. (1988). *Causes, Coping and Consequences of Stress at Work*. New York & Chichester: John Wiley.

Cooper, C. L. & Sadri, G. (1991). The impact of stress counselling at work. In P. L. Perrewe (ed.), Handbook on Job Stress. Special issue, *Journal of Social Behaviour and Personality*, **6**, no. 7, 411–423.

Cooper, C. L., Cooper, R. D. & Eaker, L. (1988). *Living with Stress*. London: Penguin Books; New York: Viking/Penguin. 2nd printing 1993.

Cooper, C. L., Sloan, S. & Williams, S. (1988). *The Occupational Stress Indicator: The Management Set*. Windsor: NFER–Nelson.

Cooper, C. L., Sadri, G., Allison, T. & Reynolds, P. (1990). Stress counselling in the Post Office. *Counselling Psychology Quarterly*, **3**, no. 1, 3–11.

Cunningham, G. (1994). *Effective Employee Assistance Programs*. Thousand Oaks CA: Sage Publications.

Dale, B. & Cooper, C. L. (1992). *Total Quality and Human Resource Management*. Oxford: Blackwell Publishers.

Davis, A. & Gibson, L. (1994). Designing employee welfare provision. In J. R. Berridge & C. L. Cooper (eds), The Employee Assistance Programme: Its Role in Organisational Coping and Excellence, *Personnel Review* **23**, no. 7, 33–45.

DeFrank, R. S. & Cooper, C. L. (1987). Worksite stress management interventions: Their effectiveness and conceptualisation. In C. L. Cooper (ed.), *Stress Management Interventions at Work*. Bradford: MCB University Press, 4–11.

Dessenne, C. et al. (1992). EAP International Survey. *EAP International*, **1**, no. 1, Autumn, 14–18.

Dessler, G. (1984). *Personnel Management*, 3rd edn. Reston VA: Relsed Publishing Co.

Dickman, J. F. (1985). Employee Assistance Programmes: History and philosophy. In J. F. Dickman, W. G. Emener & W. S. Hutchison, Jr. (eds), *Counselling the Troubled Person in Industry*. Springfield IL: Charles C. Thomas.

EAPA (Employee Assistance Professionals Association) (1992). *EAPA Press File: EAP Utilisation and Cost Benefits*. Arlington, VA.

EAPA. (1994). *UK EAPA Standards of Practice and Professional Guidelines for Employee Assistance Programmes*. London: EAPA.

EAPA (1997). *UK EAPA Guidelines for the Audit and Evaluation of Workplace Counselling Programmes*. London: EAPA.

Earnshaw, J. M. & Cooper, C. L. (1994). Employee stress litigation: The UK experience. *Work and Stress*, **8**, no. 4, 287–295.

Earnshaw, J. M. & Cooper, C. L. (1996). *Stress and Employer Liability*. London: Institute of Personnel and Development.

Edwardes, M. (1983). *Back from the Brink*. London: Collins.

Elkin, G. (1992). Industrial chaplains: Low-profile counselling at work. *Employee Counselling Today*, **4**, no. 3, 17–25.

Feldman, A. (1991). Trust me: Earning employee confidence. *Personnel*, **68**, no. 2, 7.

Fingret, A. (1994). Developing a company mental healthplan. In C. L. Cooper & S. Williams (eds), *Creating Healthy Work Organisations*. Chichester: John Wiley, 97–114.

Finn, W. (1995). Sympathetic ear. *Personnel Today*, 26 September 1995, 29–31.

Fleisher, D. & Kaplan, B. H. (1988). Employee assistance/counselling typologies. In G. M. Gould & M. J. Smith (eds), *Social Work in the Workplace*. New York: Springer, 31–44.

Friedman, M. (1980). *Free to Choose*. Harmondsworth: Penguin Books.

Friedson, E. (1970). *Profession of Medicine: A Study in the Sociology of Applied Knowledge*. New York: Dodd, Mead & Co.

Galliano, S. (1994). Counsellor criteria for EAPs. *ACW Journal—Counselling at Work*, Summer 1994, 13–14.

Geare, A. J. (1990). Job stress: Boon as well as bane. *Employee Counselling Today*. **1**, no. 3, 21–29.

Goldberg, D. P. (1972). *The Detection of Psychiatric Illness by Questionnaire*. Oxford: Oxford University Press.

Good, R. K. (1986). Employee assistance—a critique of three corporate drug abuse policies. *Personnel Journal*, **65**, 96–107.

Goodman, J., Marchington, M., Berridge, J., Bamber, G, & Snape E. (1997). Great Britain. In G. Bamber & R. Lansbury (eds), *Industrial Relations: an International Comparison*, third edition. London: Routledge, forthcoming.

Hellan, R. T. (1986). An EAP update: A perspective for the 80s. *Personnel Journal*, **65**, 51–54.

Highley, J. C. & Cooper, C. L. (1994). Evaluating EAPs. *Personnel Review*, **23**, no. 7, 46–59.

Highley, J. C. & Cooper, C. L. (1995). An Assessment of Employee Assistance and Workplace Counselling Programmes in British Organisations. *A Report for the Health and Safety Executive*. Unpublished.

Holosko, M. J. (1988). Perspectives for employee assistance program evaluations: A case for more thoughtful evaluation planning. *Employee Assistance Quarterly*, **3**, nos. 3 & 4, 59–68.

Hoskinson, L. & Reddy, M. (1989). *Counselling Services in UK Organisations*. Milton Keynes: ICAS.

Howard, J. C. & Szczerbacki, D. (1988). Employee Assistance Programs in the hospital industry. *Health Care Management Review*, Spring.

Hunt, D. D. (1989). Anglicizing an American import. *Personnel Administrator*, **34**, 22–26.

IPM (Institute of Personnel Management) (1992). *Statement on Counselling in the Workplace*. London: IPM.

Johnson, T. (1972). *Professions and Power*. London: Macmillan.

Jones, J. W., Barge, B. N., Steffy, B. D., Fay, L. M., Kunz, L. K. & Wuebker (1988). Stress and medical malpractice: Organization risk assessment and intervention. *Journal of Applied Psychology*, **73**, no. 4, 727–735.

Kahn, H. & Cooper, C. L. (1990). Mental health, job satisfaction, alcohol intake and occupational stress among dealers in financial markets. *Stress Medicine*, **6**, 285–298.

Kemp, D. (1989). Major unions and collectively-bargained fringe benefits. *Public Personnel Management*, **18**, no. 4.

Kessler, S. & Bayliss, F. J. (1995). *Contemporary British Industrial Relations*, 2nd edn. Basingstoke: Macmillan,

Kim, D. S. (1988). Assessing EAPs: Evaluation, typology and models. *Employee Assistance Quarterly*, **3**, nos. 3 & 4, 169–187.

Knott, T. D. (1986). The distinctive uses of evaluation and research: A guide for the occupational health care movement. *Employee Assistance Quarterly*, **1**, no. 4, 43–51.

Kurtz, N. R., Googins, B. & Howard, W. C. (1984). Measuring the success of occupational alcoholism programs. *Journal of Studies on Alcohol*, **45**, 33–45.

Lee, C. & Gray, J. A. (1994). The role of Employee Assistance Programmes. In C. L. Cooper & S. Williams (eds), *Creating Healthy Work Organizations*. Chichester: John Wiley, 215–242.

Legge, K. (1995a). *New Perspectives on Human Resource Management*. London: Routledge.

Legge, K. (1995b). HRM: Rhetoric, reality and hidden agendas. In J. Storey (ed.), *Human Resource Management: A Critical Text*. London: Routledge, 33–59.

Luthans, F. & Waldersee, R. (1989). What do we really know about EAPs? *Human Resource Management*, **28**, 275–288.

MacInnes, J. (1987). *Thatcherism at Work*. Milton Keynes: Open University Press.

Maiden, R. P. (1988). Evaluating Employee Assistance Programs: EAP evaluation in a Federal Government Agency. *Employee Assistance Quarterly*, **3**, nos. 3 & 4, 191–203.

Martin, A. (1967). *Welfare in Britain*. London: Batsford.

Masi, D. A. (1984). *Designing Employee Assistance Programs*. New York: AMACOM.

Masi, D. A. & Friedland, S. J. (1988). EAP actions and options. *Personnel Journal*, **67**, 61–67.

McClellan, K. (1989). Cost-benefit analysis of the Ohio EAP. *Employee Assistance Quarterly*, **5**, no. 2, 67–85.

Megranahan, M. (1990). Employee Assistance Programmes: frameworks and guiding principles. *Employee Counselling Today*, **2**, no. 3, 28–33.

Megranahan, M. (1991). Editorial. *Employee Counselling Today*, **3**, no. 4, 3.

Megranahan, M. (1993). Editorial. *Employee Counselling Today*, **5**, no. 5, 3.

Megranahan, M. (1994). Counselling in the workplace. In W. Dryden, D. Charles-Edwards & R. Woolfe (eds), *Handbook of Counselling in Britain*. Routledge, 168–183.

Megranahan, M. (1995). Presentation to *Postgraduate Course in Organisational Psychology*, Manchester School of Management, UMIST, 29 November 1995.

Miles, R. E. & Snow, C. C. (1978). Organizational strategy: structure and process. *Academy of Management Review*, **3**, 546–562.

Millerson, G. (1964). *The Qualifying Associations*. London: Routledge.

Murphy, L. R. (1988). Workplace interventions for stress reduction. In C. L. Cooper & R. Payne (eds), *Causes, Coping and Consequences of Stress at Work*. Chichester: John Wiley, 301–339.

Murphy, L. R. (1995). Managing job stress: An employee assistance/human resources partnership. *Personnel Review*, **24**, no. 1, 41–50.

Myers, D. W. (1984). *Establishing and Building EAPs*. Westport CN: Quorum Books.

Nadolski, J. N. & Sandonato, C. E. (1987). Evaluation of an Employee Assistance Programme. *Journal of Occupational Medicine*, **20**, no. 1, 32–37.

Nobile, R. J. (1991). Matters of confidentiality. *Personnel*, **68**, 11–12.

Orlans, V. (1986). Counselling services in organisations. *Personnel Review*, **15**, no. 5, 19–23.

Orlans, V. (1989). Counselling in the workplace: A review and thoughts for the future. *Employee Counselling Today*, **1**, no. 1, 3–6.

Orlans, V. (1991). Evaluating the benefits of Employee Assistance Programmes. *Employee Counselling Today*, **3**, no. 4, 27–31.

Peters, T. J. & Waterman, R. H. (1982). *In Search of Excellence, Lessons from America's Best Run Companies*. New York: Harper & Row.

Peters, J. & Smith, P. (1996). Developing high potential staff—an action-learning approach. *Employee Counselling Today*, **8**, no. 3, 6–11.

Pigors, P. & Myers, C. A. (1977). *Personnel Administration*, 8th edn. Englewood Cliffs, NJ: McGraw-Hill.

Pope, T. (1990). Good idea but what's the cost? *Management Review*, **79**, no. 8, 50–53.

Proctor, B. & Ditton, A. (1989). How can counselling add value to organisations? *Employee Counselling Today*, **1**, no. 3, 3–6.

Reddy, M. (1991). Counselling—its value to the business. In R. Jenkins and N. Coney (eds), *Prevention of Mental Ill Health at Work—A Conference*. HMSO, 50–58.

Reddy, M. (ed.) (1993). *EAPs and Counselling Provision in UK Organisations 1993*. Milton Keynes: ICAS.

Reddy, M. (1994). EAPs and their future in the UK. *Personnel Review*, **23**, no. 7, 60–78.

Roethlisberger, F. J. & Dickson, W. J. (1939). *Management and the Worker.* Cambridge MA: Harvard University Press.

Roman, P. T. & Blum, T. C. (1992). The 'cores' of employee assistance programming: Cross-national applications and limitations. *EAP International,* 1, no. 1, 4–8.

Roman, P. M., Blum, T. C. & Bennett, N. (1987). Educating organisational consumers about Employee Assistance Programs. *Public Personnel Management,* 16, no. 4, Winter, 299–372.

Routledge, P. (1993). *Scargill: The Unauthorized Biography.* London: Harper Collins.

Schabracq, M. J., Winnubst, J. A. M. & Cooper, C. L. (1996). *Handbook of Work and Health Psychology.* Chichester: John Wiley.

Schmidenberg, O. C. & Cordery, J. L. (1990). Managing Employee Assistance Programmes. *Employee Relations,* 12, no. 1, 7–12.

Schneider, R. & Cohen, N. (1991). The effectiveness of supervisor training in Employee Assistance Programs: Current practice and future directions. *Employee Assistance Quarterly,* 6, no. 1, 41–55.

Selye, H. (1975). Confusion and controversy in the stress field. *Journal of Human Stress,* 1, 37–44.

Semler, R. (1993). *Maverick!* London: Century Books.

Shain, M. & Groeneveld, J. (1980). *Employee Assistance Programs: Philosophy, Theory and Practice.* Lexington, MA: Lexington Books.

Shapiro, D. A., Cheesman, M. & Wall, T. R. (1993). Secondary prevention: Review of counselling and EAPs. Paper presented to the *Royal College of Physicians Conference on Mental Health at Work.* London, 11 January 1993.

Shaw, G. H. & Sugarman, L. (1990). Can people be sent for counselling? *Employee Counselling Today,* 2, no. 1, 9–13.

Sidney, E. & Phillips, N. (1989). *One-to-One Management: Counselling to Improve Job Performance.* London: Pitman.

Smith, A. & Jacobson, K. (1988). *The Nation's Health—A Strategy for the 1990s.* London: King's Fund.

Smith, C., Child, J. & Rowlinson, M. (1990). *Reshaping Work: The Cadbury Experience.* Cambridge: Cambridge University Press.

Smith, K. G. & McKee, A. (1993). The British Airways Employee Assistance Programme: A community response to a company's problems. *Employee Counselling Today,* 5, no. 3, 4–8.

Somerville, C. (1990). CHAT—counselling, help and advice together. *Employee Counselling Today,* 2, no. 1, 14–15.

Sonnenstuhl, W. J. & Trice, H. M. (1986). *Strategies for Employee Assistance Programs: The crucial balance.* Key Issues No. 30, ILR Press, New York State School of Industrial and Labor Relations, Cornell University.

Storey, J. (1995). Human Resource Management: Still marching on, or marching out? In Storey, J. (ed.), *Human Resource Management: A Critical Text.* London: Routledge, 3–36.

Strauss, A., Schatzman, L., Ehrlich, D., Bucher, R. & Sabsin, M. (1963). The hospital and its negotiated order. In E. Friedson (ed.), *The Hospital in Modern Society.* New York: Macmillan, 147–169.

Straussner, S. L. A. (1988). Comparison of in-house and contracted-out Employee Assistance Programs. *Social Work,* 33, 53–55.

Swanson, N. G. & Murphy, L. R. (1991). Mental health counselling in industry. In C. L. Cooper & I. T. Robertson (eds), *International Review of Industrial and Occupational Psychology,* 6, 265–282. Chichester: John Wiley.

Teasdale, E. L. & McKeown, S. (1994). Managing stress at work: The ICI–Zeneca Pharmaceuticals experience 1986–1993. In C. L. Cooper & S. Williams (eds), *Creating Healthy Work Organisations*. Chichester: John Wiley, 133–165.

Teram, E. (1988). Formative evaluation of Employee Assistance Programs by studying role perceptions and organisational cultures. *Employee Assistance Quarterly*, **3**, nos. 3 & 4, 119–128.

Thatcher, M. (1993). *The Downing Street Years*. London: Harper Collins.

Thomason, G. F. (1976). *A Textbook of Personnel Management*, 2nd edn. London: Institute of Personnel Management.

Torrington, D. P. & Chapman, J. (1978). *Personnel Management*. London: Prentice-Hall.

Trice, H. M. & Schonbrunn, M. (1981). A history of job-based alcoholism programs, 1900–1955. *Journal of Drug Issues*, **11**, 171–198.

US Department of Labor (1990). *What Works: Workplaces without Drugs*. Washington, DC: US Department of Labor.

van den Berg, N. (1991). Workplace mutual aid and self help. *Employee Counselling Today*, **3**, no. 2, 9–19.

*Walker v Northumberland County Council, 1995, IRLR*, **35**.

Williams, S. (1994). Ways of creating healthy work organisations. In C. L. Cooper & S. Williams (eds), *Creating Healthy Work Organizations*. Chichester: John Wiley.

Winstanley, I. (1995). Counselling models: Will any do in an EAP? Paper given to the *5th EAR Conference*. London: 1995.

Woollcott, D. (1991). Employee Assistance Programmes: Myths and realities. *Employee Counselling Today*, **3**, no. 4, 14–19.

*Index compiled by Geoffrey Jones*